MW00572714

Among His Slaves

George Mason, Slavery at Gunston Hall,
and the Idealism of the American Revolution

Terry K. Dunn

To Felix !
with love to a special
special ! special
friend
Terry

Copyright © 2017 Terry K. Dunn

All rights reserved. No part of this book may be used or reproduced in any manner whatsoever without written permission except in the case of brief quotations in critical articles or reviews.

Unless otherwise noted, photographs in the text of the book courtesy of the author.

Commonwealth Books of Virginia
www.commonwealthbooks.org
e-mail: info@commonwealthbooks.org
Alexandria, VA 22307
703-307-7715

Library of Congress Control Number: 2015949354
ISBN (Paperback): 978-1-943642-37-3
ISBN (Ebook - EPUB): 978-1-943642-38-0
ISBN (Ebook - PDF): 978-1-943642-39-7
ISBN (Ebook - Mobipocket): 978-1-943642-40-3

American History/Biography

Printed in the United States of America

To Keith

Who understands how important this is to me

Contents

Preface

The bust of George Mason of Gunston Hall done by artist Wendy Ross welcomes guests at the visitor's center.

$\mathcal{I}$n the last decade, a serious need for museums to address the difficult subject of slavery in America's history has become a prominent topic among historians. Points of criticism concerning museums and historic sites of many types range from no mention of slavery at all to insufficient or even misrepresentation of enslaved persons at sites where slavery was known to exist. James Oliver Horton and Lois E. Horton's edited volume, *Slavery and Public History, The Tough Stuff of American Memory*, explores this issue in depth and includes studies and perspectives on museum lapses in addressing the sensitive issues of American slavery and how these problems could be and should be better handled in the future. Their book also considers another overwhelming concern – that American history textbooks in public education are severely deficient in discussing American slavery.[1] Are public educators guilty of diluting or eliminating the teaching of the tough subjects of America's slave past? Are America's museums leaving out part of the story because it is too sensitive to discuss with visitors?

In 1998, Roy Rosenzweig and David Thelan surveyed 1500 people about their interests in learning about the past, their connections with the past, and their sources for learning about the past. The survey revealed that almost 80 percent of the participants said that they had confidence in the information they received at museum sites as truthful, whereas only about one-third in the survey expressed that confidence in high school teachers.[2] That is high praise and faith in museum education and interpreters! But are museums and historic sites only telling what they are comfortable with in the story-lines? And perhaps, as the Hortons' book reveals, are museums skipping-over the parts of the story that visitors – and interpreters – might find sensitive?

Museums have always played a critical role in supplementing the classroom experience in teaching history. Field trips provide the opportunity of "bringing history to life" or "pulling history out of the pages of a book." These excursions are real teaching opportunities and chances to encourage interest in history for

---

[1] James Oliver Horton and Lois E. Horton, Eds., *Slavery and Public History, The Tough Stuff of American Memory* (The New Press, New York, 2006), vii-xiv.
[2] Roy Rosenzweig and David Thelan, *The Presence of the Past: Popular Uses of History in American Life* (New York: Columbia University Press, 1998), 21, 32.

students - and adults as well. Museums must make the opportunity provided to excel in telling stories, providing hands-on experiences, provoking questions, and projecting issues that are relevant to the site; they should not duck sensitive issues that may be part an integral part of their story. As James Oliver Horton says:

> The history of slavery and its role in the formation of the American experience is one of the most sensitive and difficult subjects to present in a public setting. At historic plantation sites and historic houses, in museum exhibitions, in film productions, and in historic parks, public historians and historical interpreters are called upon to deal with this unsettling, but critical topic, often under less than ideal teaching conditions. Moreover, they are asked to educate a public generally unprepared and reluctant to deal with a history that, at times, can seem very personal.[3]

Horton believes the emphasis of telling the stories of America's past falls heavily on two groups: to the public historians - the docents and interpreters on the front lines of museums - as well as to the classroom educators.

Whether or not classroom texts are falling short of telling complete history in America's schools, field trips augment and support the educational experience. Interpreters and Docents, the "public historians," on the front lines of museums and historic sites, thus become the first, and likely the only, communicators of a specific site's history.

Gunston Hall Plantation is a prime example of a museum that can offer the visitor a panorama of Virginia life in the eighteenth century. Home of George Mason, author of the Virginia Declaration of Rights, Gunston Hall was also the center of life to perhaps 100-125 enslaved people. The story for school groups and visitors of all ages who visit this museum focuses on the person of George Mason, his family, and his all important writing of the Virginia Declaration of Rights. But it must also include discussion of those workers who provided Mason with the means of comfort and opportunities in the gentry life style he led - those individuals brought here and held by force and were "among his slaves," as John Mason so aptly put it. Rich sources from decades of historical research reveal much about

---

[3] Horton and Horton, *Slavery and Public History,* 36-37.

daily life for enslaved Africans and African-Americans in the Chesapeake region. Focusing on the years of George Mason's life as an elite eighteenth century plantation owner, this research provides a background for the more than one hundred enslaved individuals named in surviving Mason documents. Stories of many of these Mason-owned slaves have never been told. Although the whole picture will never be complete, understanding more about their lives enriches our knowledge of American history during a period when our emerging nation struggled with the ideological conflict of freedom in a slave society. Given the high confidence of museum visitors, "Public historians" need to get the story right.

It is challenging to tell this story as clearly and completely as possible. To do so, an understanding of the documented evidence is necessary to discuss objectively the individuals (and in some instances their families) of the enslaved Africans who lived, worked, and struggled to survive on this Chesapeake plantation. The surviving primary sources reveal names, ages, relationships, occupations, and, sometimes, behavior of the enslaved men, women, and children owned by George Mason. Many of these sources also reveal the transfer of ownership within Mason family members; they indicate the monetary values - the "business" of slavery - and, in a few cases, they illuminate the fate of an individual across time.

Sometimes our best understanding of history comes from those individuals who break the rules and get into trouble. In this fashion, several of Mason's slaves tell us important stories about themselves - and about their master. Their difficulties emphasize the omnipresent desire for freedom. The idealism of human rights - the concept of *democratic ideals* - was not lost on the enslaved. The stories of "Runaway Dick" and "Yellow Dick," emphasize the deep rooted desire for freedom; they also reveal George Mason's knowledge and use of a tightly structured legal system designed to punish slaves who broke laws; they show the importance of the monetary value of this form of "property;" and they indicate just what that loss of property meant to the owner.

Gentry women played an important, though sometimes understated, role in dealing with slavery in eighteenth century Virginia. These wives and mothers on plantations influenced decisions not only in the day-to-day activities of slaves' work and behavior, but also in the way in which they projected their values on issues regarding slaves' lives and futures. For George Mason, the influences of his mother, his mother-in-law, his wife, and his eldest daughter helped modify his changing world view toward the institution of slavery.

Gunston Hall Plantation's history places it squarely into the time line of the elite planter class that scholar and historian Ira Berlin describes as the "Plantation Generation."[4] By the middle of the eighteenth century a "mature" slave plantation system was clearly established in the Chesapeake. The primary labor source for planters had transitioned from one of indentured white laborers to enslaved black laborers. Slavery was clearly defined and designated by race. The planters, as the elite society and primary participants in the lawmaking bodies of the colony, created a legal structure around this system of racial slavery. Moreover, they molded and structured a farm model to include overseers to enforce the work to be done, punish the laggard, and reduce the amount of unstructured "leisure" time slaves had. In the Chesapeake region, the tobacco, wheat, and corn that were the mainstay crops were shipped to international markets and were highly profitable. A plantation was a business. African or African descended enslaved men, women, and children were the laborers of this business by no choice of their own and with no share of its profit.

Well before the time of the American Revolution, a complete legal structure for black slavery was in effect in Virginia. As planters expanded exports of multiple crops they became self-sufficient in food production for their families and enslaved workers. Skills among the slaves enhanced a level of plantation autonomy. Mason, like many planters, capitalized on diversified means to provide and increase his revenue. He rented land to tenant farmers, ran ferries at strategic river points, and utilized fishing rights to augment his income. But slaves, who provided the underlying labor source for his farms, were his true wealth. However, at the same time, George Mason realized that this fact undercut the idealism of the American Revolution.

This book is an attempt to do two things: First, to provide information for all who want to know more about the enslaved people of Gunston Hall. This work is based on extant primary sources and supported by secondary sources. Although many

---

[4] Ira Berlin, "Coming to Terms with Slavery in Twenty-First-Century America" in Horton and Horton, *Slavery and Public History* 19-34. Berlin argues that in the Plantation Generation, "Biographies of individual men and women, to the extent that they can be reconstructed, are thin to the point of invisibility. Less is known about these men and women than about any other generation of American slaves." (p. 11) See also: Ira Berlin, *Many Thousands Gone: The First Two Centuries of Slavery in North America* (Cambridge, Massachusetts: Belknap Press, 1998), 95-105.

Mason family documents – plantation records and correspondence – have un-doubtedly been lost, the surviving documents reveal much about the individual slaves in Mason family ownership. Additionally, a broad body of scholarship on Chesapeake slavery life enlightens our understanding of the eighteenth century plantations. On this basis we can build a strong picture of slavery at Gunston Hall. *The story is overdue.* It is time to tell the story of enslaved Africans and African-Virginians who lived on George Mason's plantation as completely as possible.

Today, many Americans of African descent have oral history traditions in their families relating to slave roots and connections. By examining the story of the *people* who were enslaved in the Mason family, there is the hope and possibility that those who have an oral history connecting them with slaves held in the Mason family in the eighteenth and early nineteenth centuries may be able to support those tradi-tions with facts.

Second, Gunston Hall's story cannot be told without addressing how George Mason's vision for human rights was paradoxically intertwined with his lifelong ownership of slaves. This paradox surrounds and overshadows his idealism, set down in writing when he drafted the Virginia Declaration of Rights which began with the words, "That all Men are born equally free and independent, and have certain inherent natural Rights...." George Mason, arguing against the slave trade at the Constitutional Convention in 1787, called "every master of slaves a Petty Tyrant." Mason, a slave master – himself a "Petty Tyrant" – manumitted none of his. The idealism of the American Revolutionary period and the expression of human rights in the Revolutionary documents stopped short of acknowledging that enslaved people of African descent were worthy of those rights, too. The paradox imbedded in the story at Gunston Hall must not be left out.

Mason's words stretched far beyond Virginia and today those words reflect the global importance of this story. As a historic site now owned by the Commonwealth of Virginia, Gunston Hall's mission states in part that it is "to stimulate continuing public exploration of *democratic ideals* as first presented by George Mason in the 1776 Virginia Declaration of Rights."[5] The exploration of our "democratic ideals" must go on.

---

[5] Author's emphasis.

Introduction

The English boxwood on the river front of Gunston Hall were planted in the 1770s and formed the original outlines for the parterres of Mason's formal garden. Today only a portion of these boxwood survive.

The Past is a Foreign Country.
Anonymous

Among His Slaves focuses on slavery at Gunston Hall, the eighteenth century home of George Mason. It brings to light a larger body of work that paints a stronger portrait of Mason's enslaved people than has been done in the past. Using the extant documents of more than eight decades of Mason and Eilbeck family members and tracing individual slaves they owned reveals much about the people who have remained anonymous through the past two centuries. We learn when many of these slaves came under ownership by the Masons, where they lived, where they worked, and what skills some had. We can identify family relationships of many slaves through inspection of these documents. And, very importantly, we can see how George Mason's attitude toward slavery changed and how it evolved. His change in attitude and his experiences with slaves is particularly critical to the discussion and evaluation of George Mason's growing abhorrence of slavery in the last years of his life. *Among His Slaves* seeks not only to bring to light Mason's slaves, but also to reveal his changing attitude toward the institution of slavery. Both provide insight as to why the author of the Virginia Declaration of Rights, freed none of the bondsmen or bondswomen that he owned.

Mason, an important, but often slighted, founding father of our nation, drafted the Virginia Declaration of Rights in late May, 1776, which he began with the statement:

> That all Men are born equally free and independent, and have certain
> inherent natural Rights, of which they can not [sic] by any Compact,
> deprive or divest their Posterity; among which are, the Enjoyment of
> Life and Liberty, with the Means of acquiring and possessing Property,
> and pursuing and obtaining Happiness and Safety.

His subsequent statements reflected the rights that so many argued were in jeopardy as Englishmen, including freedom of the press; the right of suffrage (by men who had "attachment" to the community); and the "fullest toleration in the exercise of religion."[6]

---

[6] Robert A. Rutland, Ed., *The Papers of George Mason, 1725-1792* (Chapel Hill: The University of North Carolina Press, 1970), 276-282. Mason's draft was presented and read to the committee on 27 May 1776.

The Committee at the Virginia Convention of Delegates in Williamsburg discussed his draft over the course of two weeks and effectively made minor changes. The exception was in the first statement which was rewritten after great debate to say:

> That all men are <u>by nature</u> equally free and independent, and have certain inherent rights, of which, <u>when they enter into a state of society</u>, they cannot, by any compact, deprive or divest their posterity; <u>namely</u>, the enjoyment of life and liberty, with the means of acquiring and possessing property, and pursuing and obtaining happiness and safety.[7]

The underlined words were the changes that the Committee made to allay the concerns and fears of Virginia's slave holders. In this modification, slaves (who were legally considered property) were excluded from society. Thus, only members of "society" reaped the benefits of these stated rights.

Eleven years later, as a Virginia delegate and an important contributor at the Constitutional Convention in Philadelphia, Mason became fearful that the lack of an inclusion of a similar human rights declaration in the national document was a serious omission. He voiced this concern, then, seconded a motion to write a statement which "might be prepared in a few hours," but the motion was unanimously rejected by the delegates.[8] Just before the close of the Convention, Mason wrote a long list of his "Objections" to the document. His first of sixteen objections stated that

> There is no Declaration of Rights, and the laws of the general government being paramount to the laws and constitution of the several States, the Declaration of Rights in the separate States are no security. Nor are the people secured even in the enjoyment of the benefit of the common law.[9]

On 17 September, 1787, the Constitution was signed by the delegates. George Mason declined placing his signature on the document.[10]

---

[7] Ibid., 287-291. The Virginia Declaration of Rights was approved sometime before 14 June 1776 when it appeared in the *Virginia Gazette* (Purdie) on that date. The underlined words are those added or modified by the committee and were not in Mason's original draft.

[8] Ibid., 981.

[9] Ibid., 991.

[10] Helen Hill Miller, *George Mason, Gentleman Revolutionary* (Chapel Hill: The University of North Carolina Press, 1975), 257-269. Three delegates did not sign on 17 September, 1787: George Mason and Edmund Randolph from Virginia and Elbridge Gerry from Massachusetts.

George Mason argued strenuously for the inclusion of rights for the next two years, especially during the Ratification Convention in Virginia in June 1788. Although the Constitution of the United States of America was ratified without a human rights declaration, the long, uphill battle for it concluded successfully before the end of his life. Our "Bill of Rights," the first ten amendments as they are known, was appended to the Constitution of the United States of America, in December 1791.[11]

George Mason, born into Virginia's slave-holding society in 1725, became a slave owner when he reached his majority (the age of twenty-one) and remained one all of his life. His attitude toward the institution of slavery initially fell in line with those of the early eighteenth century slave owners in what has become called the "Golden Age" of prosperous Chesapeake planters. The decades of the 1730s, 1740s, and 1750s brought established gentry families an accumulation of wealth from tobacco production. Slave populations grew from "natural increase" and the threats of insurrection of newly imported slaves declined. Political stability within the British realm carried over to its colonies. Horizons for slave-holding planters in the Chesapeake appeared secure.[12]

But over time, George Mason's own experiences as a slave master, the influences of women within the Mason and Eilbeck families (his mother, his mother-in-law, his wife Ann, and his oldest daughter), and the upheaval of events that culminated in the American Revolution, changed his attitude from one of acceptance of slave labor to one of abhorrence. In the later decades of his life, he argued for change and the curtailment of the slave trade in the new nation.

To understand this story, Mason's slaves – the people themselves – are vital. Although the surviving documents are finite in number, they nonetheless reveal much about the enslaved. Each document recorded different sets of information, but compiled they reveal: slaves' names, ages, or values; occupations or characteristics, if any; where they lived; and family connections (direct relationships in some cases and inferred by names in others.) We also learn what happened to a

---

[11] Miller, *Gentleman Revolutionary,* 285-300. George Mason died on 7 October 1792.
[12] Lorena S. Walsh, *Motives of Honor, Pleasure, & Profit: Plantation Management in the Colonial Chesapeake, 1607-1763* (Chapel Hill: The University of North Carolina Press, 2010), 624-628.

few of these slaves over time. Some documents suggest clues about how his slaves influenced him. His experiences among his "people" helped to change and modify his view of the institution over his lifetime. We cannot fully understand George Mason, the "Forgotten Founder," as one historian has called him, without carefully studying his slaves.[13]

How many slaves did George Mason own? His 1773 will included thirty-six slaves by name and referred to eleven others in mother-child relationships. This is not a complete accounting, by any means. Local tithable (or tax) lists taken in the 1780s survive. In 1782, Martin Cockburn's district census recorded that George Mason had nine white and ninety black inhabitants on his property. That year in Charles Little's district where George Mason had property at Little Hunting Creek, there were six white and thirty-eight black inhabitants. Mason's total of black inhabitants for 1782 was one hundred twenty-eight. The taxable lists for 1787 recorded that George Mason held thirty six blacks over the age of sixteen and forty two blacks under the age of sixteen; George Mason, Jr., the oldest son, held twenty-one over the age of sixteen and twenty under sixteen; Thomson Mason held two blacks over the age of sixteen and three under sixteen. The total number of slaves is one hundred twenty-four with fifty-nine over the age of sixteen and sixty-five under that age.[14] Therefore, estimates of approximately one hundred twenty-five slaves who worked in the fields and supported Gunston Hall by the time of the Revolution seem consistent with existing records.

Slave's names become a critical part of identifying individuals and relationships. Although slave owners applied names with classical characterization to many newly arrived Africans, some retained their native names. Traditional naming

---

[13] Jeff Broadwater, *George Mason, Forgotten Founder* (Chapel Hill: The University of North Carolina Press, 2006).

[14] Nan Netherton, Donald Sweig, Janice Artemel, Patrick Hickin, and Patrick Reed, *Fairfax County, Virginia, a History* (Fairfax, Virginia: Fairfax County Board of Supervisors, 1992), 35. Thomson Mason and his wife, Sarah McCarty Chichester Mason were living at Gunston Hall in 1787. Their slaves included Sally (daughter of Lucy), Joe (son of Mrs. Eilbeck's Bess), and Cupid (given by Grandfather Eilbeck) as listed in George Mason's 1773 will. The numbers reflect that Thomson's wife Sarah likely brought two slaves with her at the time of her marriage. See Appendix G. George Mason, Jr. married in 1784. Slaves counted for him in the 1787 census reflect those he received from his father (and slaves through his marriage), but provide for an overall estimate of Gunston Hall's black population in this window of time. See Appendix G. See also, Pamela C. Copeland and Richard K. Mac Master, *The Five George Masons, Patriots and Planters of Virginia and Maryland* (Lorton, Virginia: The Board of Regents of Gunston Hall, 1989), 237.

patterns in Africa reflected something about when a child's birth took place: the day of the week, the season of the year, or an event of significance that occurred. But as natural increase among slaves grew in North America, naming patterns changed to reflect kinship among the enslaved individuals. In short, slave parents chose the names for their children that reflected family members. Both male and female children were likely to have the name of a grandparent (first born children) or that of an uncle or an aunt. A parent naming a child for one of his or her own siblings had two effects for the slave community. First, it recognized the importance of kinship and extended family. Second, it may have reflected what one historian has called "functional reciprocity," that is, the binding of the family unit's responsibilities to each other. In the event of the loss of the child's parent (through death or sale), namesakes insured a level of continuity of care and concern for that child. Slave families highly valued their children. Patterns of naming them for kin not only extended family ties, it preserved memories within the fragile structure of the slave community.[15]

Slave masters recognized "marriages" and families among their slaves. But their view of family structure was different from the slave community's perspective. Virginia law defined the status of a child after the status of the mother, not the father.[16] For example, if a black woman was free, her child was free; but if the black woman was a slave, her child was also a slave. Thus, when masters "preserved" slave families, they were likely to keep slave women together with their children or their daughters, emphasizing matrilineal descent. Sons were very likely to be separated by the ages of ten or twelve. Fathers rarely fit into this picture of the slave family structure at all. To counter this, slaves used kinship names from both paternal and maternal sides of a child's family, to preserve broader family relationships.

---

[15] Cheryll Ann Cody, "Naming, Kinship, and Estate Dispersal: Notes on Slave Family Life on a South Carolina Plantation, 1786 to 1833," *William and Mary Quarterly*, Series Three, 39 (January 1982): 192-211. Cody also noted "almost a complete absence of necronymic naming" among slaves (naming a child for a deceased child) as was frequently done in white families. Although this study was conducted on a South Carolina plantation, kinship ties and naming patterns were even more significant in the Chesapeake. Philip D. Morgan, *Slave Counterpoint, Black Culture in the Eighteenth-Century Chesapeake & Lowcountry* (Chapel Hill: The University of North Carolina Press, 1998), 550-558. The importance of slave naming patterns is the basis for identification of relationships among George Mason's slaves in this book.
[16] William Waller Hening, ed., *The Statutes at Large; Being a Collection of All the Laws of Virginia, From the First Session of the Legislature, in 1619.* 13 vols. (Richmond, 1819-1823), 2:170. Virginia law did not recognize marriages among enslaved people.

Among His Slaves is set on the backdrop of the eighteenth century Chesapeake landscape. Virginia, first settled in 1607 by Englishmen who struggled to survive in Jamestown, became the largest and wealthiest of the North American colonies by the mid-eighteenth century when George Mason IV came of age. African slave labor constituted the largest portion of Virginia's wealth and that wealth was concentrated in the hands of the uppermost levels of Virginia society, its gentry and upper-middling classes. George Mason of Gunston Hall in Fairfax County, a fourth generation of Virginians, fits squarely into the gentry class. He was a Gentleman, a planter, and owner of about a hundred and twenty-five slaves.

Three generations of Mason family members preceded George Mason IV of Gunston Hall in Virginia. His great-grandfather George Mason I (1629-1686) immigrated to the Chesapeake region at the close of the English Civil War, acquired land and laborers, and established himself within the colony's government. His grandfather, George Mason II (1660-1716), built on that status, increased land holdings, and invested in African slave labor. His father, George Mason III (c.1690-1735), added to the family's holdings of land and slaves. As the oldest son, George Mason IV (1725-1792), inherited all of the accumulated family land and distinguished himself during the American Revolution as a "pure patriot" and authored the Virginia Declaration of Rights in 1776.[17]

George Mason IV was nine when his father drowned in a boating accident during a Chesapeake squall. As his father died intestate (without a will), the English laws of primogeniture passed all land to him as the eldest son.[18] He would also inherit personal property and slaves, all of which was held in trust for him by his guardians, his mother Ann Thomson Mason and his uncle John Mercer. His mother ably managed his assets until he reached twenty-one, the age of his majority.[19]

By 1750, as a young planter stepping onto the Chesapeake scene, George Mason IV held a world view that was similar to his contemporaries. Coming from a family with generational roots in Virginia, he held a place in gentry society, had wealth

---

[17] Because of the many family members named George Mason, historians have used Roman numerals to distinguish the different generations. Where clarification is necessary, that format will be used here. John Mason referred to his father as a "pure patriot" in his *Recollections*. Terry K. Dunn, ed., *The Recollections of John Mason* (Mason Neck, Virginia: The Board of Regents of Gunston Hall, 2012), 55.
[18] Copeland and MacMaster, *The Five George Masons*, 73.
[19] Ibid., 73-76.

beyond the vast majority of the colony's population, and received the education of a "proper" gentleman.[20] His position also granted him power. He held positions of authority in the local Anglican church, the Fairfax County Court, the Virginia militia, and the House of Burgesses. His education and his understanding of law provided him with the tools to control the labor of others – in short, to control his world and his environment. Thus, George Mason's world view was one of power, prestige, and promise for his future success.

The decades that ensued altered his world view considerably. George Mason, dealing with his enslaved laborers, sometimes found it difficult to make them perform to his desires. Punishments were not always successful in changing behavior. He learned that some slaves were "faithful" to his wishes or "trustworthy" when unattended. He learned – often through the women in his family – that sometimes rewards to slaves (and their children) were justified humane acts in an inhumane system of slavery.

Great Britain forced dramatic change on Virginia's planters in 1765. Faced with threats of "taxation without representation" and fearing "enslavement" to the mother country, Mason and others throughout all the British colonies rebelled against such treatment. The parallels of African slavery in British North America juxtaposed against Britain's treatment of its subjects were not overlooked as the colonists considered "revolution" against England. It was at this time that George Mason wrote his first criticisms of the institution of slavery.

The events of the American Revolution radically changed Mason's world view by the 1780s. He saw Virginia – and ultimately the United States – on a bigger, global stage, one based on the "Principles of Liberty, & the sacred Rights of human Nature."[21] Seeing the rise of this new nation full of the promise of democratic ideals, George Mason also wanted to see the United States begin to dissolve the institution of slavery.

Chapter One of *Among His Slaves* begins by tracing the earliest generations of Mason family members in the Chesapeake. These generations lived in the region

---

[20] Walsh, *Motives of Honor*, 394-395.
[21] Rutland, *Papers of George Mason*, 1199.

at a time when both slavery and indentured servitude provided labor sources for land owners who saw tobacco as a means to wealth. Historian Ira Berlin calls this the time of the "Charter Generation"[22] in slavery where servants, both black and white, moved across somewhat flexible boundaries. Freedom from servitude was possible. With less regard for color, some individuals gained free status, mostly through good fortune and survival long enough to reap its benefits. But it was also during these decades that the laws of Virginia began closing in; a legal structure gradually evolved to create the status of "servitude for life" that would be applied along the color line – to those with African heritage. This chapter examines the development of this legal slave system, looks at the Mason family slaves, and postulates how their lives may have been affected by these laws.

Chapter Two moves to broader resources to examine in greater detail the lives of plantation slaves in the Chesapeake region in the eighteenth century to better visualize the material world of this time and place. Surviving Mason family documents provide scant understanding of day-to-day life, but studies of dozens of other plantations using various sources (such as archeology) and greater numbers of extant records help to fill in the gap in understanding daily and seasonal plantation life in this region. A close look at available food, clothing allotments, housing types, and material culture provided for by the masters and obtained by the slaves themselves in various ways, paints a vivid picture of daily life in what Berlin calls the "Plantation Generation."[23] Through these studies we can better envision how slaves lived – and how they found ways to cope with oppression of slavery. Close scrutiny of extant Mason family documents then allows us to see George Mason's enslaved people against this backdrop.

Chapter Three explains Ann Thomson Mason's management of George Mason IV's inheritance and then focuses on his early years as a planter. His mother's attitude toward the enslaved laborers she both owned and managed in trust for her children and her careful use of "human resources," reveals some personal family attitudes that carried over to the next generation of Mason slave owners. George Mason saw how his mother gave (and passed down in her will) favored slaves to her daughter Mary Mason Seldon, only to have Mary's sudden death

---

[22] Berlin, *Many Thousands Gone*, 12.
[23] Ibid.

cause her to repurchase gifted slaves and add codicils to her will. He watched as his mother carefully reexamined and reevaluated these slaves' futures. Ann Thomson Mason now entrusted George Mason with one very particular slave woman.

From 1746 until 1770 when George Mason IV came into his inheritance and established his own plantation, he faced some difficult challenges as a slave master. Unexpected events taught Mason more about the people who worked and lived around him in slavery. These events challenged him to view slavery through a new lens in the decades before the Revolutionary period.

Chapter Four begins with the 1770s. Plantation life for George Mason was jolted by the sudden and unexpected death of his wife Ann Eilbeck Mason in 1773. It caused him quickly to focus on the future of his children and write an extensive will that would fill twenty-four pages in the Fairfax County Will Book. So well thought out that he never revised it, this document creates a basis for understanding more about some of the slaves of Gunston Hall and their familial connections. Additional Mason and Eilbeck family documents add to that knowledge. A subtle picture of how Mason ran his farms or quarters comes to light and many slaves' interconnections appear. Problems continued to plague him, however, and run-aways frustrated him. These years provide us with stories of' his slaves' strong desire for freedom. The enslaved, too, heard the words of idealism in the American Revolution period that resounded with "all men are created equal."

Chapter Five explores – in depth – George Mason's changing attitude about slavery. He stated his growing "detestation" of slavery as early as 1765, more than a decade before he became the draftsman for the Virginia Declaration of Rights. His written words grew ever more emphatic as time went on. Across more than two decades – from 1765 to 1788 – as Mason's distain for slavery in his writing increased, he emphasized that "the author of them conscious of his own good Intentions, cares not whom they please or offend."[24]

The Virginia gentry realized their words arguing that the colonists were slaves to Great Britain chaffed against the reality of holding African *slaves* in America.

[24] Rutland, *Papers of George Mason*, 173.

Many others called it to public attention, too, Thomas Paine especially. Referring to the Enlightenment philosophies that spurred the Revolution, Paine criticized slavery as "contrary to the light of nature" in his first pamphlet distributed in America.[25] Acknowledgement of this contradiction and its moral conflict did not go unnoticed. As the Revolution ended, the Virginia Assembly voted to pass laws closing the slave trade and allowing owners the ability to free slaves. With new laws written in 1782, the power of manumission was now returned to the slave masters and taken back from the government. It was a good start: In two successive steps, Virginia closed the external slave trade and made possible the freedom of thousands of blacks by the turn of the nineteenth century.

George Mason's own words, however, do not match actions that he could have taken to legally manumit his own slaves. Calling all masters of slaves "Petty Tyrants," he does not free any of the approximately 125 individuals he owns. How do we reconcile this paradox? Can we do so at all? How do we understand George Mason as a patriotic Virginian, founding father of the United States of America, draftsman of documents putting forth democratic ideals and human rights – and slave master until the end of his life? This chapter dissects this paradox and offers insight.

The final chapter, Concluding Thoughts, is complex. Mason's words on both human rights and slavery are profound. "That all men are by nature equally free and independent and have certain rights...," resonated in the Virginia Declaration of Rights, the document he drafted in May 1776. In the ensuing months of that year, each of the thirteen colonies adapted a variation of human rights statements into their new state governments.[26] Mason continued to argue against the institution of slavery. He vigorously supported Virginia's closure of the external slave trade and argued strenuously for total closure of the external trade for all states at the Constitutional Convention in Philadelphia in 1787. But at the Convention, Mason and other supporters of national closure were defeated. The slave trade into the United States would continue for twenty more years.[27] Mason, refusing to

---

[25] Douglas R. Egerton, *Death or Liberty, African Americans and Revolutionary America* (New York, Oxford University Press, 2009), 99.
[26] Robert A. Rutland, *The Birth of the Bill of Rights* (Boston: Northeastern University Press, 1983), 41-77.
[27] The term "external slave trade" referred to newly imported slaves from outside the United States. The "internal slave trade" between the States themselves was not altered by the Constitution.

sign the Constitution, listed among his sixteen objections: "The general legislature is restrained from prohibiting the further importation of slaves for twenty odd years...."

The influences that modified George Mason's attitude toward the institution of slavery – and the enslaved people themselves – came from the political changes and ideological thinking taking place in America, to be sure. But influences from the women in the Mason and Eilbeck families stressed their desire and means to treat some slaves in a protective manner under a legal system that defined them merely as property. This legal system remained virtually unchanged all of George Mason's life, but the women in his family showed sensitivity to their slaves' plight. Within the confines of this legal system, Mason and Eilbeck women – and George Mason himself – attempted to secure a structured future for some of their slaves.

Only George Mason's words on human rights outlived him. His anger and disapproval of slavery fell away into the footnotes of history. Even the brief spurt of idealism that reinstated a master's legal ability to free his slaves after 1782 by will or deed and generated thousands of manumissions in the Chesapeake region, soon withered. Discussion of abolition in Virginia's legislature rose in the 1790s – and then peaked in the early nineteenth century. Mason died in 1792 before his sentiments could be added to those debates. Ultimately such talk ended in Virginia.[28] Tragically, slavery in the Commonwealth of Virginia would continue until its dissolution at the end of the Civil War.

---

[28] St. George Tucker, lawyer, professor of law at the College of William and Mary, and justice on the United States District Court, published *A Dissertation on Slavery: With a Proposal for the Gradual Abolition of It, in the State of Virginia* in 1796. He presented his plan to the Virginia General Assembly; it was given little discussion. The enthusiasm of the Revolution was already in jeopardy. The manumission law of 1782 would be restricted in 1806 and anti-slavery societies faced increasing opposition in the south at the turn of the nineteenth century. See: St. George Tucker, *View of the Constitution of the United States with Selected Writings* (Indianapolis: Liberty Fund, Inc., 1999), 402-446. Also: Egerton, *Death or Liberty*, 141-146.

Abbreviated Mason Family Genealogy

Built for George Mason IV, construction on Gunston Hall began in 1755 and was completed in 1759. The Mason family lived here until 1792.

Abbreviated Mason Family Genealogy

This genealogy chart does not include children who died before their majority.

George Mason I (1629-1686)

Married   1. Mary French
         George Mason II
Married   2. Frances (Maddocks) Norgrave
         no issue

George Mason II (1660-1716)

Married   1. Mary Fowke

George Mason III	Mary Mason
French Mason	Elizabeth Mason
Nicholson Mason	Simpha Rosa Ann Field Mason
Ann Fowke Mason	

Married   2. Elizabeth Waugh
         Catherine Mason
Married   3. Sarah Taliaferro
         Sarah Mason

George Mason III (c. 1690-1735)

Married   Ann Thomson
         George Mason IV
         Mary Thomson Mason
         Thomson Mason

George Mason IV (1725-1792)

Married   Ann Eilbeck

George Mason V	Mary Thomson Mason
Ann "Nancy" Eilbeck Mason*	John Mason
William Mason	Elizabeth Mason
Thomson Mason	Thomas Mason
Sarah Eilbeck Mason	

* George Mason IV's oldest daughter will be referred to as Nancy Mason throughout this work in order to eliminate confusion between Ann Eilbeck Mason, his wife.

Chapter One: Beginnings

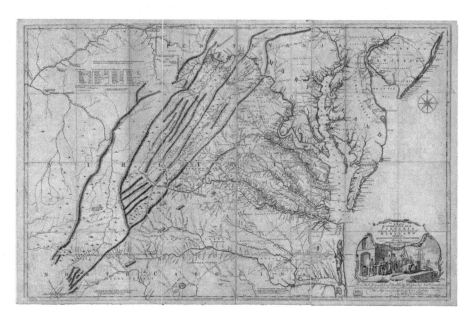

Created by surveyors Joshua Fry and Peter Jefferson, this highly accurate map of Virginia was first published in 1753. Revised two years later, it was in its sixth edition by 1775 and proved to be one of the most important maps during the French and Indian War and the American Revolution. Courtesy, Library of Congress.

$\mathcal{M}$any English immigrants who came to Virginia at the beginning of the seventeenth century sought wealth. They found it – not in the form of silver or gold as the Spaniards did in Central and South America – but in the cultivation of tobacco. By mid-century, England's civil wars forced some landowners and nobility to come to the new world to begin their lives anew; those loyal to the crown found themselves in great peril or suffering great material loss when Charles Cromwell as "Lord Protectorate" took over England's government. The Mason family of Worcestershire, England had been loyalists. George Mason (the first of that name in America) left for the Chesapeake in 1650 or 1651. He arrived at an expanding, but challenging, time in Virginia. The colony's labor force, critical to the tobacco planters, was being shaped by its laws to create two systems: one of white indentured servitude and the other of African slave labor. George Mason I arrived in Virginia at a time of opportunity; he prospered, acquired social status, and gained political power. He established the beginning of what would become a eminent gentry family spanning many generations in Virginia. Over time, his family acquired thousands of acres of land and became prominent slave owners. This is where the story of George Mason IV, gentry planter, slave owners, and author of the Virginia Declaration of Rights begins.

Virginia, the first permanent English settlement in North America, initially brought fortune seekers hoping to find the treasured gold and silver that the Spanish found in South and Central America. They were very quickly disappointed. But an unexpected crop, tobacco *(Nicotiana tabacum)* – grown by Native Americans – soon became an agricultural reprieve as the Europeans learned to cultivate and export it to a ready and eager European market. As a cash crop, however, tobacco demanded consistent care and attention to grow from seed to maturity and to process from drying, packing, and shipping.[29] Because many early white settlers saw themselves as entrepreneurs and not farmers, they sought laborers to tend

---

[29] Lois Green Carr, Russell R. Menard, and Lorena S. Walsh, *Robert Cole's World, Agriculture & Society in Early Maryland* (Chapel Hill: The University of North Carolina Press, 1991), 55-71. This provides a comprehensive discussion on tobacco cultivation in the Chesapeake.

their fields; such "unskilled" workers were always in short supply. The English attempted to coerce natives into labor, but indigenous peoples balked at servitude to white men. They held a distinct advantage living in familiar territory and could easily run away. Consequently, English men seeking a new start in Virginia gradually began to fill the need for agricultural labor. In an attempt to encourage impoverished men and women to come to Virginia, indentures (or contracts) were offered where a person could give four to seven years of their labor in exchange for passage to Virginia. Persons with financial means who paid the passage held the indenture and, according to the headright system, were granted 50 acres of land by the crown.[30] Thus, those with wealth had the opportunity to acquire land and labor simultaneously.

The African slave trade to the new world had begun in the sixteenth century and flourished. The Spanish, Portuguese, French, Dutch, Danish – and soon English – traders made large profits from cargoes of enslaved African men and women sold in South and Central America and the West Indies. Captured in war-like fashion in their homelands, these people were transported on a "middle passage" across thousands of miles of ocean and forced to labor in mines, on farms or plantations, or serve as domestics in homes.[31] Increasingly, the process of enslavement became ever more "business like" as sea captains sought to crowd more Africans as cargo into smaller, sleeker, faster ships. For these Africans, the passage carried fear, danger from disease, near starvation, and cruelty by ships' crews. Once landed, these people faced uncertain lives as planters examined the "cargo" and made their purchases.[32]

---

[30] A "headright" was a grant of fifty acres of land for each immigrant to Virginia. Originally intended to attract white settlers, it was extended to transported slaves in 1635. Headrights could be bought and sold, thus someone with the financial means could acquire hundreds of acres of land by buying up headrights. Intertwined with the indenture system, a planter could buy the indenture of a person for his labor, obtain 50 acres of land, and have the indentured servant work the land. See Warren M. Billings, *A Little Parliament, The Virginia General Assembly in the Seventeenth Century* (Richmond: The Library of Virginia, 2004), 204-206.
[31] Berlin, *Many Thousands Gone*, 17-19.
[32] Ibid., 100-105. Also, the presence of factors or "Guinea factors" in the new world is an interesting addition to understanding the slave trade and middle passage that Africans endured. These factors profited well in the multi-step business of this trade. See Nicholas Radburn, "Guinea Factors, Slave Sales, and the Profits of the Transatlantic Slave Trade in Late Eighteenth-Century Jamaica: The Case of John Tailyour," *William and Mary Quarterly*, 3d Ser., 72, No. 2, April 2015.

In the first half of the seventeenth century Virginia's colony saw growth in the population of whites, in large part because of this system using indentures and headrights. But by about 1660, changes occurred in Great Britain that reduced white emigration. Population declines and rising wages in England made greater opportunities for livelihood possible and made indentured servitude looked less inviting. Virginia planters, needing more laborers as tobacco sales boomed, now turned toward the African slave trade, already supplying thousands of African men, women, and children to the West Indies and South America. Virginia planters ultimately began purchasing slaves in increasing numbers, making slavery Virginia's most important labor source by the end of the seventeenth century.[33]

In the Chesapeake region of North America, an early record of the arrival of Africans dates to the summer of 1619 when a ship, a "Dutch man of Warr," carrying "20. and Odd Negroes" [sic] arrived in the James River. These slaves, taken off a Portuguese slave ship originally bound for Brazil, arrived on the lower James River at Point Comfort in Virginia. The ship's cargo was disembarked and sold.[34]

Great Britain gave legal status to the condition of indentured servitude, but it had no laws defining slavery. Although these Africans who arrived in the Chesapeake (and many others who followed) were taken initially as "slaves" by the Portuguese, their status in Virginia was undefined. Were they slaves or "servants?" Did the purchaser of this labor *own* the person or *"rent"* his time and muscle? Because no clear laws defined these people from Africa, some found their way to a free status, although some, like so many white indentured servants, never survived long enough to enjoy that possibility. Stories of a few of the Africans who arrived in

---

[33] Allan Kulikoff, Tobacco and Slaves, *The Development of Southern Cultures in the Chesapeake, 1680-1800* (Chapel Hill: The University of North Carolina Press, 1986), 37-44. Historian Lorena Walsh takes exception to the theory that slavery was a second-hand alternative to Virginia's labor needs. "Shortages of indentured servants...could not have forced elite planters to turn to slaves had they preferred indentured servants and been willing to pay higher prices for them, for it was the elite who had first choice of any laborers offered for sale in the colony....Those at the pinnacle of wealth and power, the councilors, took the lead in buying slaves, followed by burgesses and other county-level officeholders." Walsh, *Motives of Honor,* 141, 200-201.

[34] Engel Sluiter, "New Light on the '20.and Odd Negroes' Arriving in Virginia, August 1619," *William and Mary Quarterly,* 3d Series, Vol. LIV, No. 2, April 1997: 395-398. These Africans came from the Portuguese colony of Angola. However, an earlier record of 32 Negroes (15 men and 17 women) in Virginia is listed in a March 1619 (muster) census. See: William Thorndale, "The Virginia Census of 1619," *Magazine of Virginia Genealogy,* 33 (1995), 155-170.

Virginia in the first half of the seventeenth century are known. One tale of survival and better fortune is the story of Anthony Johnson.

Anthony Johnson, or "Antonio a Negro" came to Virginia in 1621 aboard the ship *James*.[35] He was purchased to work the tobacco fields on Richard Bennett's plantation on the south side of the James River. "Mary a Negro Woman" arrived a year later and also was sold to Bennett. Both Mary and Antonio were among the survivors of the Powhatan Indian uprising and massacre of March 22, 1622 that killed English settlers on both sides of the James River; fifty-two people were killed at the Bennett Plantation alone. Luck was a prerequisite to survival for blacks and whites alike.[36]

It is not known when Antonio adopted the name Anthony Johnson, but he and Mary married[37] and lived together for over forty years and had four children that survived. Virginia Councilman Richard Bennett appears to have been Anthony's benefactor as well as owner and at some unknown point gave Anthony his freedom (or assisted him in obtaining it.)[38] Bennett's family ties to Virginia's Eastern Shore may also explain why the Johnsons settled there in Northampton County in later years.[39] Freeman Anthony Johnson became a landowner; in 1651 he claimed 250

---

[35] T.H. Breen and Stephen Innes, *"Myne Own Ground," Race and Freedom on Virginia's Eastern Shore, 1640-1676* (New York: Oxford University Press, 1985), 7-18. See also: John Thornton, "The African Experience of the '20.and Odd Negroes' Arriving in Virginia in 1619," *William and Mary Quarterly*, 3d Series, Vol. LV, No. 3, July 1998: 421-434.

[36] Warren M. Billings, ed., *The Old Dominion in the Seventeenth Century*, 207-209, 220-224. Also: David A. Price, *Love & Hate in Jamestown, John Smith, Pocahontas, and the Start of a New Nation* (New York: Vintage Books, 2005), 200-222. For another perspective see: Helen C. Rountree, *Pocahontas's People, The Powhatan Indians of Four Centuries* (Norman: University of Oklahoma Press, 1996), 66-81.

[37] Marriage is a tenuous and ambiguous term for those of African descent in this time. That the Johnson's children were recognized in certain legal transactions lends support to the possibility they had a recognized marriage. In general, however, slaves were not allowed to legally marry under Virginia law.

[38] Billings, *The Old Dominion in the Seventeenth Century, A Documentary History of Virginia* (Chapel Hill: The University of North Carolina Press, 1975), 148-150.The Virginia County court system was formed in 1634, after which wills, inventories, and deeds were recorded. Early documents indicate instances of Africans who were freed after a period of "service." Walsh, *Motives of Honor*, 115-117.

[39] Billings, *A Little Parliament*, 35, 90-91. Richard Bennett was a member of the Governor's Council, but served as one of several elected Virginia Governors during England's Interregnum period. Bennett served from 1652-1655, the immediate years following the arrival of the first George Mason about 1651. Bennett's daughter Elizabeth married a Puritan, Charles Scarburgh, from the Eastern Shore of Virginia.

acres of land on the Pungoteague Creek.[40] Court documents also show that Johnson became a slave owner himself of at least one slave, "J[ho]no[than] Casor[,] Negro."[41] In the 1660s the Johnson family moved to Somerset County, Maryland after selling 200 acres of their Eastern Virginia land and giving 50 acres to one of their sons, Richard. All of the family members ultimately resettled in Maryland.

Anthony died before Mary, but she and her sons continued as landholders and farmers. In her will in 1672, Mary bequeathed a cow with a calf to each of her three grandchildren. This free African family of three generations lived on their own land, defended actions in court cases (and won them), and passed property on by will and gift. Their story is not only one of survival, but also reflects the early, flexible legal status of Africans who, against their will, found themselves on the opposite shores of the Atlantic Ocean in the seventeenth century.

There is an interesting codicil to the story of the Johnson family. In 1677, Anthony Johnson's son John purchased a Maryland tract of land that he named "Angola." As so many of the early seventeenth century slaves were taken from Angola, John – a first generation black man born on North American soil – likely wanted to retain the memory of his family's homeland.[42]

As Virginia's population increased in the seventeenth century, the numbers of upper-class white males grew; these men disproportionately held offices in a variety of governing positions. The total estimated population in Virginia in 1640 was 8,000 and rose to about 55,600 by 1680. The African population nonetheless remained small; Governor William Berkeley estimated that there were about 2000 Africans in Virginia in 1671.[43] However, beginning with the last quarter of the seventeenth century, as the demand for slave laborers began to boom, the black population rose rapidly. Thousands of slaves arrived in the Chesapeake, most now coming from the African Gold Coast and Bight of Biafra. Of about 100,000 people in Maryland and Virginia in 1700, 13 per cent were from Africa. By 1720, the percentage of Africans in Virginia's population alone rose to 25 per cent.[44]

---

[40] Breen and Innes, "*Myne Owne Ground,*" 11. Johnson claimed this acreage under the headright system.
[41] Ibid., 14-15.
[42] Ibid., 7-18. John Thornton, "The African Experience," 421-434.
[43] Walsh, *Motives of Honor,* 140.
[44] Ibid., 142, 200-204.

As more and more Africans arrived in Virginia, problems surfaced. Cultural and language differences disrupted the English mindset. Slaves' challenged their status by claiming Christian baptism or declaring promises of emancipation by owners. A few won their freedom; most did not.[45] Virginia's legislators, the Burgesses who were elected from each county, began to modify the legal structure to mold and define the status of Africans, put restraints on their activities, and mete out punishments for infringement of laws. They began to make a clear legal distinction between black and white; between enslaved and indentured. As a result, they developed an institution of racial slavery.

Across the seventeenth century in Virginia, the primary labor source evolved from one of white indentured servants to one of black slavery. In the decades between 1640 and 1690, structured, legalized, racial slavery developed. The transformation of this labor system can easily be seen in reading Virginia's legal statutes in these decades. Frequently begun by stating, "Whereas some doubts have arisen..."[46] law after law was adopted by Virginia's elected Burgesses to create a separate code that applied to Africans. These laws gradually created servitude for life. They forbade Africans' freedom based on baptism or Christianizing;[47] they defined a mulatto;[48] and laws decreed that the condition of a child followed the condition of the mother.[49] Punishments also reflected the division between white servants and black slaves. Africans could be whipped more or dismembered as punishment. They could be bought, sold, and willed to others, separating family and loved ones. The Burgesses passed these laws and so many more.

In 1640, one case presented to the General Court of Virginia indicates one of the early turning points in the legal code. Three servant men – two white men and one black man – ran away from their master, Hugh Gwen. All three runaways were caught and punished. The two white men ("Victor, a dutchman," and James Gregory, a "Scotchman") were each given an additional year of servitude to their terms to Gwen and also three years of service to the colony as punishment;

---

[45] Ibid., 116-118.
[46] Hening, ed., *Statutes.* See for example: 2:170.
[47] Ibid., 2:260.
[48] Ibid., 3: 250-252. The definition of a mulatto was given as a "child, grandchild, or great grandchild of a negro."
[49] Ibid., 2:170.

John Punch, "a negro," was given servitude for "the time of his natural life" to his master or his assigns.[50] The three men committed the same offence, but the black man was singled out for the harshest punishment. John Punch became a slave for the remainder of his life.

Another legal challenge also shows how the Virginia Burgesses determined what laws needed to be enacted. Elizabeth Key sued for her freedom in 1656 – and won. She was a mulatto woman, the daughter of a slave woman and a white father, Thomas Key. Key, now deceased, had specified before his death that his daughter Elizabeth was to have her freedom. Depositions taken supporting her case convinced the court

> "...That by the Comon [sic] Law the Child of Woman slave begott by a freeman ought to be free [and] That she hath bin long since Christened... [and] For these Reasons wee conceive the said Elizabeth ought to bee [sic] free...."[51]

Two English precedents supported this decision: (1) *the status of the child followed the status of the father* and (2) *Christians should not be slaves for life*. Elizabeth Key was given her freedom, but these ideas would be overturned in Virginia law in the following decade. Among a cascade of laws that came on the Virginia books between 1640 and 1690, two would be a direct reflection on the case of Elizabeth Key. In December 1662 it was enacted "that all children borne in this country [Virginia] shalbe [sic] held bond or free only according to the condition of the mother...." And in September 1667,

> "Whereas some doubts have risen whether children that are slaves by birth, and by the charity and piety of their owners made pertakers of the blessed sacrament of baptisme, should by vertue of their baptisme be made ffree [sic]...*It is enacted...* that the conferring of baptisme doth not alter the condition of the person as to his bondage or ffreedom...."[52]

---

[50] H.R. McIlwaine, ed., *Minutes of the Council and General Court of Virginia* (Richmond: Virginia State Library, 1924), 466.
[51] Billlings, *The Old Dominion,* 165-169.
[52] Hening, *Statutes,* 2:170 and 2:260.

The court case of Elizabeth Key certainly helped precipitate the passage of these laws. The legal status of a child now followed the *mother* and not the father in Virginia. And, Christian baptism did *not* give an exemption to slavery for an African or child of African descent.

Other laws quickly followed in succession. Of the many, one stipulated that the death of a slave during punishment was not a felony on the part of the master. (It was presumed he would not deliberately destroy his own property.) It was not illegal to wound or kill a runaway slave or one resisting arrest. It was unlawful for a slave to be armed with any weapon. It was unlawful for a slave "to presume to lift up his hand in opposition against any Christian."[53] Laws filled gaps in the system of slavery as the situations called for them. Still, a master had the legal right to manumit a slave, but growing numbers of free blacks in the Virginia population became worrisome. Could they encourage other slaves to seek freedom? Might freed blacks insight an insurrection? Thus in 1691, it was enacted that any emancipated slave was to leave Virginia within six months.[54] Free blacks were not wanted in the colony.

Historian Lorena Walsh describes the decades of 1640 to 1680 – the mid-seventeenth century – as the "Age of the Small Planter;" it was a critical time in the colony's development. Virginia planters began to invest substantially in an African work force. The lawmaking body in Virginia, the elected Burgesses, molded a system of laws that defined racial slavery that was separate from white indentured servitude. They developed this system of laws to protect their investment – and they defined their investment as *property*.[55]

The geographical differences in the North American colonies, however, largely defined labor needs and, as a result, created three distinctly different forms of slavery in these colonies. A non-plantation system dominated in the north where extensive farming did not take place, but domestic and skilled workers were desired. A plantation system developed in the Chesapeake colonies that required large numbers of unskilled laborers to tend tobacco plants and grow grain such as

---

[53] Ibid., 2:270, 299-30, and 481-482.
[54] Ibid., 3:86-88.
[55] Walsh, *Motives of Honor*, 122-144.

corn and wheat. Low-country planters in South Carolina and Georgia grew rice and indigo; they needed slave laborers to tend and harvest crops, but they also depended on domestic and skilled slaves in cities such as Charleston where many planters maintained principle residences. These three different forms of slavery systems can be clearly identified by mid-eighteenth century.[56]

In the Chesapeake region, Maryland and Virginia depended on slave labor at middling and large plantations where planters lived on their home "seat," overseeing outlying "quarters" or farms where tobacco and grain were grown as cash crops and animals were tended for consumption. Skilled slaves (such as blacksmiths, carpenters, and coopers) often lived near the planter's home seat; domestic slaves cooked, and tended the needs of the big house; and some slaves, selected as personal body slaves, waited on the master or other family members.[57] Throughout the colonial period, slavery existed as a legal institution and a "normal" feature of everyday life. All levels of society understood the system. The gentry and many middling planters and tradesmen generally owned slaves. They knew the laws and enforced them; the gentry in fact were the ones who wrote them. To a certain degree, lower white farmers and tenants were elevated in this caste system, although they mingled among slaves in daily life. Society defined the place of the "lesser sort" of the white population, and laws protected them from the harshest punishments that were reserved for slaves. Blacks knew their place at the bottom of the heap.

Somehow – despite all the oppression that a legal system and social divide created – enslaved people in North America survived. Moreover, the culture they created within these constraints developed a remarkable and unique blend of African traditions, European customs, and survival techniques. It is this creolized culture that has drawn historians, archeologists, sociologists, linguists, and many others into research and greater understanding of this African-American culture in recent decades.[58]

---

[56] Ira Berlin and Ronald Hoffman, eds., *Slavery and Freedom in the Age of the American Revolution* (Charlottesville: The University Press of Virginia, 1983), xvii.

[57] John Michael Vlach, *The Planter's Prospect: Privilege & Slavery in Plantation Paintings* (Chapel Hill: The University of North Carolina Press, 2002), 5-26. Vlach gives an interesting overview of plantations through paintings.

[58] Mechel Sobel, *The World They Made Together* (Princeton: Princeton University Press, 1987), 3-11; 233-242.

The relocation of Virginia's Capitol from Jamestown to the newly created city of Williamsburg in 1699 brought a comprehensive review of the colony's legal code in 1705. Slavery, with its restrictions and punishments placed on those of African descent, remained firmly in place. This judicial review clearly maintained the two legal tracks defined under law - one for the white population as indentured servants and the other for the black population as enslaved. The 1705 review of laws continued to allow a master his authority to free a slave, but in 1723, this power was transferred to the Royal Governor and his Council. Thereafter, any petition considered for a slave's manumission had to include recognition of "meritorious service" in order to consider his freedom.[59] Thus, the system of racially based slavery was now complete. The last loophole to freedom was closed. There was almost literally no way out slavery in Virginia. (See Table One.)

In the beginning, George Mason I, great-grandfather to George Mason of Gunston Hall, emigrated from England about 1651. He arrived in the Chesapeake in the period just as laws were beginning to shape the structure of slavery in Virginia. Over the remainder of his life, he purchased the labor he needed, probably both African slaves and white indentured servants. He quickly moved into the ranks of the gentry and as a legislator helped to mold and enact laws defining racial slavery across the next three decades of his life.

George Mason I (1629-1686)

George Mason I left Pershore in Worcestershire, England at the close of the English Civil War when the loyal supporters of King Charles II were defeated in Worcester.[60] Oliver Cromwell's newly formed government confiscated land and

---

[59] H.R. McIlwaine, et.al., eds., *Executive Journals of the Council of Colonial Virginia*. 6 Vols. (Richmond: Virginia State Library, 1927-1966), 4:199; 5:18; 5:55, 56, 60; 5: 140, 141;5: 191, 193; 5:195, 196; 5:214,215; 5:295, 298; 6:200; 6:290,291; 6:320; 6:334, 335; 6:450,451; 6:509; 6:526. Fewer than twenty slaves received their freedom under this process across a half century of time (1729-1773). It is interesting to note that in 1778 George Mason IV drew up the legislation to free a slave named Kitt for revealing a counterfeiting ring in Brunswick County. Kitt was freed; his owner, Hinchie Mabry, was compensated for his loss of property. Virginia Legislators would pass a law allowing owners to manumit slaves in 1782.
[60] As there are many generations of Mason family members with the first name George, many historians have given Roman numerals to the earliest six generations in Virginia to distinguish each. This method will be used here beginning with George Mason who immigrated from Pershore.

property of many Royalists. Some who had been loyal to the king simply fled England. Among many who emigrated from Worcestershire and Staffordshire to the Chesapeake region of North America were George Mason, the brothers Thomas and Gerard Fowke, and Giles Brent. These men's lives remained connected as they re-established life in the New World. George Mason I was about 22 years old when he arrived in the Chesapeake region.[61]

The first recorded document that refers to George Mason I in Virginia is in 1652 in Northumberland County where he was listed as a juryman. By 1656, now a Virginia militiaman, Captain George Mason, presented a certificate to the government stating that he had imported eighteen persons into the colony. This entitled him to patent 900 acres of land (50 acres for each person imported, including himself) in the recently formed county of Westmoreland.[62]

During these early decades of Virginia's settlement, those with financial means acquired land, accepted positions of authority in the community, purchased indentures for the labor of others, and (with luck) began to establish themselves as English country gentlemen. It was a chance for a new beginning. George Mason I ultimately established his residence or family seat on land along Accokeek Creek in Stafford County; his neighbor, Colonel Giles Brent, lived on the adjacent property. George Mason I married Mary French, another family with Pershore ties, and they had one surviving child, George Mason II. After Mary French Mason's death, George Mason I married the widow, Frances (Maddocks) Norgrave, but this couple had no children.

George Mason I served as a Stafford County sheriff and a justice of the peace and was elected a member of the House of Burgesses in the Virginia Assembly; he advanced to the rank of colonel in the Stafford County Militia during Bacon's Rebellion in 1676.[63]

---

[61] Copeland and MacMaster, *Five George Masons,* 1-10. Thomas Fowke returned to England after the restoration of the monarchy. Also: Miller, *Gentleman Revolutionary,* 4.

[62] Miller, *Gentleman Revolutionary,* 4,5. Helen Hill Miller says this is in Westmoreland County. Northumberland County was formed in 1645; Westmoreland County was formed from the western area of Northumberland in 1653; Lancaster County was formed in 1653; Stafford County was laid out in 1664; Prince William County was laid out in 1730; and Fairfax County was laid out in 1742.

[63] Copeland and MacMaster, *Five George Masons,* 13,14. Also Miller, *Gentleman Revolutionary,* 4. As a leader in the Stafford County Militia, George Mason and Giles Brent, and Gerard Fowke were fined and deprived of their offices in an incident that preceded Bacon's Rebellion.

His cash crop of tobacco brought fluctuating profits, but land leased to tenant farmers and ferry rights across the Occoquan River brought George Mason I a diversified financial base and local prestige. This status and wealth was passed down to his son, George Mason II, following his death in 1686. George Mason II was his father's only heir.[64]

During the years that George Mason I served as a Burgess, from about 1675 to his death in 1686, a number of laws building the structure of Virginia's slavery were passed. Of note were two laws: One determined the ages at which children should be considered working hands and become tithable, or taxable. It declared that "negroe children" at the age of twelve and "christian servants," or white children, at the age of fourteen became tithable. A second law concerning fears of slave insurrection was written that stated

> ...it shall not be lawfull for any negro...to carry or arme himself with any club, staffe, gunn, sword or any other weapon of defense or offence, nor to goe or depart from of[f] his masters ground without a certificate from his master...[and] that if any negroe...shall presume to lift up his hand in opposition against any christian...[will] receive thirty lashes on his bare back well laid on.[65]

George Mason I may or may not have participated in the direct passage of these laws, but as a land holder it can be presumed that he held some indentured servants and slaves as laborers on his plantation. Thus he would have had more than a passing interest in protecting his assets and would have looked favorably on such laws. It is also presumed that George Mason II inherited laborers – indentured servants or African slaves – upon his father's death, although no will or inventory has come to light.

---

[64] Copeland and MacMaster, *The Five George Masons,* 1-18, 38. Also: Kate Mason Rowland, *The Life of George Mason, 1725-1792, 2 Volumes* (New York: Russell & Russell, Inc., 1964), 1:16. No will or inventory survives to reveal the specifics of the wealth.
[65] Hening, *Statutes,* 2:479-480, 481-482.

George Mason II (c. 1660-1716)

George Mason II was born on the family's Accokeek plantation in Stafford County according to family tradition. The family's seat was located near the proposed town of Marlborough on the Potomac River.[66] As a second generation of landed Chesapeake planters, he utilized opportunities for acquiring additional property and his wealth increased primarily through raising tobacco. The crop was highly desirable in the European markets, but it posed problems for the planter in that it was both "land hungry," that is, it depleted the soil of nutrients, and was labor intensive throughout the 12 to 15 month cycle from seed to shipping.[67] As decreasing numbers of indentured servants arrived from England in the later part of the seventeenth century, planters turned increasingly to the importation of African slaves as laborers. In his lifetime, George Mason II became an established slave owner.

He also continued along the paths forged by his father solidifying his gentry status by serving in high positions in government including the House of Burgesses. With the desire for more land, he and others continued to push into the Indian territories. Rising to the rank of colonel, George Mason II fought in native uprisings on both Maryland and Virginia shores of the Potomac River. He eventually settled on land that today is known as Mason Neck after the Dogue Indians were forced from the peninsula.

George Mason II married three times. His first wife, Mary Fowke Mason, had seven surviving children: George, French, Nicholson, Ann, Mary, Elizabeth, and Simpha Rosa.[68] He had a daughter Catherine by his second wife Elizabeth Waugh Mason,

---

[66] Copeland and MacMaster, *Five George Masons,* 42-43. Also: John W. Reps, *Tidewater Towns, City Planning in Colonial Virginia and Maryland* (Williamsburg: The Colonial Williamsburg Foundation, 1972), 77-78. The House of Burgesses designated Marlborough, a proposed town on the Potomac Creek, to be a port of entry for Stafford County. George Mason II was a trustee for the town and owned its only tavern. The town failed to develop, however.

[67] As a "land hungry" crop, tobacco cultivation rapidly depleted soil nutrients (within 3-5 years) and then necessitated leaving it fallow for years before it could be cultivated again. This meant that planters required vast acreage in order to consistently plant a significant, saleable crop for export.

[68] Copeland and MacMaster, *Five George Masons,* 21. Mary Fowke was the daughter of Gerard Fowke who immigrated in the time of George Mason I. This family also owned a Maryland property known as Gunston Hall.

who died in childbirth. Only a daughter, Sarah, survived among four children born to his third wife, Sarah Taliaferro Mason.[69]

George Mason II died in 1716 during an epidemic that also took the lives of his son Nicholson and wife Sarah. In that year, his two surviving sons, George and French were already living on their own plantations on Pohick Creek. French Mason lived on the northern side of Pohick Creek and George Mason III lived at "Newtown" on the southern side. Twenty-two slaves were listed by name in his will, but did not include those he had already given to George Mason III, who received his share of the estate in an earlier deed of gift. It is not known how many slaves George Mason III acquired through deed of gift and inheritance, but it is likely that he received at least seven slaves as did his brothers, French and Nicholson. Nicholson Mason died before his father. George Mason III may have received some of the seven slaves designated for his brother. His seven slaves included: Charles, Maul, Billy, Nancy, Lucy, Nelly, and Jigg.[70]

George Mason III (c. 1690-1735)

George Mason III was about 26 or 27 years old at the time his father died. The family resided on the south of Pohick Creek in Virginia, but he had acquired additional land in Prince William County and Stafford County, Virginia and Charles County, Maryland. As in the generations before him, George Mason III served in government positions in Stafford County as sheriff, a colonel in the militia, and a representative to the House of Burgesses. He was also one of the men who accompanied Virginia Governor Alexander Spotswood on a noted expedition and exploration of the land beyond the Blue Ridge Mountains; George Mason III became known as one of the famous "Knights of the Golden Horseshoe."[71]

George Mason III married Ann Thomson in 1721. She was the daughter of Stevens Thomson, the attorney general for the colony of Virginia under Governor Francis Nicholson. The Mason family initially lived in Virginia on Doegs' Neck on the

[69] Ibid., 21-22.
[70] Fairfax County, Virginia Land Causes 2, 13-15. *Last Will of George Mason II*, Jan. 29, 1715.
[71] Miller, *Gentleman Revolutionary*, 23. Copeland and MacMaster, *Five George Masons*, 51-54.

property known as Newtown, but later relocated to Charles County, Maryland to the Stump Neck Plantation on the Chicamuxen Creek. George Mason IV was born at the Doegs' Neck home of Newtown on 11 December, 1725, Mary Thomson Mason was born in Charles County, Maryland in 1731, and Thomson Mason was born in Virginia in August, 1733.[72]

On an early March day in 1735 as George Mason III prepared to sail from his property in Virginia to return to his Maryland plantation, storm clouds gathered unexpectedly. By the time the ferry set off across the Potomac, a squall engulfed and capsized his vessel. Its principle occupant, George Mason III, drowned.[73] He was buried at Newtown on Doegs' Neck in Virginia. No other occupants of the lost vessel were recorded from this accident. How many were on board? Very likely one or more enslaved persons manned the ferry; others may have traveled with Mason that day. Did they drown as well, leaving their names – and those of their mourners – silent in the historical record?

George Mason III died intestate; that is, he left no will. According to prevailing English law, all of his property passed to his oldest son, young George Mason IV, about nine years old. His mother, Ann Thompson Mason, and his uncle, John Mercer, were named guardians of the three minor children.[74] George Mason IV's inheritance included all of his father's land in both Maryland and Virginia, or over five thousand acres. Ann Thomson Mason chose as her dower, land on the Virginia side of the Potomac and relocated her family there before the end of 1735.[75]

---

[72] Copeland and MacMaster, *Five George Masons*, 56.

[73] Ibid., 51. Miller, *Gentleman Revolutionary*, 25. Miller says he was sailing eastbound.

[74] The English laws of primogeniture stated that all real property went to the oldest son in such cases. George Mason III's sister Catherine married John Mercer of Marlborough Plantation. John Mercer was a lawyer and merchant. Mercer purchased lots in the town of Marlborough, an early planned community that was struggling to develop. He built his mansion, a mill, brewery, glass factory, and wharf there among other structures. After Mercer's death in 1768, the town plan dwindled. See Reps, *Tidewater Towns*, 77-78.

[75] Marylynn Salmon, *Women and the Law of Property in Early America* (Chapel Hill: The University of North Carolina Press, 1986), 151-156. Dower was a widow's life portion of her husband's land and property. In Virginia at the time of George Mason III's death, Ann Thomson Mason was entitled to life use of her choice of one-third of her husband's real property (land) and one-third of his slaves. Also, I am appreciative for comments and discussion in email communication with Lorena S. Walsh, 6 July 2015: "The usual practice was for the personal property (slaves, livestock, etc.) to be kept and worked undivided under the control of the administrator until the first child came of age, at which time that child would gain control of those slaves which he/she had been allotted, as well as a proportional share of other personal property."

Stump Neck Plantation

The Stump Neck Plantation in Charles County, Maryland had been the principal seat of the Mason family at the time of George Mason III's accidental drowning. Left behind were his wife, Ann Thomson Mason, and three young children: George (9), Mary (4), and Thomson (2). When the inventory to settle this Maryland estate was taken in August, the total value of all property there was in excess of £721 with the value of the slaves and indentured laborers alone at about half that amount or £353.[76] The family's primary home had sufficient furniture, linens, tableware, and cook ware to provide comfortable surroundings; more than 150 yards of various fabrics were listed that provided a substantial supply for clothing for the family and for the slaves and servants as well. Also inventoried was £75 worth of silver (listed as "336 Ozs [ounces] old plate.")

Twenty-two enslaved people made up the largest part of the plantation's value – and its work force. Included were: five men, **Rush, Dublin, Dick, Gambor,** and **Will** (all aged 30 except Gambor, 26) and five women, **Frank** ("a woman," 30), **Judith** (30), **Nan** (26), **Virgin** (40), and **Jo** (50), and three teenage girls: **Peg** (16), **Bridget** (14) and **Kit** (14). There were also young children among the slaves. Nan had just given birth the day before the inventory was taken and was listed with "her Child 1 day old." Additionally, eight more children ranged in age from 1 to 8 years old: **Sue** (8), **Dick** (4), **Jenny** (2 1/2), **Priscilla** (1 3/4), **Beck** (1), **Frank** (10), **Isaac** (7), and **Sarah** (8). Rush and Dublin were skilled men, listed as ship carpenters; Dick was a shoemaker. The other men and women probably tended the fields or did domestic chores. One was likely designated as the cook. The children may have had various jobs according to their ages and abilities.[77] Overall, the total population of enslaved adults was

---

[76] Maryland Hall of Records, Charles County Inventories 1735-1752, 13-15.Copeland and MacMaster, *Five George Masons,* 73. Inventories varied as to the amount of information taken. Many inventories provided ages, skills, and sometimes relationships among the slaves. The purpose was to give a monetary value to the decedent's property.

[77] See Appendix A. Peg, age 16, was tithable (taxable) according to the law and would be counted as a full working hand, thus an adult in this enumeration. Both African men and women were counted as tithable laborers, whereas white women were not considered tithable. Children often started work in the fields at a young age (3 or 4) to pull worms off tobacco plants or at small tasks requiring little knowledge of the cultivation process. They worked interspersed with adults or older children, possibly for only part of the day. Until a child could work a "full share" at the age of 16, they were provided half rations of food and clothing by the master. Nan's one day old child was the youngest child at the time the inventory was taken. See: Walsh, *Motives of Honor,* 22-24.

young – between the ages of 16 and 35, with the exception of Virgin, age 40, and Jo, age 50. The inventory gave no information as to the relationship of any of these slaves to each other.

It is possible that some – or all – of the men and the women listed in the inventory were slaves that George Mason III inherited from his father's estate when he died in 1716. If so, the youngest two adults, Gambor and Nan, would have been about ten years old that year. Nan might have been born in the Chesapeake, but Gambor was perhaps a newly purchased slave who endured the "middle passage" from Africa to North America.[78] George Mason III's brother, Nicholson Mason, was to have inherited a slave named Nancy, but he died before receiving his inheritance. George or his other surviving brother, French, likely became her owner. Thus, it is possible that this slave Nancy is the same person listed as "Nan" with "her child 1 day old" in the Stump Neck Inventory.

The inventory at Stump Neck also included six indentured male servants with their time left to serve: Daniel Davey (30) had six years remaining to serve; Charles Doughtery (21) had four years; James Codey (24) had six years; Richard Wote (no age given) had six years; Alexander Young, a carpenter, (35) had one and three-fourths years; and John Davis (24) had three months remaining to serve.

With the sudden death of a master, the slaves' circumstances were put into jeopardy. A man's unresolved debts required the liquidation of property for settlement of his estate – and the most easily sold property was often the slaves themselves. Laborers, both enslaved and indentured, were bought and sold on a regular basis and brought relatively consistent prices and ready capital. The biggest fear for any slave was the threat of separation from family, especially the separation of a child from his mother. Although far from complete, the surviving Mason family documents do not indicate that slaves were sold following the death of George Mason III.

Stump Neck was a working tobacco plantation and the residence of the Mason family. As such, domestic labor (cooking, dairying, laundry, sewing, child care, etc.)

---

[78] Walsh, *Motives of Honor,* 201-203. Between 1698 and 1729 Britain became the leading provider of slave laborers in the Chesapeake with more than half of the Africans coming from the Bight of Biafra. These decades were the turning point in the region to slave labor from indentured servitude. Gambor's name may be a reference to the African region of Gambia.

as well as agricultural work (tending the cash crop of tobacco, growing corn, and vegetables, and raising animals) kept the enslaved and indentured workers occupied. Rush and Dublin as ship carpenters, most likely spent much of their time building or maintaining vessels for the transport of goods and persons to and from the Maryland and Virginia shores of the Potomac River. The indentured servant Alexander Young was referred to only as a "carpenter;" perhaps his skills were primarily used in the construction and maintenance of buildings or fences. Slave Dick was a shoemaker, supplying shoes for the slaves and possibly the white family.

This community of workers – both black and white – probably lived in a few separate structures allotted to them. When their work day ended, they spent what little time remaining eating meals and attending to their own lives and those of their children. They struggled daily to survive. As a slave grew older and was unable to work a full day, he or she often watched the youngest children during work time. Among the adult slaves at Stump Neck, Jo (50), was the "elder" in the community; she may have been relieved from some of the daily work load and thus became responsible for minding the very youngest slave children. She could have also tended the slaves' garden and prepared food. As the oldest in the slave community, Jo held a place of esteem. She maintained the memory or history of the slave community and possibly knew stories of the "Middle Passage" or African home-land to pass on to the generations below her.

What were the relationships of these people to each other? The inventory lists individuals in seemingly random order and only Nan with her one-day old (un-named) child provides a family connection. Naming patterns, however, allow for speculation that Frank (10) was the child of the woman Frank (30) and Dick (4) was the son of Dick (30, the shoemaker), but no other links are apparent.[79] English, or pidgin English, may have been the main (or at least encouraged) language spoken at Stump Neck. Almost all of the slaves' names on the inventory reflect Anglican names, likely imposed on the slaves by the owner. Only Gambor's name – perhaps

---

[79] Philip D. Morgan, *Slave Counterpoint, Black Culture in the Eighteenth-Century Chesapeake & Lowcountry* (Chapel Hill: University of North Carolina Press, 1998), 451-452. Sobel, *The World They Made Together*, 158-159.

an African name - was an exception. Names like London, Parus [Paris], or Dublin reflect a master's choice of a classical name imposed on a newly purchased African.[80]

Prince William County, Virginia

The second inventory taken after the death of George Mason III in 1735 was on his Virginia property in Prince William County and reflects a smaller farming operation with fewer workers. Limited furnishings and cooking utensils, hoes, axes, grind stones, a "Musket" and a "long Gun," cattle, horses, sheep, and hogs, as well as a array of fabric and clothing items made up the principle list of itemized goods. Only thirteen names of slaves and indentured servants were listed there.[81] This inventory unfortunately provides less information describing the people than the one at Stump Neck: no ages and no skills for the individuals are given. They were designated only as "man," "woman," "boy," or "girl," but monetary values were listed for each.

London, Winsor, and **Matt** each held a value of £22; **Parus,** [meaning Paris?] was valued at £20. **Nan Wilson,** a "Mulatto woman" was valued at £19.[82] The boys, **Jack, Stephen** and **Job,** were valued at £14, 12, and 10 respectively; the girls, **Lucy,** and **Jenny,** a "Mulatto girl," were valued at £6 and 4 respectively; the decreasing values probably reflected younger ages among the children. The combined value of all the slaves was £141 or approximately half of the total inventory value of almost £304. There were three male indentured servants, but no ages or time left in service was listed for them. They included James (no last name), John Webb, and Morgan Carpenter. James and Morgan Carpenter perhaps had longer to serve with values of £7 each; John Webb's value was £5.

---

[80] Morgan, *Slave Counterpoint,* 159-170. Lorena S. Walsh, From *Calibar to Carter's Grove* (Charlottesville: University Press of Virginia, 1997), 546-547. Sobel, *The Word They Made Together,* 154-160. Many times slaves retained another name in the slave community as well as the one recognized by the owner thus rejecting the classical or geographic names.

[81] Prince William County, Virginia Will Book C, 1734-1744, 49-50. See also Appendix B.

[82] It is presumed that Nan Wilson was enslaved. It is interesting that she had a surname noted in the inventory.

Nan Wilson was a "Mulatto woman." Jenny, the "Mulatto girl," was possibly Nan's daughter. No other ties are evident, but it is of note that only one woman was living on this plantation.[83] The inventory reveals little else about the people on this Virginia property. Was there an overseer who directed the work? Or did George Mason III direct the work himself before his death, crossing the Potomac River at regular intervals to give orders, evaluate progress, and take corrective measures if needed? If so, these slaves were working somewhat autonomously at their agricultural duties. During the years following her husband's untimely death, Ann Thomson Mason filed disbursement documents in the county to show the management of the assets (the slaves) she used to support her three children as well as to preserve her son George Mason IV's inheritance.

Before the end of the year in 1735, Ann Thomson Mason moved her family from Maryland to the property on Chopawamsic Creek in Prince William County, Virginia.[84] The relocation brought her into closer proximity to John Mercer's Marlborough home. He was her brother-in-law and joint guardian to her children and as a prominent lawyer he could provide her with legal advice and guidance about the children's education. The Disbursement Records filed in Prince William County, Virginia for the years 1735 to 1742 of Ann Thomson Mason list the expenses that were incurred for her children and the income for that property that was divided into thirds for the support for George, Mary, and Thomson. As part of the income, these records list the value of the tobacco grown, or "shares made," by individual slaves during these years. Additionally, rents from tenants on other Virginia land held in trust contributed to the financial support of the children. Rents (usually paid in tobacco) provided the larger part of the income.[85]

Of the twelve slaves who made up the work force on the Virginia plantation, London seems to be the most capable and reliable worker. In the years from 1735 to 1742 he provided a "full share" in every year although he was continually sent to work lands in Maryland. Parus was also a dependable worker. In 1736, he and London were the only two slaves listed in the disbursements as bringing in their "shares;" Parus worked land in Virginia. From 1737 on, Matt and Windsor were

---

[83] See Appendix B.
[84] Copeland and MacMaster, *The Five George Masons,* 74.
[85] Prince William County Will Book C, 1734-1744, 275-290.

reported making their "shares" in the work force. Jack, probably a boy approaching 10 or 12 joined the men in 1737; Stephen, another boy, joined them in 1738. Nan Wilson, the mulatto woman, remained the only woman at the Virginia property. She was "sick" in 1737 and "mostly sick" in 1738. The disbursements show that both Drs. Tenant and Brown were paid for medicine or medical attention for Nan in those years. The reason for her illness may have been pregnancy; a notation in 1740 indicated that she now had two children, Will and Johnny.[86] The other slaves on the Virginia property were all children apparently too young to contribute to "full shares." (See Table Two.)

In addition to growing tobacco for income, the slaves also grew corn, wheat, and beans – and probably myriad other vegetables for consumption. A specific notation was made that these additional crops were not monetarily evaluated for the disbursements. The documents filed also consistently remarked that "there is no charge of Cloathing or maintaining the Negroes or for their Bedding" to the estate. These charges would have put the estate in debt. That implies that the costs of housing, clothing, and feeding these enslaved men, women, and children was more than the value of the "shares" they made. It is probable that Ann Thomson Mason supplied the slaves' needs from her dower property profits. One other major source of income was leased property. Rent was collected in tobacco and or in cash and recorded in the disbursement records. (See Table Three.)

The years 1740 and 1741 were the most productive in the disbursement documents as two of the boys apparently were now old enough to tend the fields of tobacco and Nan Wilson worked both of those years as well. Now however, both London and Matt consistently worked in Maryland at Stump Neck making their "full shares" there.

By about 1740, construction and repair began on both the Virginia and Maryland properties. Expenses for carpenters, nails, and tools at another Virginia property, Dogue's Neck (in Fairfax County), were enumerated in the disbursement papers. In 1742, two tobacco houses were constructed there, one 52 feet long and the other 30 feet long indicating increased development of the quarter on Dogue's Neck. That same year also saw the construction of two smaller tobacco houses, one 40

---

[86] Ibid. Copeland and MacMaster, *The Five George Masons*, 78.

feet long and one 30 feet long, at Stump Neck in Maryland. The slaves were probably the primary labor source for construction; Rush and Dublin at Stump Neck (the ships' carpenters) were probably tasked to work on these buildings. The indentured servant, Alexander Young, also a carpenter, had been released from his contract by this time. However, white carpenters could have been hired if needed.

The disbursement documents specifically indicate the yearly profit made on the Maryland and Virginia properties. Ann Thomson Mason carefully recorded the profit on the Maryland property her son George Mason IV inherited under the laws of primogeniture. (See Table Four.) She divided profit from the Virginia property equally among the three children for their upkeep. One thing is apparent from the disbursement records that were filed: Ann Thomson Mason learned quickly how to be a plantation manager and an accountant. She capably utilized and recorded the assets that supported her three "orphaned" children after the unexpected death of George Mason III.[87] John Mercer, her brother-in-law, co-guardian to the children, lawyer, and planter, provided support and assistance to her, but Ann Thomson Mason appears capable in performing the task of guardian.

Court documents for disbursement after 1742 apparently have not survived. George Mason IV reached the age of 21 in 1746 and took control of his inheritance. Undoubtedly, he watched the management styles of both his guardians as he became an adult. His mother provided a strong role model, monitoring details of the family's assets, carefully recording purchases for each of her children, and making decisions regarding plantation management. John Mercer, his uncle, may have provided guidance for the children's education and certainly would have given a young man with an eager desire to learn access to his own considerable library with books on law, science, history, literature, and architecture.[88] Mercer, a prominent and prosperous attorney, was also an avid land speculator and member of the Ohio Company, which may have given George Mason IV an advantage in that organization. Mason was appointed the Company's treasurer in 1750, a position which he held for the remainder of his life. However, Mercer provided a poor role model as a slave master. His management style proved highly detrimental to his work force. Historian Lorena Walsh writes:

[87] At this time, orphans were defined as children who had lost their father, not both parents.
[88] Rutland, *Papers of George Mason*, cxii-cxiii. C. Malcolm Watkins, *The Cultural History of Marlborough, Virginia* (Washington D.C.: U.S. Government Printing Office, 1967), 146-188.

By 1753, [John Mercer] had purchased a total of 112 slaves, most of them newly imported Africans, including a number from the Bight of Biafra, at a cost of more than thirty-two hundred pounds sterling....Between 1731 and 1750, 46 of the 89 slaves he had purchased by [1753] had died, and an additional 3 had been sold....Mercer's mostly imported slaves were not only sickly but also desperately unhappy. One hanged himself, and several were chronic runaways. Another sign of trouble was frequent turnover among Mercer's overseers.[89]

By the time George Mason IV reached his majority in 1746 he had watched and learned much about plantation management from his guardians. As a positive role model, his mother, Ann Thomson Mason, skillfully managed assets to provide for the needs and education for her three children. She kept separate records for the slaves' work on the lands that George Mason would inherit. She moved slaves to provide the most profitable work outcome. She dealt with the all of the laborers' needs on a daily basis and provided medical attention when necessary to the slaves. The number of slaves remained constant (or grew through natural increase) during the years that records are available. She filed her records with court officials on a regular, yearly basis.

His uncle, John Mercer, provided young Mason with a somewhat different role model in his management of land and slaves. Mercer actively speculated on and acquired new land for his plantation through the Ohio Company and likely assisted his nephew in obtaining the position of Treasurer in that company in 1749. Mercer also purchased large numbers of new slaves for his plantation at a high cost. But Mercer saw exceptionally high mortality rates among these new slaves. Young George Mason may have been aware of problems and practices at Marlborough that led to the runaways and slave deaths there.

Then, in 1746, young George Mason IV stepped onto the Virginia landscape as a land-owning, gentry gentleman and slave master. Ready to take his place in the upper level of the colony's society, the "rules" were already formed for him. Commerce and trade supported the demand for his tobacco crop and provided a means of acquisition of slave laborers from Africa. The legal structure encompassed

---

[89] Walsh, *Motives of Honor,* 514-518.

a thorough system to ensure that his slave labor force maintained its place and it upheld the punishment of his slaves if they did not comply. But – as Mason would learn more directly – slaves were human beings.

Just *how* did slaves live day-to-day and endure the oppression circumscribed on them in this tightly bound system that classified them as property and not as persons? That story is told by the enslaved people themselves. Patched together in the last half-century by archeologists, researchers, and historians, it is a remarkable story of survival.[90]

---

[90] Studies of the forced migration of Africans have calculated that approximately eleven million people were brought to the Americas in the transatlantic slave trade. For every African brought into North America, twelve or thirteen were brought into the Caribbean Islands. (Numerically, the calculations are 388,747 into North America and 4,371,000 into the Caribbean according to the figures in the Trans-Atlantic Slave Trade Data Base). Heavy mortality in the West Indies accounted for the continual need to replace laborers, whereas natural increase among slaves in North America occurred. Richard S. Dunn, *A Tale of Two Plantations, Slave Life and Labor in Jamaica and Virginia* (Cambridge, Massachusetts: Harvard University Press, 2014), 1-2. See also: www.slavevoyages.org.

Chapter Two:

Chesapeake Plantation Life in the Eighteenth Century

Construction for slave housing such as this reconstructed slave quarter at Carter's Grove Plantation (circa 2001) might be log and daub or clapboard and structures were often earth fast. They typically had a dirt floor (packed clay) which allowed for the interior pits to be dug to hold personal belongings, root vegetables, or even stolen goods to be stored and out of sight. Chimneys, also made of log and daub, were constructed such that they leaned outward from the side of the house. Thus, if they caught fire, they might possibly be pried loose and pushed away from the structure and save the house.

$\mathcal{G}$eorge Mason IV, born in 1725, lived his entire life in a slave society. A gentleman by birth, this way of life seemed "normal" in the Chesapeake region in the eighteenth century. Slaves afforded Mason and his family a source of labor and luxury. Those individuals of African descent, legally bound in this status, suffered life-long oppression, a loss of their civil rights, and lived constant fear of being sold and separated from family.[91]

Many written comments in legal documents, journals or diaries, and personal letters give insight into what slave life was like, albeit from the gentry's point of view. Occasionally, this way of life was critiqued by traveling visitors who viewed it from the outside and provided a broader world perspective. Reading between the lines, many of these comments shed truer light on the slave's perspective of life in slavery.

But getting deeper into the "real" story requires another approach. In recent decades, archeology has played a key role in this new examination of slave life from the "bottom rail," as some historians have phrased it. Evidence compiled from archeological research has revealed a clearer picture of daily life among Chesapeake slaves. Recovered material culture – the things of everyday use – in the excavated living spaces of known eighteenth century slave sites, along with a closer re-examination of primary documents and closer attention to oral history, now brings far greater understanding about slave life and slave culture in Virginia and Maryland. This new investigation paints a vivid picture of how enslaved people managed to survive (and even manipulate their oppressive conditions) and to adapt and retain some knowledge and memory of African heritage. Slaves molded and amalgamated their native customs and ideals into the English life style forced on them – all while living in an impoverished and legally restrictive environment where the reality of freedom was denied.

---

[91] Berlin, *Many Thousands Gone,* 1-14. Berlin describes *societies with slaves* as one in which slaves are only one form of labor. Throughout the seventeenth century in Virginia, African labor was a developing source along with white indentured labor. *Slave societies* were societies where master-slave relationships formed a societal model. By the beginning of the eighteenth century, Virginia had such a legal and social model; Virginia had become a *slave society.*

The study of slavery in the eighteenth century Chesapeake region is essentially a study of survival. It also reveals the elements of a uniquely African-American culture that developed in colonial America. Understanding eighteenth century Chesapeake slave life begins with examining life peculiar to that time and place; it is also the period when George Mason's plantation Gunston Hall developed and flourished.[92] Mason, his family, and the slaves they owned, experienced the "push and pull" of living in a *slave society*. This chapter looks more closely at the lives of the slaves in this time and in this region for a better understanding of their daily routines and restrictions; it helps to portray the way slaves coped and survived within this oppressive institution.

Gunston Hall is fortunate to have the surviving mansion where George Mason lived for more than half his lifetime. A finite number of letters and documents relating to Mason and other family members have also survived, but the knowledge of Mason's day-to-day plantation management through journals and records he likely kept is lost. One personal family account describing his plantation management comes from his son John who wrote his *Recollections* in the 1830s:

> Thus my father had among his slaves: carpenters, coopers, sawyers, blacksmiths, tanners, curriers, shoemakers, spinners, weavers & knitters, and even a distiller. His woods furnished timber and plank for the carpenters and coopers and charcoal for the blacksmith; his cattle killed for his own consumption or for sale, supplied skins for the tanners, curriers & shoemakers; and his sheep gave wool and his fields produced cotton and Flax for the weavers and spinners; and his orchards fruit for the distiller. His carpenters & sawyers built and kept in repair all the dwelling houses, barns, stables, ploughs, harrows, gates, &c. on the plantations & the out houses at the home house. His coopers made the hogsheads the tobacco was prized in, and the tight casks to hold the cyder & other liquors. The tanners and curriers with the proper vats &c., tanned & dressed the skins as well for upper as for soul [sic] leather to the full amount of the consumption of the estate and the shoemakers made them into shoes for the Negroes. A professional shoemaker was hired for 3 or 4 months in the year to come and make up shoes for the

---

[92] Walsh, *Calibar to Carter's Grove*, 136-137, 145-152.

white part of the family. The blacksmith did all the iron work required by the establishment such as making & repairing ploughs, harrows, teeth, chains, bolts, &c., &c. The spinners, weavers, & knitters made all the coarse cloth & stockings used by Negroes and some of the finer texture worn by the white family – nearly all worn by the children of it. The art of distilling from grain was not them among us... but [at a] few public distilleries. All these operations were carried on at the home house, and their results distributed as occasion required to the different plantations. Moreover, all the Beeves and hogs for consumption or sale were driven up and slaughtered there at the proper seasons, and whatever was to be preserved was to be salted & packed away for after distribution.[93]

While John Mason's *Recollections* provide an important primary source regarding his father's management of his slave plantation, it falls short of divulging information of day-to-day life. Many other Chesapeake planters' records do exist, however. Some give great detail and reveal much about life on tobacco plantations and combine to provide a broader – although perhaps generic – image of slavery in the eighteenth century.

Archeology at many sites provides an important component to understanding as well. Combined with a variety of primary source documentation, a more expansive portrait of daily life for the two hundred thousand enslaved men, women, and children who lived in Virginia in the eighteenth century emerges.[94] Virginia's slave system was created and supported by laws and customs that developed throughout the seventeenth century. Part of that structure required planters to provide their slaves with the basic necessities of food, clothing, and shelter. An interesting picture of these "necessities" emerges.

---

[93] Dunn, ed., *Recollections*, 63, 64.
[94] Evarts B. Greene and Virginia D. Harrington, *American Population Before the Federal Census of 1790* (New York: Columbia University Press, 1932), 141-142. Approximately 40% of Virginia's nearly half million population was of African descent by the time of the American Revolution.

$\mathcal{A}$ $\mathcal{P}$lace to $\mathcal{L}$ive

Slaves provided the vast majority of the agricultural and domestic labor in Virginia. Planters encouraged skills such as carpentry and blacksmithing among some of their slaves as needs arose, but most slaves tilled the soil and took care of farm animals. Blacksmiths, carpenters, coopers, etc., as John Mason described above, were vitally important to the maintenance of the plantation. Domestic skills such as cooking, laundering, or dairying provided slave owners with the comfort and luxury sought after in establishing a proper English life style. Skilled slaves usually lived and worked in structures close to the owner's house in smaller outbuildings made of brick, clapboard, or log construction. These buildings also provided slaves places for sleeping, eating, and socializing when work was completed for the day. As these structures were in close proximity to the master's own mansion and probably visible to visitors, they were often reasonably well constructed; some had brick or wooden floors, glass panes in the windows, secure doors (sometimes with locks), and, occasionally, interior walls that were finished with plaster or whitewash.[95]

Typically, kitchens, laundries, and even stables served as work places and home for many domestic slaves. In the most elaborate architectural plantation designs, wings or "flankers" were added to the master's house to provide the needed domestic services and housing. Examples of this extended arrangement can be seen in George Washington's home at Mt. Vernon in Fairfax County, in John Tayloe's mansion known as Mt. Airy in Richmond County, or in Thomas Jefferson's

---

[95] Cary Carson and Carl R. Lounsbury, eds., *The Chesapeake House* (Chapel Hill: University of North Carolina Press, 2013), 163-167.

Monticello in Albemarle County. Also, the accurately reconstructed two-story, kitchen-laundry-servants' hall of the Peyton Randolph house in Colonial Williamsburg, with a connector passageway to the main house, depicts this idea as well. On a majority of Virginia plantations and in its cities or towns, many slaves with special skills both lived and worked in close and watchful proximity to their white families.[96]

At Mount Vernon, George Washington's cook and her husband lived in the kitchen.[97] Joseph Ball's favored slave Aron was housed "in the Kitchin [sic] Loft" at his Morrattico plantation, remaining there until a "framed House Twelve foot Long and ten foot wide [could be] built for him...."[98] At the Randolph's Tuckahoe Plantation in Goochland County, structures close to the main house included the typical work places such as the kitchen, smokehouse, storehouse, and dairy, but also included four one-story buildings, each with two rooms, that provided domestic slave housing. A central fireplace in these buildings supplied heat to each room; the lofts above served as living quarters. From six to as many as twenty four slaves were housed in these spaces on the Randolph property.[99]

Williamsburg provides an important picture of eighteenth century housing for domestic and skilled slaves who served their master's needs. The city of nearly 2000 people included predominantly prosperous merchants, artisans, and gentry families. But fully one half of the city's population was made up of enslaved workers who tended to domestic chores or provided a wide variety of skills to their owners. Nearly all the slaves were housed within the city's numerous dependency buildings. Peyton Randolph's kitchen, laundry, and quarters (connected by a covered passage to the main house) provided space for the largest number of enslaved people in the city at the time of the Revolution. Twenty seven individuals lived and worked on the Randolph's property in the center of town.[100]

---

[96] Ibid., 128-130, 170-172. Vlach, *The Planter's Prospect*, 11-21.

[97] Sobel, *The World They Made Together*, 143.

[98] Carson and Lounsbury, *Chesapeake House*, 160-163.

[99] Clifton Ellis and Rebecca Ginsburg, Eds., *Cabin, Quarter, Plantation* (New Haven: Yale University Press, 2010), 122-126.

[100] The Virginia Almanac for the Year of Our Lord God, 1776 (Williamsburg, Virginia, 1776). The total population was listed as 1880 with 894 white persons (47.6%) and 986 blacks (52.4%). Will and Inventory of Peyton Randolph, 1775: York County, Virginia Wills and Inventories, XXII, 308-310. Carson and Lounsbury, *Chesapeake House*, 129.

Further west in the city, near the Governor's Palace, Thomas Everard's property included a separate kitchen, a two room structure with a hard packed clay or "dirt" floor that provided both a work room and a sleeping area for his slaves. George Wythe's slave cook, Lydia, had a similar two-room kitchen just across Palace Green from Everard. At the east end of town, businesses such as Wetherburn's Tavern, housed twelve slaves in a large combination kitchen-laundry building at the rear of the property. It was Henry Wetherburn's slaves who maintained his excellent reputation. They cleaned rooms, did laundry, cooked and served meals, tended gardens, smoked meats, and brandied cherries and other fruits for the tavern guests. It was at this tavern that George Mason lodged when he visited the city for meetings for the Ohio Company in the 1750s. He likely stayed there also when he served in the House of Burgesses in 1758.[101]

For skilled slaves, whether in cities or on plantations, the environment of work and daily life was one in the same; it was within proximity and under the watchful eye of the master himself. It is interesting to note that some slaves had locks on doors to their living quarters. Even with few possessions, a lock and key established a sense of defined personal space to others who lived near them – including the master or his family.[102]

Most Chesapeake slaves however – perhaps 90 percent - had no skills beyond farming and tending animals.[103] For George Mason and other planters, a majority of their slaves worked and lived on outlying farms or quarters some distance from the master's home or "seat" as it was often called.[104] Clusters of perhaps 20 to 25 slaves lived in just a few cabins made of log and daub (mud) or clapboard construction and were directed in their daily routines by an overseer.[105] The overseer, usually a paid white man, also lived at the quarter with the slaves, most likely in a separate

[101] Mary A. Stephenson, "Mr. Wetherburn's Tavern: Block 9 Colonial Lots 20 and 21," Colonial Williamsburg Foundation Library Research Report Series 226 Colonial Williamsburg Foundation Library, 1965. Wetherburn died in 1760; Mason may have found accommodations after that at another tavern or stayed with friends in the city. York County, Virginia Wills (21), 36-43.
[102] Ellis and Ginsburg, Cabin, Quarter, Plantation, 135-137. Barbara J. Heath, Hidden Lives (Charlottesville: University Press of Virginia, 1999), 62-64.
[103] Approximately half of Virginia's population was white and unskilled as well.
[104] Carson and Lounsbury, Chesapeake House, 157. The term "quarter" might refer to a building, a farm, or to a slave cabin or group of cabins.
[105] Walsh, Calibar to Carter's Grove, 19, 20; 90; 181,182.

structure with his own family, if married.[106] Constructed by slave carpenters, these buildings (usually one or two room structures with a loft area) followed typical Chesapeake construction methods. These houses provided meager shelter; they had only wooden shutters to keep out wind and rain (no glass in window openings), a packed clay or dirt floor, and unfinished interior walls with mud or rag chinking to keep out drafts.

Gunston Hall's living areas for Mason's slaves also included a cluster of log houses somewhere on the northwest side of the lawn where, "...skirted by a wood, just far enough within which to be out of sight, was a little village called <u>Log-Town</u>....Here lived several families of the slaves serving about the mansion house."[107] This unique arrangement gave some of George Mason's slaves autonomy in their lives. They effectively "commuted" to work at the master's home.

Although the slave master dictated the materials and style for construction of housing, the occupants at the quarters modified some aspects of their living spaces and even retained some African customs. Excavated archeological sites have revealed the presence of in-ground holes or pits inside slave houses. Initially referred to by archeologists as "root cellars," these pits held interesting material objects such as ceramic sherds, coins, buttons, tools, utensils, and faunal remains.[108] They frequently served as a storage place or even a hiding place for personal items. Some belongings may have been obtained legitimately through purchases or even given by masters. Some were stolen. In September 1770, Landon Carter, determined to find out which of his "servants" [meaning slaves] stole a butter pot from his dairy house, ordered "Billy Beale to search all their holes and boxes." Carter was aware of where slaves kept personal items.[109]

---

[106] Ibid., 181. Some of George Mason IV's overseers are identified. William Green was at Hallowing Point, Charles Neal was at Little Hunting Creek, and James Smith was at Dogue Neck. Two other overseers were mentioned by first names only: Charles (Neal?) and Grover. Rutland, *Papers of George Mason,* 1162, 1226,967, 1246, and 1248. Nace was listed as the "Black overseer" at the Occoquan Quarter in George Mason V's inventory. See Appendix L. Copeland and MacMaster, *Five George Masons,* 239.
[107] Dunn, ed., *Recollections,* 59. Underlining in original text.
[108] William M. Kelso, *Kingsmill Plantations, 1619-1800* (New York: Academic Press, Inc., 1984), 200-205. William M. Kelso, *Archeology at Monticello* (Thomas Jefferson Memorial Foundation: Monticello Monograph Series, 1997), 82-102. Barbara J. Heath, *Hidden Lives* (Charlottesville: University Press of Virginia, 1999), 27-43. Walsh, *Calibar to Carter's Grove,* 191-192.
[109] Jack P. Greene, Ed., *The Diary of Colonel Landon Carter of Sabine Hall, 1752-1778,* 2 Vols. (Richmond: The Virginia Historical Society, 1987), 495. Beale was an overseer.

Another custom of African retention can be seen in slave's garden fences, which were sometimes erected in a circular pattern. The yards between buildings were open living spaces and swept clean of debris and rubbish. These areas served as outdoor cooking and gathering places for the slaves who lived in the quarter. As in Africa, much living was centered outside, not inside the structures.[110]

Slave's living accommodations varied considerably whether near the master's house or far from his view. But small, important elements of African carryover in the use of interior space, within the yards between buildings, or the placement of fences made subtle, personal changes to slaves' lives.

"...for want of Good Covering a nights."

Slave owners provided some basic material needs such as clothing, shoes, food, a cook pot, and perhaps a few dishes. Certain standards became accepted as normal. As with most goods, masters provided blankets for their slaves on a rationed basis, usually one new blanket per year. Journals and accounts frequently list blankets among the items distributed along with clothing. For example, in October 1756, Joseph Ball instructed his nephew:

> Let the Negroes have Good Warm Clothing, and in Time: and let Each Bed have a New Cotton Blanket of Two Breadths and Two yards & a Quarter long; they catch their Deaths for want of Good Covering a nights.[111]

Concerned about getting good value for his money, George Washington bought large quantities of blankets at a time. In September, 1791, he wrote his secretary Tobias Lear in Philadelphia to suspend original instructions he first sent to purchase blankets there until Washington himself could inspect a shipment of "Dutch Blanketing" newly arrived in Alexandria, the "only sort of them which are applicable to my use are...'Stripped Duffells...'."[112] Then, in early October he wrote

---

[110] Heath, *Hidden Lives*, 27-43.

[111] The Letterbook of Joseph Ball (1743-1759), Library of Congress, Washington, D.C. (microfilm M-21, Colonial Williamsburg Foundation), 22 October, 1756.

[112] Dorothy Twohig, ed., *The Papers of George Washington, Presidential Series 8, March – September 1791* (Charlottesville: University Press of Virginia, 1999), 25-27. Washington's letter was dated 26 September, 1791.

Lear, "I by no means like the prices, or quality, of the Blankets in Alexandria and scarcely know what Judgement [sic] to form of those in Philadelphia: but if while hesitating between the two I should miss both, it would be bad indeed, as my People would in that case be in distress the ensuing Winter."[113] Washington finally deferred to Lear to decide on the quality of the Philadelphia goods. Lear wrote that he considered the Philadelphia blankets a good choice as they were "said to be from Yorkshire, from whence the best and most substantial course woolens are imported...."[114] Lear confirmed the purchase for Washington of one hundred of the "largest" and "best quality" and one hundred of the "middle size, but good quality" blankets.[115] For Washington – the owner of the largest number of slaves in Fairfax County, Virginia – and other planters to be sure, a large purchase of two hundred blankets was not to be taken lightly.[116]

Slaves' bedding varied considerably. A slave could sleep on the floor, on the ground, or perhaps on straw piled in a corner with a blanket for cover. Some masters ordered construction of beds (built up off the ground) within the slave's quarters.[117] A few had actual mattresses (stuffed with anything from straw to feathers). One runaway slave "took with him a good feather bed, blankets, cotton sheets, and a blue rug...."[118] Joseph Ball's man Aron had an impressive list of possessions including

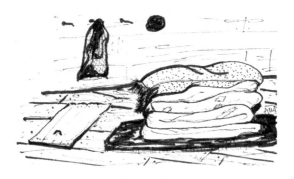

---

[113] Ibid., 57, 58. Letter dated 7 October, 1791.
[114] Ibid., 70-73. Letter dated 11 October, 1791.
[115] Ibid.
[116] Fritz Hirschfeld, *George Washington and Slavery, A Documentary Portrayal* (Columbia: University of Missouri Press, 1997), 16. In an inventory that Washington took in 1786, there were 103 slaves in his ownership and 113 dower slaves for a total of 216 slaves at Mount Vernon.
[117] Morgan, *Slave Counterpoint,* 114. Walsh, *Calibar to Carter's Grove,* 90.
[118] Lathan A. Windley, compiled by, *Runaway Slave Advertisements, Volume 1, Virginia and North Carolina* (Westport, CT: Greenwood Press, 1983), 365.

a "Large Matress [sic] stuffed well with flocks and stitched with tufts, and a bolster filled with feathers, the Mattress & Bolster both besides their Ticks having Ozenbrigs cases; and two new coverleds, and other old Bedclothes...."[119] Fine bedding indeed! But it was not to be placed on a fine bedstead; Ball directed that "one of the worst of my old Bedsteads [be] cut short & fit for his Mattress...."[120]

Foodways

Within the farm quarters slaves cooked and ate their meals when time was allowed or the workday was done. Great attention has been given recently to slave food-ways: the foods they prepared and ate as well as the cooking and serving utensils they used. Archaeological evidence reveals substantial information on both the diet and the objects used in food service. Slaves on large Virginia plantations generally possessed imported English dishwares. Ceramic sherds found at the slave quarter at Carter's Grove Plantation outside Williamsburg included a dominance of undecorated creamware (about 85%), as well as white salt-glazed stoneware and delftware.[121] "Mulberry Row" excavations at Thomas Jefferson's home Monticello also revealed mainly creamware and pearlware ceramic items.[122] These ceramic wares were imported goods from England. Plates and bowls were the most frequently found type of vessel at Carter's Grove and typical pieces included a

---

[119] Ball, *Letter Book*, 23 April, 1754.
[120] Ibid.
[121] Patricia Samford, "Carter's Grove Slave Quarters Study" (Unpublished: Department of Archaeological Research, Colonial Williamsburg Foundation, Williamsburg, VA, 1988), 4, 5.
[122] William M. Kelso, "Mulberry Row: Slave Life at Thomas Jefferson's Monticello," Archaeology, (September-October, 1986), 32. Considerable Chinese export porcelain, including fifteen matching underglazed blue plates, was also found at that site.

"Queen's" rim soup plate (c. 1760) and an octagonal salt-glazed stoneware plate.[123] Most of the ceramics found in these archeological sites showed unusually heavy usage. They were generally noticeably stained and scratched; often the ceramic glaze was completely worn away.[124] The sherds reveal, however, that regardless of such heavy usage, dishwares were rarely chipped on the edges. This is of significance because of a generally accepted idea that planters handed down broken or discarded dishes. Rather, it seems that larger plantation owners may have either passed down less fashionable dishware as they replaced it with newer English styles, or that inexpensive dishware was actually purchased for the intended use of the slaves. It is also possible that slaves bought some dishware for themselves.[125]

Bone handled knives, two-pronged forks, and spoons were commonly found on these sites, with spoons being the dominant utensil. Wine bottle glass was also quite common.[126] In his studies of Chesapeake plantation buildings and slave sites, historian John Vlach determined that iron pots were the most frequent cooking vessel that slaves used. Frying pans, skillets, stew pans, spits and racks were also common on slave sites, although andirons were conspicuously absent.[127]

Slaves' diets in eighteenth century Virginia varied. Although the weekly ration for an adult slave usually consisted of a peck of corn and a pound of meat (frequently beef or pork), most Virginia planters allowed their slaves a plot of ground to garden for themselves. They frequently granted free time to the slaves during the weekly schedule to tend their own gardens as well. Sunday was the acknowledged day off. Slaves grew a wide variety of crops: "water Melions," "Irish Potatoes," cabbages, turnips, beets, peas, beans, pumpkins and sweet potatoes, to name just a few.[128] These gardens contributed to variety in their diet and also became a source of income as produce was often sold or bartered.

---

[123] Samford, Carter's Grove Slave Quarters Study, 7; and direct communication with Patricia Samford. Queen's ware was a marketing term used by Josiah Wedgwood. After Britain's Queen Charlotte purchased Wedgwood's creamware, he gained permission to refer to the ceramic ware as "Queen's Ware."
[124] Ibid., 6.
[125] Ibid. Kelso, "Mulberry Row,"32.
[126] Samford, "Carter's Grove Study", 4.
[127] John Michael Vlach, "Afro-American Domestic Artifacts in Eighteenth Century Virginia," *Material culture,* 19 (1987): 8.
[128] Morgan, *Slave Counterpoint,* 134-142. Stacy Gibbons Moore, "Established and Well Cultivated," *Virginia Cavalcade* 39 (1989):74.

Additionally, slaves were allowed to keep chickens – generally known as dunghill fowl – and they were considered to be the "general chicken merchants."[129] Trading (or outright sale) of the chickens and eggs might be with the master himself. Other foodstuffs such as oysters, fish, and items raised in the slaves' own gardens found their way to the master's table by such means. The slaves' market economy often extended to local communities of poor whites and sometimes included stolen items from the plantation.[130]

Slaves commonly bartered for alcohol (rum or brandy) and were occasionally offered this as an incentive by the masters.[131] In 1770, Landon Carter tried to discourage alcohol barter and consumption among his slaves by giving his men only one shirt a year instead of the usual two: "My people always made and raised things to sell and I obliged them to buy linnen [sic] to make their other shirt instead of buying liquor with their fowls."[132] Two years later, Carter expressed concern that the legislature did not attempt to stop the trade of "night shops" where this slave economy was carried out.[133] But by 1777, Carter's attitude had mellowed. "My Poor Slaves raise fowls, and eggs in order to exchange with their Master now and then; and though I don't value the worth of what they bring, Yet I enjoy the humanity of refreshing such poor creatures in what they (though perhaps mistakenly) call a blessing," he wrote in his diary.[134]

[129] Morgan, *Slave Counterpoint*, 359.
[130] Ibid., 359-361, 366-369.
[131] Ibid., 415.
[132] Ibid., 131.
[133] Greene, *The Diary of Colonel Landon Carter*, 649.
[134] Ibid., 1095-96.

Planters may have readily allowed slaves to have gardens and chickens to supplement their diets because doing so reduced the financial burden of feeding them. George Washington plainly indicated just that when he gave instructions to Anthony Whitting: "It is not my wish or desire, that my Negroes should have an oz. of [corn] Meal more, nor less than is sufficient to feed them plentifully. This is what I have repeated to you over & over again...." As did many slave masters, Washington had established a standard ration for adults and children; slaves were to get only that.[135]

Archaeological evidence points to multiple sources of protein in slave diets. A study at Kingsmill Plantation emphasized that the domestic meats (beef and pork) provided as weekly rations were not high quality cuts, but rather meat from skulls, necks, feet, lower limbs, backs, and ribs. Slaves could and did utilize varied parts of animals for their diet. However, evidence of faunal remains found at archeology sites indicates additional sources of protein beyond the meager rations that masters provided. Slaves, opportunistic hunters and skilled fishermen, collected and ate local fish, shellfish, wild animals (raccoon, squirrel, and opossum), wild fowl, and turtles.[136]

Recent archeological discoveries at Gunston Hall to the east of the mansion where "Negroe quarters" were known to have been located provide similar indications of supplemental foodways patterns.[137] Thus far, the predominant faunal remains of fish, shellfish, and birds appear to be a major addition to the food for Mason's slaves. As on other Chesapeake plantation sites, sherds of white salt-glazed stoneware (showing several pattern styles) were a principle type of ceramic slaves used, along with tin glazed earthenware and red ware. Of interest in the Gunston Hall "east yard quarter" site are findings of a lock mechanism, gun flint, and lead shot. Perhaps some of Mason's slaves were more than "opportunistic" trappers or hunters of additional food.[138]

---

[135] Philander D. Chase, ed., *Papers of George Washington, Presidential Series January-May 1793* (Charlottesville: University of Virginia Press, 2005), Vol. 12, 634.
[136] Morgan, *Slave Counterpoint*, 134-145.
[137] Dunn, ed., *Recollections*, 59.
[138] Personal communication with Gunston Hall Archeologist David Shonyo, August, 2016. Similar patterns of distribution of the artifacts at the "east yard quarter" site to those of the "house for slaves" at Mount Vernon have been noted. The identification of a brick lined privy on this east side of Gunston Hall is also being investigated. The location of the slave housing known as Log Town described in John Mason's *Recollections* has yet to be discovered, however.

A combined examination of the main food sources and primary implements available to slaves indicates a general pattern of food preparation at these plantation sites. The predominant cooking utensil was an iron pot and the primary eating utensils were bowls and spoons; the food sources included grain (corn), a broad spectrum of vegetables grown in the slaves' own gardens, wild animals, fish, and domestic meats of poor quality. Evidence indicates that slaves' main meals probably consisted of one pot cooking: stews, porridges, or soups. Using currently available foods on any given day, a variety of meats and vegetables provided a steady, comparatively nutritious diet. Such cooking also allowed maximum flexibility for meal times as work would be regulated by the master or overseer, not the slaves themselves. A simmering food pot over a courtyard fire provided food throughout the day. Slaves ate when time, chance, and the overseers allowed.

Rations of Clothes

Virginia planters provided their field slaves with a yearly clothing ration, but it was generally given out on a semi-annual basis in summer and winter. A standard yearly allotment of adult clothes for males would have included: a waistcoat and breeches, a pair of summer breeches, two shirts, a pair of hose and a pair of shoes. Females generally received: a jacket and petticoat, a summer petticoat, two shifts, a pair of hose, and a pair of shoes.[139] Robert Carter of Nomini Hall specifically directed that the summer clothes would be furnished the first Monday in June and winter clothes the first Monday in December. But Virginia planters had a reputation for being tardy in delivering slaves' clothing. After giving instructions for clothing distribution to his slaves, Joseph Ball wrote:

> And all this must be done in Good Time; and not for the Winter to be half over before they get their Winter Cloths, and the Summer to be half over before they get their Summer Cloths; as the Common Virginia Fashion is.[140]

Young children were given less. One or two shirts or shifts of poor quality materials were provided; baby clothes were often made of old, recycled fabrics. Joseph Ball

---

[139] Ibid., 125-127. Linda Baumgarten, " 'Clothes for the People,' Slave Clothing in Early Virginia," *Journal of Early Southern Decorative Arts* Vol. XIV, No. 2 (Nov. 1988):40-45.
[140] Ball, *Letterbook*, 14 Feb. 1743/44.

instructed, "Let the Breeding Wenches have Baby Cloths; for which you may tear up old Sheets, or any other old Linen, that you can find in my house...and let them have Good Midwives; and what is necessary."[141] New cloth might sometimes be used for baby clothes such as the "...piece of Linnen for the purpose of Baby clothes for the Negroe Women. Viz. 26 yards of Dowlas..." that Washington designated.[142]

Sometimes clothing was bought ready-made, such as men's fearnothing (or fear-nought) jackets, monmouth caps, and stockings. But most often, fabric was imported and a majority of the slaves' clothing was made locally. There was a world-wide textile trade in place before the American Revolution, with much cheap cloth coming from Europe and the British Isles. Coarse linens (known as Osnaburg and rolls) were produced largely in Germany and Scotland; inexpensive wool (called plains, plaids, and, ironically, "cotton") came from England, Scotland, and Wales.[143] During the period of the Revolution, however, planters attempted to produce all their coarse goods. John Mason recalled,

> "My father had among his Slaves...shoemakers, spinners, weavers & knitters...his Sheep gave wool and his Fields produced cotton & Flax for the Weavers & Spinners...his cattle supplied skins for the shoemakers...."[144]

Regardless of the planters' desires for self-sufficiency, the cloth trade with Europe resumed quickly after the war. In 1788, George Mason wrote to Thomas Jefferson in France:

> I have desired Capt. James Fenwick...to send over some Patterns of coarse Goods...to his Brother and my Son; to see if such can't be manufactured in France, as cheap as in Great Britain: the consumption of these Articles in the Middle and Southern States is immense...You will observe that the coarse woolens are what we buy for our Slaves....[145]

---

[141] Ibid.

[142] Christine Sternberg Patrick, ed., *Papers of George Washington, Presidential Series 1 June-31 August 1793* (Charlottesville: University of Virginia Press, 2007), Vol. 13, 297-298. Dowlas was a coarse linen fabric.

[143] Baumgarten, "Clothes for the People," 40-45.

[144] Dunn, ed., *Recollections*, 63.

[145] Rutland, *Papers of George Mason*, 1124-1125.

At about this same time Washington noted that, "I manufacture a sufficiency [of coarse woolens] to clothe my out-door Negroes," but he added that he was "obliged to buy about 200 ells of Ticklenburg for present use...."[146]

Many times planters hired tailors or seamstresses to make clothing. Nathaniel Burwell at Carter's Grove paid "Mr John Grymes (Taylor [sic])" for making "35 suits for Crop People." He recorded an additional payment to Grymes "for puting [sic] Pockets in them."[147] Francis Taylor of Midland Plantation in Orange County frequently mentioned clothing preparation for his slaves in his diary:

> Nov. 30 [1795] I rode to Barbours Store--Bought Woolen Cloths for Negroes
>
> Dec. 9 [1795] Polly Edwards...came here and Cut out[?] Coats & breeches for my 5 negro men
>
> Dec. 28 [1795] ...Bot 4 doz small buttons of Pedlar
>
> Aug. 7 [1796] ...I gave the Negro men a felt hat each
>
> Oct. 27 [1798] ...Cut off a Shirt for each of my negroes German Ozna.
>
> Dec. 18 [1798] Sary [a slave] about making Mens Cloaths[.][148]

Washington, always concerned with efficiency, worried when his slaves sewed less than their usual nine shirts per week. He also disliked the adoption of newer styled trousers as they would require more cloth to make than breeches.[149]

Frequently, however, the planters gave fabric to their slaves or "cut off a shirt" and expected them to make their own clothing. Landon Carter's Betty "cut out" 10 boy's suits and 40 men's and women's suits in November 1763 which were probably distributed to the slave women who would to sew the clothes for the slaves in the quarter - all in their spare time after the master's work was completed.[150] Thomas

---

[146] John C. Fitzgerald, ed., *The Writings of George Washington from the Original Manuscript Sources 1745-1799* (Washington D.C.: United States Government Printing Office, 1939) Vol. 29, 111-112. An ell was an English unit of length equal to 45 inches.
[147] Walsh, *Calibar to Carter's Grove*, 190.
[148] "Francis Taylor Diary, (1786-1799)," Southern Historical Collection, Louis Round Wilson Special Collections Library, University of North Carolina: passim.
[149] Baumgarten, "Clothes for the People," 65. Trousers or "trowsers" were pants for men without a kneeband. Washington instructed that they be made shorter to use less fabric.
[150] Greene, *Diary of Landon Carter*, 242.

Jefferson gave his slaves seven or eight yards of linen and five to seven yards of wool on an average each year for the adults (children were only provided about half that amount); he also provided thread.[151]

Domestic slaves and those who served as personal body servants spent most of their work time in and around the master's home. Their appearance reflected the master's station. Generally, their clothing was of better quality fabric. Hand-me-downs from the white family to favored slaves occasionally supplemented their allotment. Joseph Ball frequently sent old clothing back to Virginia from England and instructed his nephew (and manager) to distribute the items to specific slaves. Aron was a consistent recipient.[152]

Where did slaves get additional clothing? Some bartered for cloth or clothes; some purchased clothing or cloth outright in stores or shops with money made from tips, earnings, or the sale of goods (such as vegetables, chickens, or baskets etc.). Runaway ads reflect that many slaves stole clothes, especially before attempting to run away. Some received hand-me-down clothing from the master's house, although evidence suggests that in Virginia, this was reserved for favored or close personal slaves.[153] Joseph Ball's favored slave Aron arrived in Richmond County with a barrel, a chest, and a box that not only included his elaborate bedding, but also a large wardrobe of clothing: "Three suits...Two pair of new shoes...several

---

[151] Robert C. Baron, *The Garden and Farm Books of Thomas Jefferson* (Golden, Colorado, Fulcrum, Inc., 1987), 262-267. See the year 1794 as an example.
[152] Ball, *Letterbook*, 3 June, 1749 and 18 July 1755.
[153] Baumgarten, "Clothes for the People," 38, 39.

pair of stockings, a pair of boots, and Twelve shirts[,] Eight of which are New...."[154] Ball frequently designated items that were to go to other slaves by name. "The Grey wastecoat [sic] & breeches with brass buttons, and the hat to poor Will[,] the stuff shirt to Mingo[,] and the Dimmity Coat and Breeches and the knife in the pocket to Harrison...."[155]

Livery also distinguished many prominent domestic slaves from others. Personal male slaves frequently wore livery in Virginia to show the status of the slave's owner. George Washington, Robert Carter, Landon Carter, and George Mason had slaves outfitted in livery. Typically styled as a man's three piece suit, the fabrics chosen might reflect the colors in a gentry family's coat of arms. "Livery lace" (of silver or gold thread) trimmed the coat sleeves, collar, or shoulders. George Mason's man James wore livery that was ordered from Carlin's in Alexandria.[156] For the slaves who wore livery, it was a uniform which indicated a slave's standing in the hierarchy as established by the white culture. James attended to George Mason's personal needs, traveled with him, and likely made purchases or tended to small errands while Mason was in Alexandria or Williamsburg. Whether James' livery created a comfortable personal identity for him within the black community is not known.[157]

Shoes, also rationed yearly, were typically only given to adult or working hands. Jefferson's farm records clearly indicate that children were overlooked in the distribution of shoes. They went barefoot. Many plantations had black shoemakers. George Mason had a shoemaker among his slaves who made shoes for the black population while a white shoemaker was hired periodically to make shoes for the Mason family members.[158] John Tayloe at Mt. Airy had two shoemakers, Joe and Ruffin, as well as "a boy" learning the trade or working with them. Not only were they employed making and repairing "coarse shoes" and the "peoples shoes" [sic] at Mount Airy, but Tayloe also effectively ran a shoe shop for his neighbors. The

---

[154] Ball, *Letterbook,* 23 April, 1754
[155] Ibid., 30 June, 1749.
[156] Baumgarten, "Clothes for the People," 33-37. William Carlin's Account Book, Alexandria, Virginia , Oct. 8, 1772. Microfilm (National Museum of American History Library), 72. Entry reads, "To making [sic] yr man James Livery Lac d £1.5.0." On June 16 that year Carlin also charged Mason for "altering pr Plush Bretches to James £0.1.6." Walsh, *Calibar to Carter's Grove,* 190-191.
[157] Dunn, ed., *Recollections,* 52, 53.
[158] Ibid., 63.

shoemakers' time was always occupied; numerous other chores such as tanning, dressing, and currying leather or mending saddles and bridles were noted among their activities.[159]

It is apparent, however, that many slaves had more than their allotted yearly garments from the variety of clothes described in runaway slave advertisements:

> "RAN away last April...a Mulatto slave belonging to Samuel Selden, jun. named Peter Deadfoot...[he] is extremely fond of dress...[but] his holiday clothes were taken from him...."[160]

Slaves at Carter's Grove plantation and other plantations had clothes they only used for "Sunday best."[161] Skilled slaves especially seem to have had many clothes, possibly purchased with money made from tips or earnings using their own skills. For these individuals, clothing might indicate a rise in their status within the black community; clothes could also represent a powerful symbol of identity.[162] Runaway ads reveal the wide variety of styles, colors, and fabrics in slave's clothes:

> "**Sancho**...carried with him a broadcloth Coat mixed with something of a violet colour, [and] a blue duffil coat."[163]

---

[159] Susan Borchardt and Ellen Donald, transcribers, "John Tayloe Uncatalogued Plantation Records: Slaves," Virginia Historical Society, (Gunston Hall Library, Gunston Hall, Mason Neck, VA, 1987), passim. John Tayloe found it necessary to take his shoemakers away from their usual work for an entire week to go to the Mill Dam and build flood gates. It appears most of his male labor was concentrated there until that task was completed.

[160] *Virginia Gazette*, (Rind), 22 September 1768. Samuel Seldon Jr. was the nephew of George Mason IV; he was the son of his sister, Mary Mason Seldon.

[161] Walsh, *Calibar to Carter's Grove*, 191. Morgan, *Slave Counterpoint*, 131.

[162] Baumgarten, "Clothes for the People," 57-59. In general, about one eighth of the ads list male slaves wearing trousers, not breeches; and a few female slaves had "gowns" among their clothing, an upper class garment.

[163] Windley, *Runaway Slave Advertisements*, 325.

George...had on a dark blue Cloth coat, cape and cuffs of red, and carried off with him... a London brown cloth coat neatly made, fine ruffled shirts, [and] silk hose....[164]

[A] new **Negro boy** about...fifteen years old...had on when he went away, a new brown Bearskin Jacket with large white Metal Buttons, old blue Breeches with lining, [and] country knit brown Stockings....[165]

Jack is well clad in a new coat, waistcoat, and breeches, of red duffil, and has a new gray fearnought great coat....[166]

Nanny...took with her a calico waistcoat and petticoat [and] one blue plains [waistcoat and petticoat]....[167]

[A] likely **Virginia Born negro fellow**...carried with him a new Suit of blue or purple Negro cotton....[168]

The small amounts of money obtained by slaves may have provided extra cloth for the meager clothing allotments. Some individuals wanted special items for "best" at Saturday gatherings; these could be stored or hidden in the holes or pits within the quarters. Masters understood that the allotments were meager and insufficient, but they relied on the slaves to either make do or find ways to supplement their clothes – just as they did their food.

Other Aspects of Slave Life

Sundays were customarily considered free time for the slaves in Virginia. They tended gardens and took care of their own necessary chores of life. Saturday nights became "gathering" times for slaves to meet, often walking long distances to be with family and friends. Nicholas Cresswell, a British traveler in America in 1774, spent time in Nanjemoy, Maryland and observed slaves in such circumstances. He wrote:

[164] Ibid., 202.
[165] Ibid. 127.
[166] Ibid. 249.
[167] Ibid. 247.
[168] Ibid., 160, 161.

Mr. Bayley and I went to see a Negro Ball, Sundays being the only days these poor Creatures have to themselves, they generally meet together and amuse themselves with Dancing to the Banjor. This Musical instrument (if it may be so called) is made of a Gourd something in the imitation of a Guitar with only four strings and play'd with the fingers in the same manner. Some of them sing to it which is very droll musick indeed[.] In their songs they generally relate the usage they have received from their Masters or Mistresses, in a very Satirical stile and manner. Their poetry is like the Music [,] Rude and uncultivated. Their Dancing is most violent exercise, but so irregular and Grotesque, I am not able to describe it. They all appear to be exceedingly happy at these merry makings and seem as if they had forgot or were not sensible of their misserable [sic] condition.[169]

Dancing, singing, and music were part of slaves' lives to help ease the drudgery and sorrow of slavery. The rhythms and instruments - such as the banjo, "Banjor," or "banjer" - and drums carried over African cultural traditions.[170] One remarkable watercolor image survives showing such a time in a slave quarter. The painting entitled *The Old Plantation* depicts Africans in South Carolina about 1800 gathered for dancing with music being played on drums and a banjo-like instrument. Evidence of special grooming of hair and clothes clearly indicates the slaves' desire to transform their lives into people - not laborers.[171]

---

[169] Harold B. Gill, Jr. and George M. Curtis III, Eds., *A Man Apart, The Journal of Nicholas Cresswell, 1774-1781* (New York: Lexington Books, 2009), 11.

[170] Morgan, *Slave Counterpoint*, 580-587.

[171] Susan P. Shamus, *The Old Plantation, The Artist Revealed* (Williamsburg, Virginia: The Colonial Williamsburg Foundation, 2010), 8-12.

Runaway ads support the fact that many slaves were able to play a variety of musical instruments and also had them in their possession.[172] The most common instrument played was the violin or fiddle; slave masters recognized their talents and frequently hired their slaves to play for entertainment or dances in the great houses. William Fearson's runaway slave was known as "FIDDLER BILLY;" numerous ads referred to slaves such as *Peter, Daniel, or Bob* who played the fiddle, danced well, sang for entertainment, and were comfortable performing for their white audiences. Sambo revealed his talents as a maker of fiddles as well.[173] Other instruments were noted in slave ads. Dick, who ran away from George Mason V, could beat a drum "pretty well."[174] And, William Allason's slave Mark could "...blow the French Horn, play the fiddle [and] whistles many tunes...."[175] As Olaudah Equiano wrote of his native Africans, "We are almost a nation of dancers, musicians, and poets. Thus every great event...is celebrated in public dances, which are accompanied with songs and music suited to the occasion."[176]

Slaves saved their better clothes, or "holiday clothes," for these Saturday night-into-Sunday gatherings. "Girls never failed to put on their garment of gladness, their bracelets, and chains, rings and earrings..." English traveler John Davis wrote.[177] Luxury items found at slave archeological excavations such as jewelry, combs, and mirrors support their desire to enhance their personal appearance.[178]

Curiously, relatively large quantities of buttons have been found in archaeological digs at slave sites. Their presence reflects a cultural importance of a very common item at the least. Linda Baumgarten suggests that buttons were used for adornment on slave clothing or even possibly used as jewelry.[179]

---

[172] Interestingly, musical instruments in slave quarters do not appear in inventories. Vlach, "Afro-American Domestic Artifacts," 16.

[173] Morgan, *Slave Counterpoint*, 591-593.

[174] *Virginia Journal and Alexandria Advertiser*, 15 July, 1784. See also Chapter Four.

[175] Morgan, *Slave Counterpoint*, 592.

[176] Olaudah Equiano, *The Interesting Narrative and Other Writings* (New York: Penguin Books, 2003), 35. See also: Vincent Carretta, *Equiano the African, Biography of a Self-Made Man* (Athens: The University of Georgia Press, 2005), 1-9. Carretta argues that Equiano was likely born in America, not Africa.

[177] John Davis, *Travels of Four Years and a Half in the United States of America During 1798, 1799, 1800, 1801, and 1802* (New York: Henry Holt and Company, 1909), 400.

[178] Walsh, *Calibar to Carter's Grove*, 191-198.

[179] Heath, *Hidden Lives*, 52-53. Baumgarten, "Clothes for the People," 59.

"The Old Plantation." This rare eighteenth century image portrays slaves in time away from work. Individuals are dancing and playing instruments that have an African origin, including a banjar (or banjo), a drum, and a "shegureh," which appears as a long scarf. It is a gourd inside a net. Shells or bone woven into the net create rhythmic sounds when shaken. Credit: The Colonial Williamsburg Foundation. Gift of Abby Aldrich Rockefeller.

Another interesting personal artifact appears in nearly all of the Carter's Grove pit sites – sherds of imported and domestic pipes. Pipe sherds were also a prominent artifact found at "Mulberry Row" at Monticello and Mount Vernon. As with other ceramics, pipes showed heavy usage and in a least one case, the stem was whittled to remake the mouth piece on a very short stem, quite close to the bowl.[180] Joseph Ball often sent along old pipes with the clothes he handed down to his slaves: "I have sent an old cloth wastecoat [sic] for Harrison and a parcell [sic] of foul [used] Pipes [to] dispose of to my folks as you think fit..."[181] Other artifacts indicate a varied material culture among slaves: marbles, Jew's harps (or jaw's harps), scissors, colored pharmaceutical or toiletry glass, beads, locks, keys, clock parts, gun parts and ammunition, and money.[182]

Slaves obtained money from several sources such as their minor status as "chicken merchants," selling produce or baskets, providing their skills to the local community, or receiving tips, particularly at holiday time. Philip Vicars Fithian carefully recorded his gratuities to various slaves. "I gave yesterday to the Shoemaker a bit - & and a Bit to the Wash woman; half a Bit to her little Girl; & half a Bit to Nelson the Boy who waits on our School...."[183] Norfolk, Williamsburg, Alexandria, and numerous towns provided a market venue that many slaves were able to use to their advantage.[184] At least two of Mason's slaves used their skills to make money in the neighborhood of Gunston Hall. Nace, Mason's black overseer at Occoquan, was occasionally paid by neighboring Martin Cockburn for "breaking horses." Gunston Nell was a midwife and delivered babies at Cockburn's plantation on more than one occasion. She was paid twelve shillings, also the going rate for a white midwife.[185] Theft, of course, was always an additional possibility for obtaining money.

---

[180] Heath, *Hidden Lives*, 56-58.

[181] Ball, *Letterbook*, 12 Feb 1756.

[182] Colonial Williamsburg, Department of Archaelogical Research, "Artifact Inventory, Carter's Grove Slave Quarters Excavation" (Unpublished, Colonial Williamsburg Foundation, Williamsburg, VA, 1991), passim.

[183] Hunter Dickinson Farish, ed., *Journal and Letters of Philip Vickers Fithian* (Charlottesville: University Press of Virginia, 1983), 96. A Bit was an eighth of a Spanish Milled Dollar. A silver coin used throughout the colonial period, the Spanish Milled Dollar was frequently cut into halves, quarters, or eighths to provide small change needed.

[184] Morgan, *Slave Counterpoint*, 252-254, 358-361.

[185] Martin Cockburn Ledger, Library of Congress. Nace was paid 9 shillings in 1771 for "breaking a colt" and £1.16 for "breaking a young horse" in 1779. In 1790 Gunston Nell was paid twelve shillings for "delivering Leah" on February 21 and twelve shillings/six pence for delivering "Megar of a girl" in November. Walsh, *Calibar to Carter's Grove*, 174-175.

But, beyond archaeological findings, the possession of money by slaves is further evidenced by merchant's records of slave purchases. The records of John Glassford & Co. in Colchester, Virginia list the accounts for "Negro Jack belonging to Mr Lintons [sic] Estate" and "Negro Sue belong [sic]to Mr Grayson." Jack's purchases frequently included rum, but he also bought shot and flints indicating his possession of a weapon. In payment, Jack ran errands, built furniture and coffins, and sold eggs to Glassford. Sue sold vegetables and chickens in payment for the goods she purchased which on one occasion included a lock for a chest.[186] Thomas Jefferson's slaves at Poplar Forest utilized the New London store of John Hook to purchase cloth, shoes, food, cider, whiskey, and a wide variety of personal goods and paid in cash, goods, or labor.[187]

Clock parts have also been found in archaeological sites and their discovery raises a curious point. Historian Mechal Sobel has commented on the Anglo-Saxon attitudes of the use of time to measure efficiency. Educated, "enlightened" planters - William Byrd II, Landon Carter, Thomas Jefferson, George Washington, and certainly George Mason as well - were all concerned about the quantity and quality of work done within specific periods of time. Planters continually attempted to increase their plantations' (and hence their slaves') efficiency. A watch or clock reflected one way of measuring efficiency. Sobel estimates that perhaps ten percent of the eighteenth

---

[186] John Glassford & Co., Records for Virginia, Colchester Store, Ledger B (1760-1761), folios 114 and 79, Library of Congress. (Colonial Williamsburg Microfilm M-1442.8)
[187] Heath, *Hidden Lives*, 50-53.

century population, including some slaves, could have had timepieces in Virginia.[188] For most people, however, owning a timepiece, might indicate not only a mechanical regulation of the day, but also serve as a status symbol.[189]

Legally, slaves were not allowed to own or use guns.[190] Yet advertisements indicate that guns were frequently stolen by slaves attempting to run away. Archaeological findings confirm that slaves had access to guns and ammunition. Possession of firearms, free time for hunting, faunal evidence of wild animals supplementing the diet, and archaeological findings now indicate that at least some slaves had guns, regardless of laws forbidding them, and whether sanctioned by the slave masters or not.[191]

From the middle of the eighteenth century until well after the Revolution, the "Great Awakening" in religion encouraged reading and writing among poorer whites and slaves. In 1761, Samuel Davies wrote, "The poor Slaves are now commonly engaged in learning to read; some of them can read the Bible; others can only spell...."[192] Ads for runaways sometimes remarked whether a slave could read, write, or cipher, but few could do all three. In Fredericksburg in 1772 James Mercer advertised for a runaway, his slave named Christmas, a waiting man who "...has waited on me from my Infancy..." and had been inoculated for smallpox, could read and spoke "with great Propriety."[193] Runaway Talbot (or Tally) could also read and "generally carried about him a new testament or psalter."[194] Sarah Floyd's slave Charles ran away from her Charles City property in 1769. In an ad, she noted that he was a sawyer and a shoemaker; and, more importantly, she noted, "The said fellow reads very well, and is a great preacher, from which I imagine he will endeavor to pass for a free man."[195] In an attempt to escape slavery, skills such as

---

[188] Sobel, *The World They Made Together*, 21-29. Dunn, ed., *Recollections*, 52.59. George Mason's personal servant, James, could have been a possible candidate for owning a timepiece as he lived at "Log-Town," waited on Mason at Gunston Hall, and also traveled with Mason.

[189] Sobel, *The World They Made Together*, 65-66.

[190] Hening, ed., *Statutes at Large*, 3:447-462, XXXV.

[191] Dennis L. Pogue, "Slave Lifeways at Mount Vernon:An Archeological Perspective" in Philip J. Schwarz, Ed., *Slavery at the Home of George Washington* (Mount Vernon, Virginia: Mount Vernon Ladies' Association,2001) 119.

[192] Sobel, *The World They Made Together*, 184. Underlining in original text.

[193] Windley, *Runaway Slave Advertisements*, 111.

[194] Ibid., 235.

[195] *Virginia Gazette*, (Rind), Feb.16, 1769.

reading and writing could make a crucial difference. Being able to write a pass to allude to one's freedom of movement in Virginia was a first, critical step in making that attempt.

Surviving artifacts from slave sites and documentary evidence from a variety of sources clearly reveal that slaves found it necessary to supplement what their masters provided for their existence. Indeed, many planters came to expect slaves to plant additional crops, raise chickens for barter or sale, and supplement their clothing allowances. Consequently, slave life varied considerably for individuals. This variability also gave way for limited self-expression within the African-American culture that was emerging in the eighteenth century, most noticeably in regard to clothing and personal appearance. Many slaves found a creative pathway to express feelings and emotion through music and dance. African American culture evolved and grew from these varied, though limited, means of self expression. Continued archeology at Gunston Hall may more clearly indicate how George Mason's slaves lived day-to-day as measured against this broad Chesapeake picture.

The word slavery is itself a generic term. It can only be best understood as what occurred for enslaved individuals in a particular time and place. This study attempts to reveal what life was like in the Chesapeake region of North America, in the eighteenth century, and in a plantation setting where so many Africans and their descendents were forced to live – a plantation setting like Gunston Hall.

As we look at slavery in this context, what is remarkable is the way in which people utilized the meager means at their disposal to manipulate and alter their conditions. They bargained, stole, tricked, and maneuvered their way into lessening their state of oppression. None of this ever diminished the desire for freedom, however. Runaway ads confirm that. Nor did the eighteenth century Chesapeake slaves completely sacrifice a world they were forced to leave behind. The cross-over of elements and values from the English culture that dominated their lives in the Chesapeake still included African ideals, customs, and language. For some, these persisted in day-to-day adaptation; for others they persisted in only in memory.

Chapter Three:

The Slaves of Gunston Hall, 1746-1770

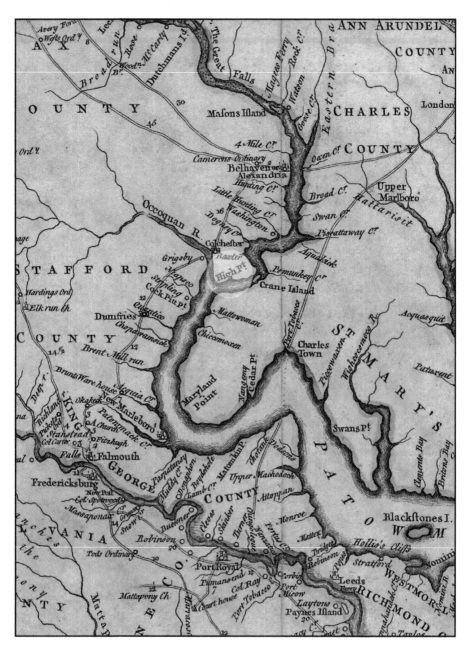

On the Fry-Jefferson map this section of the Potomac or "Patowmack" River shows the region where the Mason and Eilbeck families lived. Gunston Hall was located on the peninsula noted as "High Pt." Mason's mansion was not yet erected at the time this map was drawn. Courtesy, Library of Congress.

$\mathcal{G}$eorge Mason IV came into his majority and inheritance in 1746. Possessing land in both Maryland and Virginia, he ultimately decided to develop several parcels on what is today known as Mason Neck in Virginia as his principle working quarters and home plantation. His marriage in April 1750 to Ann Eilbeck, the daughter and only child of William and Sarah Eilbeck from Charles County, Maryland, solidified his plans. The Eilbeck family lived on Mattawoman Creek and were neighbors and close associates of George Mason III's family, although there appears to be no arrangement in the marriage of Ann Eilbeck to George Mason IV. [196] It was by all indication a marriage of great affection between them. The future looked bright as the young couple married and George Mason IV began a promising career as a prominent Chesapeake planter. To commemorate their marriage, portraits of Ann and George Mason were commissioned by the well known artist John Hessalius. [197] The ensuing two decades – from 1750 to 1770 – would be busy, fulfilling, and generally happy ones for the couple. But they would also be challenging years for the young planter as he developed his plantation business and learned first-hand the problems of being a slave master. To his initial inheritance, slaves were added in a number of ways during the next two decades. This chapter looks at the addition of slaves to Gunston Hall and issues George Mason IV encountered as a slave owner.

George Mason IV's mother, Ann Thomson Mason, had taken her dower land in Prince William County, Virginia. She continued to use the slave laborers to support herself and her two younger children, Mary and Thomson after 1746. Mary Mason married Samuel Seldon in April 1751, just one year after George Mason married. She was twenty years old. In August of that year, Thomson Mason was admitted to the Middle Temple at the Inns of Court in London to study law. He was called to the bar in November 1754, the year he reached his majority.

---

[196] George Mason and Ann Eilbeck were married on April 4, 1750 in Charles County, Maryland by Mason's close friend The Reverend John Moncure. The *Maryland Gazette* reported the marriage on May 2, 1750 describing the bride as "a young lady of distinguished merits and beauty and a handsome fortune." See Copeland and MacMaster, *The Five George Masons,* 90. Ann Mason undoubtedly brought slaves with her into the marriage, but no document survives to mention who they might be.
[197] The individual portraits of George and Ann Mason were painted by John Hessalius circa 1750. Copies of the originals (now lost) were made by Dominic Boudet circa 1811.

Ann Thomson Mason managed her dower property and the assets designated for her children extraordinarily well. She never remarried and as a *feme sole*[198] under the law, she controlled the labor of the dower slaves and slaves held in guardianship for her children to provide the financial means to purchase land and slaves for herself and to invest in land and slaves for both her daughter and younger son. She willed all of her three children slaves.[199]

George Mason IV possibly moved some of his slaves from his Maryland land at Stump Neck to Virginia as he began to develop the "Mason Neck" properties, first to Dogue Neck and later to Gunston Hall. He also began to acquire additional slaves in 1753 – probably through purchases from slave ships in the region. In August of that year, seven slave children were "adjudged" for their ages and recorded in the Fairfax County Order Book for Mason for future tithable, or taxable, purposes. These children included **Oronoko**, 12; **Synharp**, 11; **Juba**, 11; **Kato**, 10; **Beck**, 9; **Jenny**, 8; and **Agniss**, 8.[200] (See Table Five.)

Because tariffs on slave purchases were lower in Maryland than in Virginia, Chesapeake planters were buying slaves in Maryland and moving them across the Potomac to reduce the overall cost of buying a new slave.[201] Although George Mason's brother Thomson became involved in the slave trade in the Chesapeake region in later years, there are no indications that George Mason bought other slaves until 1767 when a record in John Glassford & Company's account book notes that he was charged £56.15 "to Ship Jenny for a Negro fellow sold to you."[202] Plantation records for George Mason have not survived, but it is probable that most of the slaves added to his work force across the years were through "natural increase" – or slave women having children. As Virginia law defined the status of a child as determined by the status of the mother, it provided great benefit to the slave owner.[203] A slave woman's child became the slave owner's property, too.

---

[198] This legal term *feme sole* was extrapolated from the French, *femme seule,* meaning a woman alone. It referred to a widow in English law. *Feme couvert* referred to a woman protected under the law by her husband or father. See Salmon, *Women and the Law of Property,* xv.

[199] Dower was the right of a widow to a life use of her husband's property. Virginia laws included the use of land and slaves. See Salmon, *Women and the Law of Property,* 142, 4-6.

[200] Fairfax Order Book, Fairfax County, Virginia, 1749-1754, 21 August, 1753, 436.

[201] Donald M. Sweig, "The Importation of African Slaves to the Potomac River, 1732-1772," *William and Mary Quarterly,* Oct. 1985, 507-524; Walsh, *William and Mary Quarterly,* 2001, 147.

[202] John Glassford & Co. Piscataway, Maryland Ledger, Nov. 30, 1767. Transcription in Gunston Hall files.

[203] Hening, ed. *Statutes at Large,* 2:170.

Throughout the 1750s Mason was busy with diverse business and personal concerns. Construction of the family's seat, the story and a half brick mansion that would be both home and center of his plantation dealings, began. Although the carpenter-joiner William Buckland did not arrive in Virginia from London until the fall of 1755 to plan and oversee the completion of the formal interior designs of the house, general construction of the building started much earlier.[204] Unskilled laborers, young and old, both black and white, were needed to dig a foundation, fell trees, mix local clay soil to mold and fire bricks, or burn oyster shells to make mortar. Mason likely hired professional white brick masons, carpenters, and an undertaker – someone who "undertook" building construction – to direct the raising of the building. William Bernard Sears is the only other identifiable carver beside William Buckland known to do work on the interior of the house, but plasterers, wallpaperers, joiners, blacksmiths, and others (primarily white workers) frequented the site in the 1750s.[205] Among Mason's skilled enslaved people in that decade were probably carpenters, blacksmiths, and others who may have worked along-side the hired tradesmen. They remain anonymous.

The Trouble with Slavery

George Mason also learned difficult lessons in dealing with some aspects of slavery during these early years. On April 16, 1754, Fairfax County records indicate that George Mason filed a complaint against "his Negro slave Dick for stealing and [being a] runaway." Dick, about 23 years old, was sentenced to have "one ear to be nailed to [the] pillory and cut off."[206] Virginia's legal statutes prescribed mutilation such as this for someone who committed a second offence for stealing a hog. Dick likely

---

[204] Copeland and MacMaster, *Five George Masons*, 96-100.

[205] Carson and Lounsbury, *Chesapeake House*, 82. Luke Beckerdike, "William Buckland and William Bernard Sears: the Designer and the Carver," *Journal of Early Southern Decorative Arts* Volume VIII, Number 2 (November 1982): 8-9.

[206] The monetary value of items stolen by slaves determined whether the slave was tried in a local county court or the oyer and terminer court in Williamsburg (established in Virginia in 1692 for values over twenty shillings.) Hog stealing – a frequent occurrence - was a misdemeanor and tried in a county court. A first offence was punished by whipping; a second by mutilation; and a third by hanging. Hening, *Statutes at Large*, 3: 173-179. Philip J. Schwartz, *Twice Condemned, Slaves and the Criminal Laws of Virginia, 1705-1865* (Union, New Jersey: The Lawbook Exchange, LTD., 1998), 20, 72-78. Fairfax County, Virginia Court Records, 1749-1801, 22.

had been punished for an earlier offence by receiving 39 lashes laid on at a public whipping post. Now, after this more severe punishment was invoked, the sheriff was to return Dick (minus one of his ears) to his owner – George Mason. Dick managed to escape from the sheriff. He ran west, possibly following the general route that is today Braddock Road. Dick became an outlaw.

On August 15 that year, George Mason again returned to the court and "[p]etitioned [for an] allowance for Negro Dick who died in the custody of [the] person carrying him to the office after being outlawed. Certified Negro valued at £40."[207] Dick had escaped. He ran. Now he was dead. What happened? When – and how – did he die?

The answers to these questions are buried deep in the *Journals of the House of Burgesses*, the government records of the colony of Virginia. The Fairfax County Court had placed a valuation on Dick; as he died while still in custody by the county, he was considered lost property. Mason petitioned the colony – the House of Burgesses in Williamsburg – for reimbursement of £40. On Monday, May 5, 1755, Mason's petition was read in the House of Burgesses. It stated:

> That his Negro Slave Dick, having run away and committed many Felonies, was in due Form of Law outlawed, and being taken up by some of Captain Mackay's Company, was by them delivered to one Daniel James, in perfect Health: That as the said James was carrying the said Slave to the Constable, he pulled him off his Horse, and in struggling to make his Escape received some Hurt, and refusing to go any further, the said James tied him with a Rope to his Horse Tail, and in that Manner dragged him to the next House, where he in a few Minutes expired....[208]

Dick was dead as a result of his capture. Mason asked for reimbursement "as this House shall see fit." The House of Burgesses, after hearing Mason's petition, referred it to the Committee of Claims for review.[209] The next day, Tuesday, May 6, the Committee of Claims reported back to the House of Burgesses with its findings and a more detailed account of the happenings.

[207] Fairfax County, Virginia Court Records, 1749-1801, 145.
[208] H.R. McIlwain, ed., *Journals of the House of Burgesses* (Richmond, Virginia), May 5, 1755.
[209] Ibid.

The Committee's findings were: George Mason's slave Dick ran away in April 1754 and committed "some Crime, for which he was tried and one of his Ears cut off, by order of the Court of the County of Fairfax...." They further reported that on April 27, Dick ran away again and was outlawed; he was apprehended on May 24 by officers of Captain Mackay's Company who were marching to the Ohio.[210] Dick was handed over to Daniel James to return the runaway slave to local authorities and provide his return to George Mason. Dick attempted to make yet another escape. Daniel James struck the slave "two or three blows" and he fell down and could not or would not go any further. James then tied Dick with a rope to his horse's tail and dragged him to the house of Samuel Jenkins where Dick died.[211]

A coroner's inquest followed the incident and Samuel Jenkins served as a witness. The coroner's jury found no wounds or bruises on the slave's body "sufficient" to kill him. Daniel James told the jury that he saw Dick take something out of his pocket; he swallowed it and then began vomiting. Daniel James stated that he believed the slave had poisoned himself. The jury, however, "did not take much Notice" of what James said.[212] The Committee of Claims was convinced that Samuel Jenkins' testimony corroborated the story of Daniel James and the attempted escape of slave Dick. They therefore recommended that George Mason be reimbursed £40 from the public funds for the loss of his property.

The House of Burgesses, however, disagreed with the interpretation of the Committee of Claims. After hearing the Committee's report, they voted to reject Mason's petition for reimbursement. George Mason received *no* public funds for his loss of property.[213] The reasons for the House of Burgesses' rejection are not recorded, but presumably they believed that Dick did poison himself and in taking his own life absolved the public of the responsibility for his loss.

---

[210] Capt. James Mackay, a British Army Commander of an Independent Company from South Carolina, was moving his unit to the Ohio territory. There, Capt. Mackay's men would join George Washington in June at the battle of Great Meadows. But, en route, Mackay's men encountered Runaway Dick, apprehended him, and then turned him over to Daniel James. W.W. Abbot and Dorothy Twohig, eds., *The Papers of George Washington Colonial Series I, 1748-August 1755* (Charlottesville: University Press of Virginia, 1983), 77, 91-92.

[211] McIlwain, *Journals of the House of Burgesses,* May 6, 1755.

[212] Ibid.

[213] Ibid.

Who was this enslaved man Dick who sought escape and lost his life in the attempt? He may have been one of the slaves on the Maryland property of George Mason III in 1735. In the 1735 inventory taken at Stump Neck, a slave boy, Dick, is listed. In 1754 he would likely have been in his mid 20s.[214] Now, perhaps on the Virginia property of George Mason IV, could he be the frustrated enslaved individual who stole, ran away, suffered mutilation, and ran again? It is possible. If so, his misfortune grew as he ran west through several Virginia counties and stumbled into the path of British officers moving west at the beginning of the French and Indian War.

Dick, knowing that he was "outlawed," surely feared he would be hanged. He made an attempt to escape, but did not succeed. Beaten by Daniel James, he was tied and dragged an unknown distance to the home of Samuel Jenkins where he died. Was he beaten or dragged to death? Or, did he have some form of poison in his pocket? If so, where did he obtain it? It seems unlikely that a young slave man carried around "poison" in the event he needed to feign illness or kill himself. Nonetheless, it appears that the members of House of Burgesses chose to believe that Dick took his own life over the coroner's inquest's dismissal of Daniel James' poisoning theory and their recommendation that Mason be reimbursed for the slave's value.

George Mason must surely have been disappointed in this decision. As a young planter (Mason was only 30 years old when he filed his petition), he used the proper recourse available to petition for his loss of "property." George Mason was equipped with legal knowledge and determination to resolve an issue over a recalcitrant slave. The decision by the members of the House of Burgesses disabused the idealism of this young gentry planter. It was a lesson Mason would surely remember. Three years later in 1758, Mason successfully stood for election to the House of Burgesses to represent Fairfax County.[215] Undoubtedly he hoped to use his understanding of law constructively in that office. But the political atmosphere disappointed him while there. He never ran for that office again. George Mason was known for his dislike of committee work and his strong desire

---

[214] Maryland Hall of Records, Charles County Inventories 1735-1752, f. 13-15,3 See Appendix A.
[215] Miller, *Gentleman Revolutionary*, 63,68.

for keeping a "private Station" as opposed "to the troubles and Vexations of Public Business."[216] His earlier encounters with the House of Burgesses may have initiated a basis for that attitude.

Within the slave community at Gunston Hall and in neighboring communities as well, Dick's death must have reverberated with the story as it found its way to them through the "grapevine." Knowledge of Dick's public punishment at the pillory was meant to be a deterrent to slaves' criminal activities in the entire region; such punishment was meant to frighten others with the idea of direct infliction of pain and a lasting physical mark. But in the end, learning of Dick's escape from the law and his ultimate, unexplained death only reinforced to slaves the reality of the constraining bonds of the institution of slavery and the power of slave masters and the law.

Ann Thomson Mason Makes Gifts and Bequests

George Mason's mother, Ann Thomson Mason managed her dower well. One example of her management skills can be seen in the detailed disbursement documents discussed in the previous chapter. Another example is seen in the variety of documents she filed in county courts to provide the means to her ends in plans and distribution of her personal assets. In December 1756, a document filed in Stafford County, Virginia, Ann Thomson Mason and her son Thomson Mason signed an agreement regarding twenty slaves as a debt of Rose Bronough.[217] The money raised from the labor of these slaves was to pay off the debt which Thomson Mason (Rose Bronough's executive administrator) assumed. The slaves, however, were housed and held by Ann Thomson Mason. Thomson was to take ownership of these slaves after fulfillment of the debt, but the documents allowed Ann Mason to retain five slaves, Dublin, Stepney, Yellow Jenny, Bridget, and Ancilla for her "use & benefit" for the remainder of her life.[218]

---

[216] Rutland, *Papers of George Mason,* 159.
[217] Rose Bronough is Simpha Rosa Enfield Mason, wife of Capt. Jeremiah Bronough in Stafford County, Virginia. She was sister-in-law to Ann Thomson Mason.
[218] Stafford County Virginia, Liber P, Deed Book 1755-1764, 153-156. (Reel 6, Library of Virginia, Richmond, Virginia.) This debt may have occurred at the time of Jeremiah Bronough's death in 1749 and the settlement of his estate.

Also in December 1756, Ann Thomson Mason had filed a "Deed of Gift and Bill of Sale" for her married daughter Mary Mason Seldon that included twenty slaves. The deed noted that nine of the individuals were "already in her [Mary Mason Seldon's] possession." Those nine were: Will, London, Limerick, Sue, Grace, Bess, Lucy, Judy, and Esther.

London was the man who had consistently worked his "full share" (in Maryland) throughout the years that reimbursement documents were filed in Prince William County. By this time he was 15-20 years older (perhaps in his 40s); he may still have been working the fields and undoubtedly was a man that Ann Thomson Mason considered a reliable worker. Lucy, possibly the "girl" in the 1735 Stump Neck inventory, was now a young woman in her twenties; she could work the fields or may have done domestic work. Judy could likely be the daughter of Judith (30) in 1735 at Stump Neck. Sue, a girl of 8 in that 1735 inventory was now perhaps in her late 20s; she also would likely have been a capable worker in the fields or about the house.[219]

The other eleven slaves listed in the Deed of Gift were: Sampson, George, Charles, Peter, Job, Rush, Pegg, Hannah, Poll, Nan Oldgate, and Letty.[220] Rush may be the ship's carpenter living in Maryland in 1735, older now, but still a man with important skills. Job may be the slave referred to as the boy Job on the 1735 Virginia inventory; he would be in his thirties at the time of the deed's writing. Peg, a teenager in 1735, could be the slave Pegg, also in her thirties, in the deed. Both Job and Pegg were likely seen as strong, capable workers. Nan Oldgate is probably the woman Nan listed in 1735 with her one day old child.[221]

Mary Mason Seldon died unexpectedly on 5 January 1758 just thirteen months after her mother wrote this deed of gift. The untimely loss of her 27 year old daughter caused Ann Thomson Mason immediately to revise her plans and revoke the 1756 deed of gift. On 8 February 1758, she filed a deed giving ten slaves to her two-year old grandson, Samuel Seldon, Jr. They include: George, Charles,

---

[219] Although Ann Thomson Mason initially had dower rights (right of usage) of slaves, it appears that she also used her resources to purchase slaves and land of her own.

[220] Stafford County, Virginia Deeds, Liber O 1748-1767, 433-456.

[221] Although unnamed, this child of Nan's may be Letty. Both Nan Oldgate and Letty receive preferential consideration in the several documents written by Ann Thomson Mason prior to her death.

Peter, Rush, Pegg, Hannah, Thomas (Hannah's child,) Poll and Nan Oldgate. She omits Job and Letty who were listed in the earlier deed.

One year later, on 24 January 1759, Mary Mason Seldon's husband, Samuel Seldon, Sr., filed a document in Stafford County stating that "...it is Doubtful in whom the Right of the s[ai]d Girl named Letty will vest after the death of the s[ai]d Ann Mason" and therefore Samuel Seldon arranged to sell "...the s[ai]d Negroe Girl Letty and her future Increase..." to Ann Thomson Mason for the sum of £40.[222] It seems apparent that Letty was an important slave to Ann Thomson Mason in order for her to essentially repurchase her in this way.

On 4 March 1760, Thomson Mason sold his mother Ann Thomson Mason six slaves for the "consideration" of £200. They were: Bridget, Ancilla, Anthony, Lucy, Alice, and Milly – and their future increase.[223] Bridget and Ancilla are two of the slaves from the Rose Bronough transaction discussed above. Although no ages or relationships are indicated in this document, it is possible that Anthony, Lucy, Alice, and Milly are "increase" – that is, the children of Bridget and Ancilla.

Five months later on 25 August 1760, Ann Thomson Mason wrote her will. To George Mason IV she bequeathed nine slaves: Bridget, Ancilla, Anthony, Sabrina, Lucy, Alice, Milly, Letty, and her son, Jamey[224] To her grandson Samuel Seldon, Jr., Ann directed that her Executors purchase "a likly [sic] young Negroe wench not Exceeding 20 years of age, with one male child...in lieu of Negroes Letty & her son Jamy..." To her granddaughter Mary Seldon she willed "a Negro girl named Jemima (the daughter of Pegg)....[225]

Two years later, after still more consideration, Ann Thomson Mason made a revision and added a codicil to her will. On 5 November 1762, she changed the path of Letty and her son yet again.

> "...I now at the request of my said son [George Mason] give the said
> Negro Letty & Jammy her son, to my Executors in trust, for my Grandson

---

[222] Stafford County, Virginia Liber P Deed Book, 1755-1764, 210-211.
[223] Ibid., 254-255.
[224] Letty's son, Jamey, was born between January 1759 and August 1760.
[225] Stafford County Will Book O, 1748-1767, 433-439.

Sam'l Seldon & heirs and if Samuel Seldon should die without issue [to my] Grand Daughter Mary Seldon & her heirs & in case my Grand Daughter should also die without issue before she arrive at the age of 21 the said Negroe Letty in trust for my son George Mason & the Negro Jammy in trust for my Grandson Thomson Mason, son to my said son George Mason..."

She also willed Samuel Seldon, Jr. her slaves Monsser and Corragio. And, finally, she stated:

It is also my earnest request & desire that the Mulatto wench named NAN OLDGATE who had been a useful slave in the family may not be sold, or exposed to Hardship as she is past her Labour, and that if possible she may be allowed to live with my son George Mason who I hope will use her with Humanity.

Of the four children that were born to Mary Mason Seldon, two died before Ann Thomson Mason's will was written. Mary Mason Seldon (b. Oct. 1754-d. 17 Sept. 1787) and Samuel Seldon, Jr. (b. 30 Apr. 1756-d.?) were living at the time of Ann Thomson Mason's death on 13 November 1762 and were mentioned in their grandmother's will.[226]

Several aspects of these numerous document changes are of note. First, Ann Thomson Mason had been planning and executing purchases over time in order that she would have the legal capability to will slaves (and land) to her daughter Mary and son Thomson who were left out of an inheritance because their father died intestate and the laws of primogeniture were invoked. Second, her initial plans were disrupted by the unexpected death of her daughter Mary. This untimely tragedy in the family caused Ann Thomson Mason to reevaluate how she would write her will. It ultimately led to her making multiple decisions and filing multiple documents as she did so. Third, these changes and the documents

---

[226] Mary Mason Seldon's two children that died before 1762 were Miles Carey Seldon (b. 24 Nov. 1751 – died before Aug. 1760) and Samuel Seldon, the first child of that name, (b. 23 Mar 1753 – d. 19 Apr 1753). In a personal conversation with Gunston Hall Genealogist Genevieve Jones, she expressed the belief that the second child named Samuel Seldon (known as Samuel Seldon, Jr.) did not live to reach his majority. No information has been obtained to determine the year of his death.

' On Saturday the 13th Day of *November*, Died at her House in *Stafford* County, in the Colony of *Virginia*, Mrs. ANNE MASON, Widow and Relict of Col. GEORGE MASON. To give her true Character at Length, would, to those who had the Pleasure of her Acquaintance, be unnecessary; and by Strangers, would be thought Flattery. Let it suffice therefore to observe, that She discharged her Duty, in the several Characters of a Wife, a Parent, a Mistress, a Friend, a Neighbour, and a Christian, with that distinguished Lustre, which every one would wish to imitate; but Few have ever equalled. Providence was accordingly pleased to reward her Virtues in this World, by gratifying her in the Accomplishment of the First and Dearest Wish of her Heart (the Happiness of her Children.) And after preparing her by a long and painful Illness, which She bore with exemplary Resignation; permitted her, in the Sixty-third Year of her Age, to exchange the transitory Pleasures of this World, for those never-fading Joys, which Goodness, like hers, may reasonably be assured of meeting with in the next.

The obituary of Ann Thomson Mason appeared in the Maryland Gazette on 23 December, 1762.

that were written leading up to her will (and finally including a codicil just days before her death), reveal that certain slaves – particularly several women and their children – were of great concern to Ann Thomson Mason as to their fate after her death.

Among the slaves she gave great consideration to were Bridget and Ancilla, from the Rose Bronough transaction. From Thomson Mason's sale to his mother to the inclusion in her will to George Mason IV, these two female slaves were favored. It is possible they were domestic slaves, with whom Ann Thomson Mason had a close association. She sought to protect them and keep them together, along with their "increase" for as long as possible. Were these women related to each other? Perhaps sisters? The reasons for their favored status could be many, but what is clear is that Ann Thomson Mason gave their future a great deal of thought.

Nan Oldgate, Letty, and Jamey posed the greatest concern for Ann Thomson Mason as to their fate as these documents reveal. Nan Oldgate is first mentioned in the deed of gift to Mary Mason Seldon, but after Mary's death, Nan Oldgate is transferred to Mary's son, Samuel Seldon, Jr. Upon reconsideration, Ann Thomson Mason adds a codicil to her will and leaves Nan Oldgate to George Mason with the charge to "use her with humanity." Letty, also initially given to Mary Mason Seldon, is sold back to Ann Thomson Mason by Mary's husband after her death. Samuel Seldon, Sr. specifically states in this deed of sale that its purpose is to "prevent as much as possible...Controversies or disputes" as to the ownership of Letty. Ann Thomson Mason decides to will Letty and her son to George Mason, but finally changes that bequest in a codicil: Letty and Jamy are to be held in trust with George Mason for Samuel Seldon, Jr.

These three slaves, Nan Oldgate, Letty, and Jamy, received the most preferential status of any in the documents Ann Thomson Mason filed. Although it is speculative, it is highly likely that there is a family connection among the three of them. Nan Oldgate may be the slave woman Nan (26) who had just given birth to a child one day before the 1735 inventory was taken at Stump Neck. Perhaps the child was – a girl. Perhaps it was Letty. In 1756, Letty would have been 21 years old. It is of note that when Ann Thomson Mason decides not to will Letty to Samuel Seldon, Jr., she specifically requests that a "wench" of 20 years of age with one son be purchased for him instead. At this time in the documentation, Letty would be about that same age. Jamy, Jamey – or James as he is later listed – is a mulatto child. It is possible that these three slaves (Nan Oldgate, Letty, and Jamy) were mother, daughter, and grandson. They were undoubtedly favored by Ann Thomson Mason as she went to such great lengths to provide for their future.

William Eilbeck Makes Gifts and Bequests

Ann Eilbeck Mason's father, William Eilbeck, filed his will in Charles County, Maryland in July 1763. He bequeathed all his Charles County land and personal property to his wife Sarah Edgar Eilbeck and his land in Prince Georges County to his only child, his daughter Ann Eilbeck Mason. In that document he also willed each of the six grandchildren in the Mason family a slave child.[227] The provision of giving a grandchild a slave child of approximately the same age was not unusual among the gentry families.[228] The slave girl Penny was transferred to his oldest granddaughter Ann, or "Nancy," Mason (as she was known) at about the time the will was written in 1763. Nancy Mason was eight years old; Penny was perhaps a year or two older than Nancy. His will designated that slave Dick (age 14) was be given to George Mason, Jr.; Cato (age 9) to William Mason; Cupid (age 8) to Thomson Mason; Priss (age 7) to Sarah Mason; and Nan (age 5) to Mary Mason. (See Table Six.)

The intent of giving a gentry child a gift of a slave child was most likely to encourage a bond from a young age between the two so that the slave would prove a "faithful" personal body servant to the white master or mistress as they grew into adulthood. In the case of Penny, this may have proved true. In subsequent documents discussed more fully later, we learn that Penny remained with Nancy more than forty years. Although it is not certain that Penny was a personal servant to Nancy in adulthood, she was the first slave Nancy owned. Penny likely traveled with Nancy as a girl, helped her dress, brushed her hair, and spent many hours in her company. Penny would have known much about Nancy's personality – both good

---

[227] Maryland Hall of Records, Annapolis, Maryland. Testamentary Proceedings, Liber 41 1764-1766, fold. 220 and 378. Only six of the Mason children were living at the time William Eilbeck wrote his will. He died on 26 July 1764.
[228] Walsh, *Motives of Honor*, 513-514; Morgan, *Slave Counterpoint*, 514-515.

and bad – and consequently learned about her desires and wants. This close association could have helped Penny gain bargaining power for things that she desired as well.

Where did slave children sleep, eat, and live when thrust into such roles as a child companion? Some may possibly have been taken into care by slaves in the child's new environment, living with the cook, the laundress, or one of the slave "nurses." This new black "family" thus became "fictive kin" to a child removed from his or her true mother, father, siblings, and other relatives. Sometimes a slave child stayed with the white child (now the owner) to gain familiarity and perform necessary chores. In such cases, the slave child would likely have slept on a pallet (mattress) on the floor of the white child's room, but would have taken meals wherever other slaves were eating. Time spent playing together as young children would eventually instill an understanding of their true relationship to each other: the white child was superior and the black child was subordinate. Color mattered; status was easily defined – it was as simple as seeing the color of one's skin. It would be a life-changing lesson learned by the slave child at a very early age.[229]

George Mason IV served as Executor to William Eilbeck's estate when his father-in-law died on 26 July 1764. Eilbeck's inventory, taken in November 1765, reveals he was a wealthy man with the total value of his estate at over £2200 that included 40 slaves.[230] William's widow, Sarah Eilbeck, inherited his Charles County plantation known as Mattawoman; she would ultimately will this plantation to her grandson William Mason – her husband's namesake – in 1780.[231]

---

[229] Eugene D. Genovese, *Roll, Jordon Roll, The World the Slaves Made* (New York: Vintage Books, 1976), 515-519.
[230] The inventory included 12 men, 11 women, 7 girls, and 10 boys with a combined value of £1238, more than half the value of the total estate. No value was given for Penny already in the possession of Nancy Mason.
[231] Charles County, Maryland Wills, Liber AF, Number 7, 582-585, 578.

The Decade Closes with a Mystery

Late in 1767, an insurrection involving the poisoning of several overseers (where some persons died), took place in or near Alexandria, Virginia. Although similar accounts of the incident appeared in several newspapers in other colonies as well as in the February 1768 Annual Register in London, only a few details of this event are known:

> From Alexandria, Virginia we learn that a Number of Negroes there lately conspired to poison their Overseers and that several persons have lost their lives in Consequence thereof: that some of the Negroes have been taken up, four of whom were executed about three Weeks ago after which their Heads were cut off and fixed on the Chimneys of the Court House and it was expected that four more would soon meet with the same Fate."[232]

Incidents such as poisonings or arson terrified the white population; public executions and the gory display of the heads of the executed served as a drastic warning and intended deterrent to any other slaves with similar intentions. But whose slaves were involved?

There is tantalizing documentation indicating that at least some of the slaves involved in this gruesome event were slaves owned by George Mason. More than a year after the newspaper account filtered through the colonies, George Washington wrote to his neighbor John Posey stating that George Mason was "disappointed of [not] receiving £350 of the Public for his executed Negroes...."[233] One thing appears certain: George Mason had slaves that were executed. Why? What had they done? Were these slaves involved in the poisoning incident reported in late 1767? What exactly had happened? And – was George Mason denied reimbursement for "lost property" yet again from the colony?

---

[232] *Pennsylvania Gazette*, December 31, 1767.
[233] John C. Fitzpatrick, ed., *The Writings of George Washington from the Original Manuscript Sources 1745-1799* (Washington D.C.:U.S. Government Printing Office, 1931-1937), Volume 2, 507. See also, Helen Hill Miller, *George Mason Constitutionalist* (Safety Harbor, FL: Simon Publications, 2001), 271.

Another year later, two additional clues in the ledger of Mason's friend and neighbor Martin Cockburn provide more insight. On 21 April 1770, Cockburn entered into his ledger:

> To House & Plantation Expenses
>
> > for my order on the Treasury for value of a Negroe fellow executed for Felony [£] 50.0.0[234]

On 16 May 1770 Cockburn made another entry regarding the same matter:

> To Capt. William Carr
>
> > Rec[eive]d of him in full for my order on the Treasury as above
> >
> > N.B. rec[eive]d of him the above £50 of my own and [£]350 on Acc[oun]t of Colo. Mason which I paid to him the same day & gave Capt. Carr a rec[eip]t for the whole[235]

George Mason was paid £350 from the public treasury in 1770. That was the exact amount Washington mentioned. According to the newspaper account, as many as eight Negroes were executed. Each of the eight slaves would have had an average value of £50, a realistic monetary value for adult working slaves (male or female) in this period.

As most of the money went to George Mason and seven of his slaves were involved in some "Felony," – a "poisoning" – did it occur on a property of Mason's and, if so, which one? How was the crime discovered? Why is there so little information about the incident? Certainly slave owners would want as little "publicity" as possible about such a serious act; slave insurrections, if widely known, might invite other similar incidents. But it is hard to imagine how such a frightening situation with not one, but possibly two public executions (as indicated by the newspaper accounts), could not invoke more written commentary in newspapers or at least in personal correspondence.... No other connection to this incident has come to light.

---

[234] Cockburn Ledger and Account Book, 21 April 1770.
[235] Ibid., 16 May 1770.

In 1770, more than two decades after George Mason's tenure as a Virginia gentry planter closed, he had experienced much as a slave master. He had overseen the construction of his mansion, Gunston Hall using much of the slave labor he purchased or inherited. He had prosecuted a slave thief, only to have him die while in the custody of the law. Mason's attempt at reimbursement from the House of Burgesses of Colonial Virginia for the slave lost while in custody failed, and he lost both money and "property." The Mason family suffered the loss of George Mason's mother and Ann Eilbeck Mason's father and as a result of both of their wills, slaves were incorporated into Mason's property holdings, adding responsibilities of oversight and management. Additionally, Mason may have experienced the fear of a poisoning among slaves he apparently owned. This time he was financially reimbursed for his "property" loss, but the event must have been frightening – for the white community and for the black community as well.

It was also during the latter part of these two decades that George Mason would begin to put in writing his sentiments about the institution of slavery. In 1765 during the Stamp Act crisis he wrote:

> The Policy of encouraging the Importation of free People & discouraging that of Slaves has never been duly considered in this Colony, or we shou'd not at this Day see one Half of our best Lands in most Parts of the Country remain unsetled [sic], & the other cultivated with Slaves; not to mention the ill Effect such a Practice has upon the Morals & Manners of our People: one of the first Signs of the Decay, & perhaps the primary Cause of the Destruction of the most flourishing Government that ever existed was the Introduction of great Numbers of Slaves - an Evil very pathetically described by the Roman Historians - but 'tis not the present Intention to expose our Weakness by examining this Subject too freely.[236]

George Mason was "duly considering" all that it meant to be a slave master. He saw slavery's bad effects on society and feared this as one of the first signs of moral decay. His sentiments would grow stronger and become more public in the

---

[236] Rutland, *Papers of George Mason,* 61, 62. This statement began a scheme drafted by George Mason to circumvent the need for taxed documents by landlords in 1765. The plan became unnecessary as Parliament rescinded the Stamp Act, but Mason's sentiments about slavery in Virginia were on record.

next two decades. During the first half of his adult life, Mason came into his own as a husband, father, planter, and slave master. He gradually pulled all of these roles into perspective, making decisions, choices, and statements that reflected his personal growth and maturity in the time that a young nation was developing and maturing as well. George Mason became a critical leader of a new nation in the next two decades. His analytical thinking also challenged the acceptance of a century and a half of slavery in North America. Although his outspoken anger toward slavery would grow, his personal actions seemingly stood still.

Chapter Four:

The Slaves
of Gunston Hall,
1770-1792

Gunston Hall's kitchen, a reconstructed building on the original site, reflects both a work place and housing for the cook and her (or his) family.

$\mathcal{B}$y 1770, George Mason was engaged in running Gunston Hall plantation as a full-fledged business. He probably had a sufficient number of slaves to work the four outlying quarters (Hallowing Point, Dogues Neck, Occoquan, and Pohick) with about twenty assigned to each location. Overseers also living at the quarters maintained the work routine and the discipline.[237] Near the mansion, outbuildings supported the domestic needs of Mason's family. A kitchen, close to the mansion and the kitchen well, was in daily operation. Other domestic structures included a dairy where soft cheeses, butter, milk, and cream were kept; a separate laundry; a smoke house; and possibly a storehouse.[238] George Mason also maintained an ice house on the east side of the property.[239]

Ann Mason, following English methods and using English cookbooks – or "receipt" books as they were then known – planned the daily dinner served at two o'clock at Gunston Hall. Ann used the first floor bed chamber as her office for planning and directing various domestic activities in the morning hours. Dinner included a first course of three or more meat dishes (beef, ham, chicken, etc.), perhaps a soup or fish, and numerous side dishes (vegetables, "salatt", pies, and breads); a second course possibly followed with additional meat and side dishes. The final course was a dessert course of syllabubs, jellies, fruits, sweetmeats, and perhaps nuts.[240] During the morning hours of preparation, Ann Mason could access the

---

[237] Overseers, usually paid white men, served as managers on farm quarters, directing the work and administering discipline as needed. On Mason's quarters several are known by name: Groves was the overseer at Dogues Neck in 1791; William Green was at Hallowing Point in 1789 and 1791; Fugate was at Pohick [?] in 1791; and Nace was the slave overseer at Occoquan when the inventory was taken there in 1797. See Rutland, *Papers of George Mason,* 1248, 1162, 1226, and 1246 respectively. See also: Appendix L and the map on p. 162.

[238] Cary Carson & Carl Lounsbury, *Chesapeake House* (Chapel Hill: The University of North Carolina Press, 2013), 156-203. Rather than a separate store house, Mason may have used the English basement at Gunston Hall for the storage of cloth for slave clothing, shoes, etc., and some food stuffs including his wine.

[239] Personal conversation with Gunston Hall Archeologist David Shonyo.

[240] Possible cook books or receipt books in Ann Mason's possession include Hannah Glasse, *The Art of Cookery Made Plain and Easy* or Elizabeth Raffold, *The Experienced English Housekeeper.* Both of these books included suggestions for menus or placement of dishes on the dining table. Although Virginia housewives utilized English books to guide them, customs may have dismissed the second course. Receipts were also modified in Virginia because of different food stuffs available and also because of African influences by slave cooks. See also Mary Randolph, *The Virginia Housewife or, Methodical Cook* (New York: Dover Publications, Inc.), 3-7 for a discussion on early nineteenth century cooking. I am very grateful to B.L.Trahos for her suggestions on eighteenth century cook book references.

kitchen from the mansion by way of the side passage to confer with the cook on the progress of the meal or possibly make changes to the menu. Cooking and baking began at day break and required an experienced cook who was an enslaved woman – or man – plus several assisting hands. Often slave children picked vegetables from the garden, plucked feathers from chickens, or did myriad unskilled chores to aid the cook. Ann Mason herself likely spent time in the kitchen, especially when new receipts were tried. Many ingredients came from the stores inside the mansion. John Mason described "The Closet" in the first floor bed chamber as an upper pantry that held the more expensive, imported foodstuffs such as sugar and a variety of spices (cinnamon, nutmeg, pepper, etc.) as well as the tea, coffee, or chocolate served as beverages. Those special ingredients needed for meal preparation were given out in the measured amounts for the receipt.[241]

As each food item was prepared, it was placed on a shelf or "dresser" in the kitchen. When mealtime drew near, slaves set up drop-leaf tables in the dining room to accommodate the family, the children's tutor, the governess, visitors, and travelers who were dining on any given day. The food was carried from the kitchen to the table. Using the images provided in the receipt books as a guide, Ann Mason placed serving dishes of food symmetrically about the center of the table in the proper English style of service. When guests and family arrived to dinner, they would likely marvel at the bounty they were about to enjoy in a picturesque setting. George Mason served a toddy to the men before dinner and offered a blessing before eating.[242] Then, seated at the dinner table, each person would be asked to serve the food closest to them while the individuals passed their dinner plates to be filled.[243] Young slave men waiting at the table in the manner of footmen served beverages (cider, wine, or possibly beer), removed plates and food at the completion of the main course, placed the second course if there was one, and last, removed the tablecloth before bringing the dessert course to the table.[244] Leftover food would be returned to the kitchen to be served for a late-night supper. The last of

---

[241] Dunn, ed., *Recollections*, 47. See as reference to upper pantries, Terry K. Dunn, "The More Precious Stores for the Table" research paper, Gunston Hall Library.
[242] Dunn, ed., *Recollections*, 52.
[243] Julia Cherry Spruill, *Women's Life & Work in the Southern Colonies* (New York: W.W. Norton & Company, 1972), 65-74.
[244] Ibid. See also, Sara Paston-Williams, *The Art of Dining* (London: The National Trust, 1999), 254-263; and Philip Morgan, *Slave Counterpoint*, 246.

the days' food was offered for breakfast the next morning, perhaps with a fresh pot of tea. This domestic ritual of two o'clock dinner required the hands of many enslaved people from day break until termination of the social activities of the day.[245]

By 1770, George Mason probably housed most of the domestic and skilled slave workers in buildings within the vicinity of the mansion; John Mason mentioned that workers' buildings on the east side of the main house were screened from view by a row of cherry trees.[246] Inside the mansion itself, slaves who tended the youngest children's needs were kept busy throughout the day and into the night. Cleaning and housekeeping duties went on with "house servants" or "house maids" (perhaps "House Poll" or "House Nell") moving about all areas in the home using the winder stairs in the side passageway.[247] Some white indentured servants may have lived among the slaves in similar structures. Mason's hired Scottish tutors most likely lived in the school house located on the west side of the mansion. Mrs. Newman, the family's governess, likely had a room on the mansion's second floor.[248]

George Mason maintained the room known as the Little Parlor – just across the side passage from the first floor bed chamber – as his work place and office. As his sons became older they were tasked to copy letters for their father or deliver letters or parcels to neighboring planters for him. No doubt they were learning his business ethics along the way. Although none of Mason's plantation ledgers appear to have survived, he, like other gentry men, most likely kept records of daily occurrences, farm production, sales, and purchases – and all work involving his slave force. Three of Mason's sons followed in his footsteps and became planters; two established business ventures. Learning management from their father was an important part of their early education.[249]

---

[245] Surviving primary documents do not reveal who was the Mason's enslaved cook. However, George Mason V's will lists "Cooke Charles" at his Lexington property. It is highly likely that Charles was the son of the man or woman who was the primary slave cook at Gunston Hall. See Appendix K.

[246] Dunn, ed., *Recollections*, 59.

[247] Morgan, *Slave Counterpoint*, 244. Carson and Lounsbury, *Chesapeake House*, 139.

[248] Dunn, ed., *Recollections*, 22, 45. Mr. McPherson, Mr. Davidson, and Mr. Constable were hired as tutors; Mrs. Newman was a hired as a governess for the girls. The dates of employment of these individuals are not known. Philip Vickers Fithian, the tutor at Nomini Hall lived in the school house along with several of Robert Carter's sons. See Farish, ed., *Journal and Letters of Philip Vickers Fithian*, xxv-xxxii.

[249] George Mason V, William, and Thomson maintained plantations as their principle ventures. John and Thomas had apprenticeships leading them into businesses.

Sudden Changes

In 1773, personal tragedy struck the Mason family. In December 1772, Ann Mason delivered twin boys prematurely. James and Richard were baptized immediately, but both died the next day and were buried in the "new Burying Ground" at Gunston Hall.[250] The entry in the family Bible tells the rest of the story more poignantly. Ann Eilbeck Mason, "occasioned by a long illness" during this pregnancy, did not improve over the winter months. On 9 March 1773, Ann Eilbeck Mason died "of a long, slow fever." She too was buried in the new family burying ground "without the common parade and ceremony of a grand funeral," as she requested.[251] John Mason, only seven years old at the time of his mother's death, remembered seeing her coffin lowered into the grave "by cords covered by black cloth." He also remembered

> ...that there was a large assemblage of friends & neighbors of every class and of the slaves of the estate present...that the children and servants [slaves] passed each other in tears & in silence & spoke in whispers...[252]

John Mason, as young as he was at the time of this tragedy, was indelibly marked by this event. He recalled the foreboding of her illness, the invitations to his mother's bedside to sip some of the weak milk punch prescribed by Dr. Craik, and her final charges to him which included that he "be kind to the servants...."[253] In April, a funeral sermon was preached at Pohick Church by the family's friend, the Rev. Mr. James Scott. Among many who attended this service was Martha Washington. George Washington paid his condolences to George Mason at Gunston Hall several days later.[254]

Domestic life had to continue. Nine children were left in need of daily care. Nancy Mason, eighteen years old at the time of her mother's death and "blessed with her mother's amiable disposition," was the oldest girl and took over running the

---

[250] Copeland and MacMaster, *Five George Masons*, 115.
[251] Rutland, *Papers of George Mason*, 481-482.
[252] Dunn, ed., *Recollections*, 49.
[253] Ibid.
[254] Miller, *Gentleman Revolutionary*, 100.

household. Her father would later write that she was "...mistress of my family and manages my little domestic matters with a degree of prudence far above her years."[255]

George Mason IV, deeply mourning his wife Ann's loss, faced this unexpected reality of life and turned toward an important task. Within two weeks of her death he wrote his will. In it he gave to each of his nine children bequests of his land, furniture, money, and slaves. In the document he referenced thirty-six slaves by name and eleven others by a maternal connection.[256] His will provides us with a central timeline to possibly trace many of these enslaved individuals. In examining surviving documents, looking principally at slave names and scattered notations of slave relationships, we can speculate on the ancestors of some; for others we can identify their progeny; in a rare few instances we can see multiple generations of slave families.[257]

No document survives indicating that George Mason freed any of the slaves he owned. When he wrote his will in 1773, Virginia was an English colony under Crown rule. Its laws prohibited a master from freeing his slaves. Only a petition approved by the Royal Governor and his Council could grant manumission, ostensibly for meritorious service within the colony.[258] Mason's slaves – perhaps as many as 125 individuals – would pass into the ownership of his five sons and four daughters.

---

[255] Copeland and MacMaster, *Five George Masons*, 116.

[256] See Appendix: G.

[257] This analysis is based largely on slave naming patterns. Although Philip Morgan advises that many Chesapeake slaves named children more frequently after fathers than mothers, patterns in the Mason slave listings reflect the use of mothers' (and other maternal line) names for children. Morgan also emphasizes the carryover of sibling names in slave families; this is indicated in Mason slave naming patterns. See Morgan, *Slave Counterpoint*, 451-2; 546-551. For additional discussion of Chesapeake slave naming patterns see also, Anne Elizabeth Yentsch, *A Chesapeake Family and Their Slaves* (Cambridge: Cambridge University Press, 1994), 367-368; and Walsh, *Calibar to Carter's Grove*, 159-170.

[258] Less than two dozen individuals were given freedom through this process in the half century between 1723 and the Revolutionary War. None seem to have been for meritorious service, but rather petitions offered because of favoritism by the master and granted because of political favoritism of the slave owner by the Council.

Slaves Bequeathed in George Mason's 1773 Will

To George Mason (V): 1753-1796; m. Elizabeth Mary Ann Barnes Hooe 1784.

Alice – Alice was one of four enslaved girls willed to George Mason IV by his mother. It is possible that some or all of these girls (Alice, Ancilla, Lucy, and Milly) were sisters. One boy, Anthony was included in this group and may be a brother to one or all of them. All of these children were born before 1760. George Mason IV willed Alice (now probably over the age of sixteen) to George Mason V, but Alice does not appear in any of his later documents. However, a woman named Alice, age forty five (valued at £35), is listed on the Prince William County property of Thomas Mason in 1800. If this is the same Alice, she could have been sold to Thomas Mason after George V's death in 1796. If so, she moved across the Occoquan River to Thomas' Woodbridge Plantation.[259] See Appendix: C, D, G, N.

Bob Dunk – There is no reference to the name Bob Dunk or Dunk in any other record. Nothing else is known of this individual. See Appendix: G.

Yellow Dick – Dick, a mulatto, was a runaway slave – not once, but twice. Already in the possession of George Mason V in 1784, an advertisement listed a reward for his return after he ran the first time. Apparently caught, Dick ran away two years later and ads were placed for him again in 1786 and 1787. Born about 1762, Dick was a "waiting man" first at Gunston Hall and then at Lexington Plantation. Working inside these homes, he likely heard much news and information about the Revolutionary War and discussion about Virginians' "enslavement to the British." There was also talk at this time among the gentry, their visitors, and travelers speculating that slaves might be emancipated. Disappointed of receiving his freedom, Dick may have taken matters into his own hands and decided to run away. (See additional discussion below.) See Appendix: G.

---

[259] There is a distinct Mason-Eilbeck family history of selling and exchanging slaves within the family. Paperwork supports a few of these instances, but many documents have not survived. With several of George Mason IV's sons dying young, it is possible that slaves and other property were sold to resolve debts. It is also possible that family members bought slaves for that purpose.

Bob (son of Occoquan Nell) – Bob (born about 1765) and his sister Nell were children of a woman named Nell living at the Occoquan Quarter. Bob was living at Lexington in 1797. See Appendix: G, L.

Peter (son of Great Sue) – Peter (born about 1767) was living at the Dogue Neck Quarter in 1797. His parents are possibly *Old Susan* (as she may now have been known) and Peter who are both listed as "past labor" and also living at the Dogue Neck Quarter. Peter had a sister named Sarah (see below) who was willed to George Mason's daughter Elizabeth. "Great Sue," "Old Susan" and "Sue" who was listed as eight years old in 1735 may all be names for the same individual. If so, "Old Susan" was about sixty-nine years old when listed in the Dogue Neck inventory. See Appendix: A, D, G, L.

Judy – A slave woman Judith, age thirty, was listed in the Stump Neck inventory of George Mason III in 1735. Sometime before 1756, Ann Thomson Mason gave her daughter Mary Mason Seldon a number of slaves including one named "Judy," possibly Judith's daughter. Judy was in the possession of Mary Mason Seldon at the time of her death and thus became the property of her husband, Samuel Seldon, Sr. However, it is possible Judy was sold or exchanged and subsequently became the property of George Mason IV. No other family connections to this individual are known. See Appendix: A, C, G.

Lucy – "Lucey," born c. 1730, may be the mother of the girl Lucy, one of the several slave children willed to George Mason IV by Ann Thomson Mason. By 1773, Lucy may be a mother herself as Mason's will included "Sally (daughter of Lucy)." See below. In 1797, Lucy (born c. 1759) was listed as age thirty eight and was living on the Dogue Neck quarter. See Appendix: B, C, D, G, L.

Dick (given by Grandfather Eilbeck) – This slave named Dick (born in 1749) was the boy of sixteen listed in William Eilbeck's 1765 inventory and was one of the slave gifts to his grandchildren. In the Eilbeck inventory, Dick's low value of £15 may indicate poor health or an incapacitation that occurred after William Eilbeck wrote his will 1763. He appears in no other documents. (Cato, for example, who was willed to William Mason, was nine years old and valued higher at £26 in 1765.) See Appendix: E, F, G.

Tom – Tom (born about 1747) is listed in the 1797 Lexington inventory of George Mason V. Tom is a carpenter and was probably one of the slaves who lived with his family at Log Town.[260] See Appendix: C, G, L.

Liberty – Liberty (born about 1747) also a carpenter, is listed in the Lexington inventory of George Mason V. Approximately the same age as Tom, he too probably lived at Log Town.[261] Although neither Tom nor Liberty may have helped to build Gunston Hall in the 1750s, both young boys would have seen its construction. Also, one or both boys may have been family members (sons or nephews) of the skilled slave carpenters or workmen who did build Gunston Hall. Slaves with skills frequently passed them down to their children.[262] See Appendix: G, L.

To William Mason: 1757-1818; m. Ann Stuart 1793.

Milly (daughter of Kate) – No extant documentation to Milly as the daughter of a slave named Kate survives. Mattawoman Kate (45) and Milly (12) in the inventory of William Eilbeck taken in 1765 are possibly these individuals. If so, "Milly (daughter of Kate)," remained on the Maryland property as William Mason inherited his Grandfather Eilbeck's Mattawoman Plantation. In 1819 William Mason's inventory lists Milly, a girl, eight years old; she is possibly a descendent of "Milly (daughter of Kate)." See Appendix: F, G, H, R.

Sampson (son of Mrs. Eilbeck's Bess) – Bess, the most highly valued female slave at the Eilbeck's Mattawoman Plantation, had seven children. Her son Sampson was three years old in 1765. An adult male slave named Sam on that plantation was possibly Bess' husband and Sampson's father. William Mason inherited that property and in 1819, there is a boy named Sampson, 10 years old, living there who might Sampson's grandson and Bess' great grandson. See Appendix: F, G, R.

Cato (given by Grandfather Eilbeck) – Cato was a slave child nine years old when he was willed to William Mason 1763. In 1819, Cato, still living on the

---

[260] Dunn, ed., *Recollections,* 59.
[261] Ibid.
[262] Morgan, *Slave Counterpoint,* 215.

Mattawoman Plantation in Maryland is (incorrectly) estimated to be fifty-six years old. Cato was probably born c. 1754 based on his age at the time of William Eilbeck's will. That would make him approximately sixty-five years old in 1819.[263] See Appendix: E, F, G, R.

To Thomson Mason: 1759-1820; m. Sarah McCarty Chichester 1784.

Sally (daughter of Lucy) – Sally, probably the other daughter of the slave "Lucey," was the sister of Lucy (above). Thomson Mason's inventory taken in 1821 lists a woman Sarah as age 60 (born about 1761) who could be "Sally" (a nickname for Sarah). See Appendix: B, C, D, G, S.

Joe (son of Mrs. Eilbeck's Bess) – Joe, Sampson's brother, was another child of Bess at the Eilbeck Plantation in Maryland. Joe was "1 yr 7 mo" [one year and seven months] old according to William Eilbeck's inventory in 1765, making his date of birth April 1764, if accurate. Joe is not listed in Thomson's inventory and probably did not survive to the year 1821.

In a 1791 letter, George Mason IV refers to "Joe" as the bearer of "a portmanteau, saddle, and mail pillion" sent to John Mason (in Baltimore?)[264] Thomson Mason and his wife resided at Gunston Hall for several years (1784-1788) while their house at Hollin Hall was under construction; by 1791 they were probably in their (still uncompleted) new home.[265] Joe, the son of Mrs. Eilbeck's Bess, resided at Gunston Hall for at least several years. Twenty seven years old in 1791, it is possible that George Mason "borrowed" Joe for such an important errand – after he perhaps completed an errand that brought him to Gunston Hall. Joe had established a considerable level of trust to travel as far away as Baltimore. See Appendix: F, G.

Cupid (given by Grandfather Eilbeck) – One of the six slave children willed by William Eilbeck to his grandchildren, Cupid, a boy of eight, was a gift to Thomson. As there are no further references to Cupid (born c. 1757), he likely did not survive until 1821. See Appendix: E, F, G.

---

[263] That would make Cato's age in closer to 65 in 1819.
[264] Rutland, *Papers of George Mason*, 1251.
[265] Copeland and MacMaster, *Five George Masons*, 236, 237.

To John Mason: 1766-1849; m. Anna Maria Murray 1796.

Harry (son of House Poll) – Poll is one of the slaves given to Mary Mason Seldon by her mother, but her whereabouts after Mary's death are not known. It is possible that "House Poll" was a slave woman who came with Ann Eilbeck when she married George Mason in 1750. This is the only mention of Harry. See Appendix: C, G.

Peg (daughter of Chloe) – Cloe was about 60 years old in 1792 and living at Stump Neck, Maryland.[266] Cloe/Chloe had at least two children, Peg and Bess, both of whom may have been acquired by George Mason after his mother's death. He willed Peg (daughter of Chloe) to John Mason and Bess (daughter of Cloe) to Nancy Mason. Among Nancy Mason's documents can be seen eight of Bess' children, including Bess' daughter, Chloe. Thus, this possible family lineage includes: a mother (Cloe), daughters (Peg and Bess), and granddaughter (Chloe). See Appendix: A, D, J, G, I, O.

To Thomas Mason: 1770-1800; m. Sarah Barnes Hooe 1793.

Jack (son of House Nell) – One of House Nell's two children, Jack, was born about 1768. Jack appears again in the 1800 inventory of Thomas Mason. Now, thirty two years old, he is a rough carpenter, but has lost sight of one eye. He is valued highly at £82. House Nell, or Gunston Nell as she was probably known also, was a midwife.[267] See Appendix: G, N.

Daphne (daughter of Dinah) – Daphne, age twenty eight, is listed in the inventory of Thomas Mason in 1800. Born about 1772, her mother Dinah is living at the Hallowing Point quarter in 1797 and is now age fifty five. See Appendix: G, N, L.

---

[266] Age estimates in inventories were highly arbitrary. It is possible Cloe was actually born after that 1735 inventory was taken.
[267] Cockburn Ledger & Account Book, 21 February 1790, 30 November 1790. Nell was paid 12 shillings for delivering Leah on February 21st and 12 shillings/4 pence for delivering Megar in November of that year. These payments were commensurate with white midwife payments of the time.

To Ann (Nancy) Mason: 1755-1814; m. Rinaldo Johnson 1789.

Bess (daughter of Cloe) – Bess was one of the slaves that Ann Thomson Mason gave to her daughter Mary but later likely reclaimed or repurchased after Mary's death in 1758. If so, Bess was now given to Nancy Mason, the oldest granddaughter of Ann Thomson Mason. Records trace Bess for more than 31 years. She is the mother of eight children: Frank, Lizzy, Dick, Chloe, Nancy, Margaret, Priss, and Delia. All of these slaves are recorded in the contract George Mason IV writes for Nancy Mason in 1789 to secure her property to her in her marriage to Rinaldo Johnson. In 1804, Nancy Mason Johnson wills this entire slave family to her son.[268] Bess and her eight children remain together for over three decades. See Appendix: C, D, G, I, O.

Frank (Bess's child) – Frank, born before 1773, is one of the eight children of Bess (daughter of Cloe) listed above.

In the 1735 inventory taken at Stump Neck in Charles County, Maryland, a slave named Frank (age 30) is specifically noted to be a woman. It is possible that Frank is the mother of Peg (16), Frank (10), and Cloe (likely born after the 1735 inventory was taken). If so, the tracings of four generations in this slave family may include: Frank, her children Peg, Frank, and Cloe; her grandchildren Peg/Pegg and Bess (daughters of Cloe); and her great-grandchildren, Frank and Chloe (the children of Bess). See Appendix: A, D, G, I, J, O.

Mulatto Priss (daughter of Jenny) – Jenny may be the girl adjudged to be eight years old in 1753.[269] She is the mother of two girls, Mulatto Priss and Little Jenny, both born before 1773. Mulatto Priss apparently does not survive until 1789 when Nancy Mason's marriage contract is written. See Appendix: G.

Nell (daughter of Occoquan Nell) – Nell was the sister of Bob and Vicky. Bob remained at the Lexington Plantation of George Mason V. Vicky probably moved to King George County when Elizabeth Mason married William Thornton.

[268] In the 1804 document, Mary is listed rather than Margaret. It may be a different child and Margaret did not survive, or it may be a nickname.
[269] Fairfax County, Virginia Order Book 1749-1754, 436. On 21 Aug 1753 seven slaves were adjudged as to their ages for George Mason IV. (See Table 5)

Nell seems to have been dealt a bad hand by the fates: perhaps inadvertently she was not included in the marriage contract that George Mason wrote for Nancy. Nancy inherited Nell, but became part of the property controlled by Rinaldo Johnson. Nell was later sold.[270] See Appendix: G.

Penny (given by Grandfather Eilbeck) – Penny was one of the six slave children given by Grandfather Eilbeck to his grandchildren. The documents show that Penny was with Nancy Mason for more than forty years. Although her age is not listed in William Eilbeck's inventory, slave children given as gifts were often close to the age of the white child. Nancy was about seven or eight years old when she received Penny.[271] Penny was born c. 1755.

In the surviving documents that list Penny, or Penelope as she was also known, and other slaves that Nancy Mason (Johnson) owned, Penny was always listed alone. She apparently had no children. Originally born in Maryland at the Eilbeck plantation of Mattawoman, Penny was moved to Gunston Hall in Virginia to be with Nancy sometime before 1763. Where she lived on the property is not known. However, in 1789, when Nancy married Rinaldo Johnson, Penny moved back to Maryland where she now lived on the Johnson's property in Prince George's County. She was finally closer to her own family members in neighboring Charles County after twenty six years. See Appendix: E, G, I, O.

To Sarah Mason: 1760-1823; m. Daniel McCarty, Jr. 1778.

Hannah – Ann Thomson Mason first gave Hannah to Mary Mason Seldon, but after Mary's death she transferred "Hannah and her son Thomas born since" (born about 1758) to Samuel Seldon, Jr. As he probably died before his majority, Hannah and other slaves bequeathed to him may have been dispersed to others.[272] If so, Tom would have been about 15 years old in 1773. Hannah and Tom would have resided at Cedar Grove Plantation (not far from Gunston Hall) after Sarah Mason's marriage to Daniel McCarty, Jr. See Appendix: C, D, G.

---

[270] This story will unfold in the further discussion of Nancy Mason's slave holdings. See pages 115, 116.
[271] Slave children given as gifts were likely expected to become personal servants, gaining trust and companionship with the white child as they grew up together. See Morgan, *Slave Counterpoint,* 380.
[272] Nan Oldgate was one of those slaves.

Venus (daughter of Beck) – In 1753, when George Mason IV had seven slaves adjudged for their ages in Fairfax County, Beck was estimated to be nine years old. In 1773, Beck, about twenty nine, was the mother of Venus, Rachel, and Mulatto Mima. In 1797, Beck, fifty, is living at Lexington Plantation. A fourteen year old girl named Beck is also listed that year at the Hallowing Point quarter. She could be another generation in that family.[273] No other references to Venus are found. See Appendix: G, L.

Mulatto Mima (daughter of Beck) – One of Beck's three daughters, this is the only mention of Mulatto Mima. Two of the three sisters (Venus and Mulatto Mima) remained together at Cedar Grove.[274] See Appendix: G.

Priss (given by Grandfather Eilbeck) – Priss, was born in 1758. One of the Eilbeck slaves, she was willed to Sarah by her grandfather. A child companion at Gunston Hall, Priss later lived at Cedar Grove, but nothing further is known. See Appendix: E, F, G.

To Mary Mason: 1762-1804; m. John Travers Cooke 1784.

Ann – No connection to this slave is made in any other documents. She may have been a slave brought into the marriage by Ann Eilbeck Mason. See Appendix: G.

Nell (daughter of House Nell) – Sister to Harry and Jack, Nell may have been the child of a slave that Ann Eilbeck Mason brought with her after her marriage in 1750. Nothing else is known about this slave. See Appendix: G.

Little Jenny (daughter of Jenny) – Sister to Mulatto Priss, her mother, Jenny, is probably the slave adjudged as eight years old 1753.[275] See Appendix: G.

---

[273] Fairfax County, VA Order Book 1749-1754, p. 436.
[274] A sister of Venus and Rachel, Mima's father was white. This distinction of color was very important to slave masters in documenting slaves in runaway ads, wills, inventories, etc. Mulatto was a defined legal term in Virginia. Hening, *Statutes*, 3:252.
[275] Fairfax County, Virginia Order Book 1749-1754, 436.

Nan (given by Grandfather Eilbeck) – Nan, born in 1760, was only three years old when willed to Mary Mason to be her companion and probably moved to Gunston Hall when she was about five. Nothing else about her is known, but all of the four slaves willed to Mary Mason would have moved south to Marlborough when Mary married. See Appendix: E, F, G.

To Elizabeth Mason: 1768- before 1797; m. William Thornton 1789.

Vicky (daughter of Occoquan Nell) – Vicky was the third known child of Occoquan Nell. Elizabeth Mason probably resided in King George County after her marriage and moved her slaves there. See Appendix: G.

Sarah (daughter of Great Sue) – Great Sue (or Old Susan as she may have later been known) and Peter had two children, Sarah and Peter. Old Susan and Peter, both "past labor" and their son Peter (30) were living at the Dogue Neck quarter in 1797. In 1789 Sarah moved to King George County when Elizabeth Mason married. See Appendix: G, L.

Rachel (daughter of Beck) – Rachel was one of the three girls born to the slave girl Beck who was adjudged to be nine years of age in 1753.[276] Nothing else is known about Rachel. See Appendix: G.

Two additional slaves that were not named in George Mason's 1773 will but appeared in other documents are of interest and importance; they are **James** and **Nace.** James was George Mason's personal body servant and the only slave that John Mason named in his *Recollections.* His omission in Mason's 1773 will is curious and is considered below. Likewise, Nace was not named in the will, but is revealed in other documents as a capable and trusted individual who was given increased responsibility by George Mason. (See Table Seven.)

[276] Ibid.

James

The most prominent person among the domestic slaves at Gunston Hall was **James,** a mulatto man, who served George Mason as his personal body servant. John Mason, in his *Recollections* said that James traveled with his father, prepared his clothing and wigs, and lived with his own family in the slave quarters at Log Town, some distance from the mansion house. James definitely had George Mason's trust. He also was dressed appropriately for the position he was given. He wore livery which distinguished him whether at Gunston Hall or wherever he traveled with Mason. James was a visibly prestigious slave serving George Mason.

It is very probable that James, the mulatto son of Letty (Ann Thomson Mason's highly favored slave woman), was this personal servant to George Mason. But the story is convoluted.

Initially, in 1756, Ann Thomson Mason gave the slave woman Letty to her daughter Mary Mason Seldon in a deed of gift. Mary died two years later and Ann now re-arranged her "gifts" of slaves. In order to secure Letty's ownership to Ann Thomson Mason, Samuel Seldon, Sr. (Mary's husband) deeded Letty back to Ann, possibly at Ann Thomson Mason's request. In 1760, Ann wrote her will; Letty and "Jamey" her son were bequeathed to George Mason IV. However, in 1762, Ann changed her mind; in a codicil, she now willed Letty and her son "Jammy" to her grandson, Samuel Seldon, Jr., *but with the provision that these two slaves were to be kept "in trust" with George Mason IV at Gunston Hall.*

Ann Thomson Mason died on 13 November 1762 and an inventory of her Stafford County, Virginia property was taken. Letty was listed as a woman valued at £75 (the highest valued slave in the entire inventory). "James, Letty's mulatto son," was a boy valued at £30.

Ann Thomson Mason's grandson, Samuel Seldon, Jr., was born in 1756; as a boy he attended school at Gunston Hall with his Mason cousins. Young Samuel boarded at Martin Cockburn's plantation known as Springfield in 1768 and 1769. However,

Samuel Seldon, Jr. is believed to have died before he reached his majority (age 21 in 1777).[277]

From 1763 until an unknown date, James (also known as Jamey or Jammy) was held in trust for Samuel - and lived on the property of George Mason IV at Gunston Hall. James presumably was being groomed as a personal body servant for young Samuel. By 1772, James was wearing livery. In the Alexandria account book of William Carlin, George Mason was charged in June and again in October 1772, for "altering pr. Plush Bretches to James" and "makeing [sic] y[ou]r man James Livery Lac[e]d." In 1773, another suit was made for his "man James."[278] Where was Samuel Seldon, Jr.in 1772? Was he still attending school and boarding nearby? Was he deceased by this time? We do not know.

James received training or instruction in curling and cleaning wigs, possibly in Williamsburg at Richard Charlton's wig shop where Mason occasionally shopped. John Mason specifically noted that his father's wigs "were dressed & prepared by his man James, a mulattoe [sic] man, who attended his person and traveled with him."[279] In early February 1778, George Mason returned home from Williamsburg after a lengthy session in the House of Delegates which produced significant legislation to aid the Revolutionary War. En route home he wrote to his cousin James Mercer that he was unable to stop in Fredericksburg to see him because of

> ...the Accident of my Servant's falling sick on the Road; which detained me four or five Days at Hubbard's [Ordinary] & obliged me, at last, to leave him behind me, & hire a Servant to this Place [Bellevue Plantation in Stafford County, the home of Thomas Ludwell Lee].[280]

This sick servant was likely James, now quite possibly George Mason's personal servant. Surely anxious to return to Gunston Hall, Mason spent nearly a week with his ill person before reluctantly leaving him behind. Nothing else is known of this event.

---

[277] There is no knowledge of him after the 1769 reference in Martin Cockburn's ledger for payment for board. Martin Cockburn Account and Ledger Book, 19 May, 1769. Former genealogist and researcher Genevieve Jones believed Samuel Seldon, Jr. died before his majority. Personal communication.
[278] William Carlin Account Book, 8 October 1772, 12 June 1773.
[279] Dunn, ed., *Recollections*, 52.
[280] Rutland, *Papers of George Mason*, 426.

Did this boy James, groomed to attend Samuel Seldon, Jr. (but who likely never got the chance to serve him) ultimately become the personal servant to George Mason IV? It seems highly probable.

Although Ann Thomson Mason's codicil made provisions for James should her grandson die before reaching his majority, it is possible that George Mason arranged to purchase James after the (early?) death of Samuel Seldon Jr. Letty's mulatto son James is the only recorded slave that fits the description John Mason gives of his father's personal servant in his *Recollections*.[281] Ann Thomson Mason gave considerable attention to this slave and his mother Letty in her documents. Her concern for their future undoubtedly was impressed on George Mason.

John Mason accompanied his father to Philadelphia in 1787 and was in close correspondence with him until George Mason's death in 1792. John knew his father's personal habits and described several in his *Recollections*. John had distinct memories of James. It made a strong impression on him that "James...& his family and those of several Negro carpenters" were allowed to live autonomously at Log Town, the little village just out of sight, behind a woods, at Gunston Hall.[282]

James does not appear in George Mason IV's will of 1773. Perhaps Samuel Seldon, Jr. was still living in that year. Or perhaps James was not legally under the ownership of George Mason at the time he wrote the document. Manumission by a master became legal in Virginia in 1782. If any slave would be emancipated, would it not be James? No record of such an event exists. Nor did George Mason IV set up any special arrangements in a will or document to provide for James's protection as his brother Thomson Mason did for his man Jack. *(See below.)*

---

[281] In the codicil to her will, Ann Thomson Mason specified that in the event of Samuel Seldon, Jr.'s death before reaching his majority, the slave James was to be willed to his sister. It is possible George Mason arranged for James' purchase from Samuel Seldon, Sr. It should be noted that there was a custom of "exchanging" slaves of similar value within the Mason and Eilbeck families. Also, although several slaves named James do appear in other family documents, none of these individuals were described as mulatto, a designation that was almost uniformly noted. For example: *James*, age 22, (b.c. 1775) is listed in the 1797 inventory at Occoquan; Thomson Mason wills a slave named *James* to his wife who is probably the same slave James, age 46, (b.c. 1775) in Thomson's 1821 inventory; and *James*, age 22, (b.c. 1778) is listed in the 1800 inventory of Thomas Mason.
[282] Dunn, ed., *Recollections*, 59.

We can speculate what possible fates could have befallen James. George Mason could have allowed James to "run away" or to "free himself" as Thomas Jefferson did when he allowed several Hemings slaves to leave Monticello.[283] Or, Mason could have arranged with one of his sons for James to have his freedom at some future time by a separate deed or document that is now lost. Or, he could have given James his freedom while in Pennsylvania in 1787, possibly providing him with a written document for James's safety in that "free" city.[284] Or James may have died, the end of his life unrecorded. Much about James continues to remain a mystery.

Nace

Another enslaved man, **Nace,** had talents and skills that George Mason recognized, fostered, and trusted. Residing at the Occoquan Quarter, Nace was apparently quite capable in handling horses. In 1771, Nace (about twenty four years old) was paid nine shillings by Martin Cockburn for "breaking a colt" at nearby Springfield Plantation. Nace continued to earn money from Cockburn; in 1779 he earned £1.16 for a similar task. This was more than three times the pay of 1771, perhaps because of Nace's increased reputation and skill level.[285] At some point, Nace became the overseer at the Occoquan quarter because of his ability and earned trust. Planters occasionally appointed slaves as "foremen" at a farm or quarter, but the Occoquan Inventory in 1797 clearly listed Nace as a "black overseer." While this was typically a paying job for a white man, it is more likely that Nace received increased benefits (additional food or clothing rations, or possibly his own horse) for compensation rather than money. Nace, clearly a responsible enslaved man, was most likely the person John Mason referenced when he stated:

---

[283] Lucia Stanton, *Free Some Day, The African-American Families of Monticello* (Monticello Monograph Series: Thomas Jefferson Foundation, 2000), 116-117. Sally Hemings' daughter Harriet and son Beverly "left" Monticello after they turned twenty-one, probably together. Jefferson gave Harriet money on her departure and put her on the stage going north. Ellen Coolidge wrote, "It was [Jefferson's] principle ...to allow such of his slaves as were sufficiently white to pass for white men, to withdraw from the plantation; it was called running away, but they were never reclaimed."

[284] John Mason wrote favorably about James in his *Recollections*. If James had run away while in Philadelphia, John probably would not have mentioned him at all. To have recorded that George Mason gave a slave freedom while in the city would be controversial in the 1830s when John was writing his memoir.

[285] Martin Cockburn Ledger, 21 December 1771, 30 April 1779.

My Father kept no stewart [sic] or clerk about him. He...superintended, with the assistance of a trusty slave or two, & occasionally some of his sons, all the operations at or about the home house....[286]

It is also of note that while John Mason was residing in Bordeaux, France in the early 1790s, George Mason moved John's "Sorrell horse" to the Occoquan Quarter under Nace's care until John returned to Virginia. Mason no longer entrusted this obviously important horse to the care of those slaves to whom he referred as "the rascals at Gunston Hall."[287]

Mrs. Eilbeck's Illness

Sarah Edgar Eilbeck, George Mason's mother-in-law in Charles County, Maryland, remained on her Mattawoman plantation after William Eilbeck's death in 1765. On February 4, 1775 she wrote her will while facing a serious illness: breast cancer. George Mason and his oldest daughter Nancy quickly went to her home as soon as they were notified that she was to have surgery. On February 6, Mason wrote to George Washington:

> Poor Mrs. Eilbeck has had a Cancer on her Breast for several Months, which has increased so much lately as to affect the whole Breast; upon which the Doctors have determined that there is a Necessity for extirpating it imediatly [sic], by amputation of the Breast, before any of the Roots or Fibres of the Cancer affect the Vital Parts; & when I came Home Yester[day] from Alexandria, I found a Messanger here, desiring me to go over to-day upon this Occasion, wth. my Daughter Nancy. I apprehend such an Opperation [sic] must be a very dangerous one, & therefore shall not care to leave Mrs. Eilbeck for two or three Days after it is perform'd.[288]

Mason stayed for more than a week and returned home on February 16, but continued to have grave concern about her recovery. He wrote to Washington again the following day:

---

[286] Dunn, ed., *Recollections*, 64.
[287] Rutland, *Papers of George Mason*, 1274. This letter, written near the end of Mason's life, was possibly his last to John.
[288] Rutland, *Papers of George Mason*, 213.

I return'd from Maryland but last Night, not being able to leave Mrs. Eilbeck sooner, & don't know how quickly I may be called there again, as I think she is far from being out of Danger, & the Doctor has some Apprehensions of a Mortification.[289]

Nancy Mason most likely remained with her grandmother for some time helping her through what must have been a frightening ordeal. Sarah Eilbeck did recover and lived another five years, presumably without further treatment or surgeries for the cancer. Mason's surviving papers give no additional information on her interim health. She died in December 1780. Sarah Eilbeck's will was probated in February 1781. She willed her property, Mattawoman, to William Mason. She also made specific bequests of slaves to three of her grandsons and to all of her granddaughters.[290]

Sarah Eilbeck's Bequests

To William Mason:

Ben – Born about 1741, Ben was a carpenter at Mattawoman Plantation. See Appendix: F, H.

Penroth or Penrith – He was born about 1725. See Appendix: F, H.

Frank – He was born about 1757. See Appendix: F, H.

Will – No additional information is known about him. See Appendix: H.

Peter – He was born about 1749. See Appendix: F, H.

Clem – Born about 1743. Clem may be one of the slaves "exchanged" with Sarah Eilbeck by George Mason as discussed below. See Appendix: F, H.

Jack – He was born about 1758. See Appendix: F, H.

---

[289] Ibid., 220.
[290] Charles County, Maryland Wills, Liber AF, Number 7, 578, 582-585.

[Mrs. Eilbeck's] Bess – Born about 1740, Bess was the mother of at least seven slaves. Her children included sons, Sampson, Joe, and Tom; her daughters were Nell, Kate, Henny, and Beck. Sam, a man on the Mattawoman Plantation who was born about 1743 may have been the father of one or more of her children. See Appendix: F, H.

Nell – Bess's daughter was born after 1765 and before 1775. See Appendix: F, H.

Kate – Bess's daughter was born after 1765 and before 1775. See Appendix: F, H.

Henny – Bess's daughter was born about 1774. See Appendix: F, H, R.

Beck - Bess's daughter was born about 1779. See Appendix: F, H, R.

Doll - Born about 1747, "Dolly" a child born in 1817, might be a grandchild of Doll. See Appendix: F, H, R.

Milly – Born about 1753, a child named Milly born in 1811 could be her grandchild. See Appendix: F, H, R.

To John Mason:

Tom – Bess's son was born after 1765 and before 1775. See Appendix: F, H.

To Thomas Mason:

James, son of Moll – Moll was born about 1744. James, age 22 in Thomas Mason's 1800 Inventory, would have been born about 1778. See Appendix: F, H, N.

To Nancy Mason:

Arecasa – Born about 1751, Arecasa had other names (Arecajah, Cage) used across time.[291] One of the best documented slaves in the Mason family records, she had four, or possibly five, children and two grandchildren that remained with her across a span of thirty nine years. Her children included Nace, William

---

[291] Cage is likely an African name or derivative referring to Monday. See Sobel, *The World They Made Together*, 158.

(or Bill), Kate and Sarah. Chansy had two daughters Mary Ann and Juda who were grouped together with Caga's adult children in the will that Nancy Mason Johnson wrote in 1804. It is not possible to determine whether Chansy was Arecasa's daughter or the wife of one of Arecasa's sons. See Appendix: F, H, I, O.

Nace – Arecasa's son and first child, Nace was born after 1765 and before 1775. He may have been named after a slave man, Nacy (perhaps his father), on the Mattawoman Plantation. Nace remained with his mother and siblings in Maryland until after 1804.[292] See Appendix: F, H, I, O.

To Sarah Mason:

Jenny – Born about 1746, this slave woman had at least three children (Sue, Robin, and Jesse) who remained with her in Sarah Eilbeck's will.
See Appendix: F, H.

Sue – Jenny's daughter was born about 1763. See Appendix: F, H.

Robin – Jenny's child. See Appendix: F, H.

Jesse – Jenny's child was born about 1769. See Appendix: F, H.

To Mary Mason:

Moll – Born about 1744, Moll's three children, James, Hannah, and Billy, were separated in Sarah Eilbeck's will. Billy remained with his mother because he may have been the youngest of the three children. See Appendix: F, H.

Billy – Moll's son was born after 1765 and before 1775. See Appendix: F, H.

To Elizabeth (Beth) Mason:

Hannah – Moll's daughter was born after 1765 and before 1775.
See Appendix: F, H.

---

[292] Nace appears to be a relatively common slave name. The Nace owned by Nancy Mason is not the enslaved overseer at the Occoquan Quarter.

According to Sarah Eilbeck's will, some slave family members were kept together and others were willingly separated. Moll's children, for example, were split up among three Mason family members, Thomas, Mary, and Elizabeth. Other individuals, such as Bess, the highest valued female slave on the Eilbeck property at £50 in 1765, remained together with all of her daughters. (See Table Eight.) Were slaves who were more closely associated with the white family such as Bess (who may have been the cook or a personal body servant) given preferential treatment?[293] Because some slaves were not seen daily in the master's house or worked in the outlying quarters and fields, their interfamilial relationships may not have been highly considered by the owner. Could Moll have been a field slave – or one who had remote duties from the main house such as a dairy maid? If so, was Moll's lesser position reflected in the insensitive decision to remove two of her children from her?

Additionally, it is interesting to note that seven slaves in the inventory of William Eilbeck were born within approximately a decade of each other: Bess (1740), Ben (1741), Clem (1742), Moll (1744), Jenny (1746), Peter (1749), and Arecasa (1751). Mattawoman Kate is 45 years old (born circa 1720) and is likely the mother of some (perhaps all?) of these individuals. Pamonkey Kate, "very old," might be Mattawoman Kate's mother.[294]

The Decade of the 1780s

George Mason remained a widower for seven years, but in the winter of 1780 he was considering remarriage. In February, Mason wrote to James Mercer:

> This cold weather has set all the young Folks to providing Bedfellows. I have signed two or three [marriage] Licences [sic] every Day since I have been at Home. I wish I knew where to get a good one myself; for I find cold Sheets extreamly [sic] disagreeable.[295]

---

[293] Mrs. Eilbeck's Bess' sons included: Sampson, Joe, and Tom. Her daughters were: Nell, Kate, Henny, and Beck.
[294] See Appendix: F.
[295] Rutland, *Papers of George Mason*, 617-618.

George Mason soon found his "Bedfellow." On Tuesday, April 11, 1780, he and Sarah Brent of Woodstock in Stafford County, Virginia were married by the Reverend Mr. James Scott of Dettingen Parish, Prince William County, Virginia. Mason was 54 years old; Sarah Brent Mason was 50.[296] Three days before the wedding they signed a marriage agreement with each maintaining their own property and describing her dower rights if he predeceased her. As there were no children born of this union, the slaves (and their increase) belonging to Sarah Brent before her marriage were returned to her after George Mason's death in 1792 as stipulated in the contract.[297]

The last decade of Mason's life was happy and busy on the domestic front. George Mason saw a majority of his children marry as well as the births of several grandchildren. The first child to marry was Sarah Eilbeck Mason who married Daniel McCarty, Jr. in 1778 and they settled at Cedar Grove Plantation in Fairfax County. In 1784, Gunston Hall would be a-buzz with the weddings of three more Mason siblings. In April, George Mason V married Elizabeth Mary Ann Barnes Hooe. Their new home was located at Lexington Plantation in close proximity to Gunston Hall. Thomson Mason married Sarah McCarty Chichester; this couple lived for several years at Gunston Hall while their Fairfax County home, Hollin Hall, was constructed. Two of their children, son Thomson and daughter Ann, were born at Gunston Hall. Then, in November, Mary Thomson Mason married John Travers Cooke and the couple made their home at Marlboro, the former plantation of John Mercer.

No family is without its losses. In a poignant letter to his daughter Sarah Mason McCarty, George Mason expressed his condolences to her on the loss of a baby daughter in 1785 writing that

> "...it is our duty to submit with all the resignation human nature is capable of to the dispensation of Divine Providence which bestows upon us our blessings, and consequently has a right to take them away."[298]

George Mason's brother, Thomson Mason, also died in 1785. He lived at Raspberry Plain in Loudoun County, Virginia, but owned land in Stafford and Prince William

---

[296] Ibid., 620-622.
[297] Ibid.
[298] Ibid., 810.

Counties also. Educated in law at the Inns of Court, Middle Temple, in London, Thomson practiced law in Virginia, served in the House of Burgesses during the colonial period and continued service in the Virginia Assembly afterward. Among his many business dealings, Thomson was a known slave trader. He advertized "...a Cargo of Choice, Healthy, Likely Slaves...from the Rivers Gambia and Senegal" in Africa in the *Maryland Gazette* for sale in the 1760s.[299]

Leonard-Town, *June* 26, 1762.
JUST IMPORTED,
From *the Rivers* GAMBIA *and* SENEGAL, *on the*
Coast of AFRICA,
A CARGO of Choice, Healthy, Likely
SLAVES; consisting of MEN, WOMEN,
BOYS, and GIRLS; which will be Sold by the
Subscriber, at his House near *St. Mary's* Court-
House, for Bills of Exchange, Sterling, *Virginia*
or *Maryland* Currency.
The Sale to begin on Monday the Fifth Day of
July, and continue till all are sold.
THOMSON MASON.

Thomson Mason, George Mason IV's brother, was known as a dealer in
slaves. This ad was placed in the Maryland Gazette on 1 July 1762. It is
not known whether George Mason bought slaves from his brother.

Whether his brother George Mason bought slaves from Thomson is not clear. George Mason did purchase a slave from the "ship *Jenny*" through the firm of Glassford & Piscataway in Alexandria and also had seven slaves adjudged for their ages in 1753, possibly newly imported slaves.[300] Thomson inherited slaves from his mother in 1760, at least five of whom were still surviving in 1785 when his Stafford County property was inventoried.[301]

---

[299] Sweig, "The Importation of African Slaves to the Potomac River, 1732-1772," *William and Mary Quarterly*, Oct. 1985.
[300] Copeland and MacMaster, *Five George Masons*, 110-111. See Glassford & Piscataway Ledger, 30 November, 1767.
[301] Stafford County, Virginia Deed Book, Liber P, 1786. These slaves include Milly, Pegg, Tony, Silvia, and Sam, a ship's carpenter. See also Appendix C.

Thomson Mason's will in 1784 distributed slaves to his (second) wife and children, but also gave detailed, specific instructions regarding his highly favored slave, his "Negro boy Jack." Jack was "allowed to settle" on 40 acres of Thomson Mason's land (in any one of the three counties: Loudoun, Stafford, or Prince William County), to tend a crop for himself, to have a barn built of "Loggs" (20 feet square), and to be given animals, tools, and a supply of various grains. He was allowed to have "one month's work of an able negro man" so that he could "put his little farm in order." Jack was also to have £6 annually and the use of the land for his lifetime, but he would hold the "Stock forever." Most importantly, Jack was *subject to the control of no person whatsoever.* Thomson Mason gave this pseudo-freedom to Jack "as grateful acknowledgement of the Remarkable fidelity and Integrity, with which he has conducted himself to me for twenty years upward."[302]

Why was this complicated and elaborately detailed reward given for his "Remarkable fidelity?" Why not just emancipate Jack? The newly written laws of Virginia in 1782 now allowed a master to free a slave through a will or deed simply by filing it with the county court. Why did Thomson Mason go to the specific outlining of this plan instead? One plausible answer lies in Thomson Mason's thorough knowledge of law in Virginia. An older law remained viable despite the new manumission law of 1782; freed slaves were required to leave Virginia within six months. Although this law seems to have been selectively enforced, Jack was in jeopardy if freed, but chose not to leave the state. He could be re-enslaved in that case. In effect, Thomson Mason provided Jack with the best protection he knew how. He gave him pseudo-freedom.

The Rascals of Gunston Hall

The Revolutionary War greatly disrupted planters' lives as thousands of slaves deserted to the enemy during wartime and inflation continued to plague a return to profitable plantation business afterward. Virginia's enactment of a manumission law in 1782, inspired by the idealism and enthusiasm of the Revolution, allowed tens thousands of blacks to begin new lives as free people in the Chesapeake

---

[302] Stafford County, Virginia Deed Book, Liber P, 308-322. Jack's age is not known. Author's emphasis in quote, but he was likely over 45. The law of 1782 provided for manumission of male slaves between 21 and 45 and "of sound mind." If not, the person manumitting him was responsible for his support.

region. For more than two decades, many northern Chesapeake communities, cities such as Baltimore, and bordering states where manumission and abolition was a growing philosophy gave way to increasing numbers of free blacks.[303] Although many slave owners took advantage of Virginia's new manumission law, George Mason did not.

For slaves who were disappointed and did not receive their manumission, the decision to run toward freedom beckoned. Knowing that free black communities existed offered a possibility for a runaway to "blend in" among them and perhaps live as a free person. It was a dangerous decision. It meant leaving family and loved ones behind - forever. But for some enslaved men and women, the desire for freedom was too strong to ignore. In short, some slaves would attempt to "free themselves" if their owner did not.

One of the Mason slaves who got tired of waiting for manumission was a house servant, a mulatto "waiting man," named Dick. Born about 1762, he was a teenager during the war years. Dick likely spent many hours each day in the Mason dining room serving beverages to guests, removing and replacing prepared dishes on the table, and listening to conversation among the gentry men and military officers who visited George Mason. The colonists loudly proclaimed they were treated as "slaves to Britain," and wanted "freedom from the mother country." These conversations encouraged optimism for Dick and those who were truly enslaved; these words inspired hope that they might also see freedom. Perhaps also hearing about the change in Virginia's manumission law, Dick anticipated freedom. But it did not come. He decided to take matters into his own hands.

In the summer of 1784, Dick ran away from the Mason property and persuaded Clem to join him. An ad was placed for their return:

> Ran away from the subscriber... Dick...a stout lusty mulatto fellow, about
> 22 years of age, has large features and eyes, a very roguish down look,
> beats a drum pretty well, is artful and plausible, and very well acquainted in
> most parts of Virginia and Maryland, having formerly waited upon me.[304]

---

[303] Berlin, *Many Thousands Gone*, 278-279.
[304] *Virginia Journal and Alexandria Advertiser*, July 15, 1784.

The slave in the ad was "Yellow Dick," as he was named in George Mason's 1773 will, one of the ten slaves given to George Mason V. The younger Mason, now married, took his inheritance early. In 1784, as his rightful owner, George Mason V placed an ad for Yellow (or mulatto) Dick's return. He suspected that Dick had stolen clothes and presumed that he was headed toward Baltimore or Philadelphia by boat. Dick did not go that far and apparently was captured just across the Potomac River in Charles County, Maryland in early 1785. A deposition taken later revealed that the "said slave Dick" had a pass signed by a "Certain William Smoot" in which Dick declared himself to be a free man in Fairfax County, Virginia by the name of Thomas Webster. Mason sued Smoot for his part in harboring a fugitive, and although the outcome of this case is not known, Dick apparently was apprehended.[305]

Now back in Virginia after his attempted escape, Dick likely faced a severe punishment. The memory of his punishment may have faded, but Dick's desire

TEN POUNDS REWARD.
Fairfax county, Virginia, July 5, 1784.
RAN away from the subscriber, about six weeks ago, two slaves, viz. DICK, a stout lusty mulatto fellow, about twenty-two years of age, has large features and eyes, and a very roguish down look; he beats a drum pretty well, is artful and plausible, and well acquainted in most parts of Virginia and Maryland, having formerly waited upon me. CLEM, a well set black negro lad, of about nineteen years of age, has a remarkable large scar of a burn, which covers the whole of one of his knees. 'Tis impossible to describe their dress, as I am told they have stolen a variety of cloaths since their elopement. I suspect they have made towards Baltimore or Philadelphia, or may have got on board some bay or river craft. I will give the above reward to any person who will bring them to me in Fairfax county, or secure them in any gaol, and give me notice so that I get them again, or five pounds for either of them.
GEORGE MASON, jun.

George Mason V placed an ad for two runaway slaves, Dick and Clem, in the Virginia Journal & Alexandria Advertiser on 15 July 1784.

---

[305] Charles Simms Papers, Library of Congress, Reel 61, Item 34620, In January 1785, Dick appears to be in the custody of William Farr and Philip Smith who no doubt turned Dick in for the reward. Clem is not mentioned in any of the depositions taken. His whereabouts is not known. Smoot was being sued for the value of slave Dick.

for freedom did not. He ran away again. In September 1786 another ad was placed for him:

>...Dick[,] a very lusty well made Mulatto fellow, about 25 years of age, has bushy hair or wool, which he generally combs back, large teeth and eyes, a grum down look when spoken to, is a subtle artful fellow, well acquainted with Virginia and Maryland, beats a drum pretty well, and formerly a waiting man....He ran away some time ago, when he worked on board a bay craft by the name of Thomas Webster.[306]

The search became ardent. This ad, and another the following year, further stated that George Mason and George Mason Jr. (George Mason V) expected Dick to

TEN POUNDS REWARD.

RAN away a few days ago from the Subscribers living in Fairfax County, Virginia, viz. DICK a very lusty well made Mulatto fellow, about 25 years of age, his bushy hair or wool, which he generally combs back, large teeth and eyes, a grum down look when spoken to, is a subtle artful fellow, well acquainted both with Virginia and Maryland, beats a drum pretty well, and formerly a waiting-man: He took with him a light lead coloured country cloth coat, with white metal buttons, a short green ditto, a white cloth waistcoat, a red ditto faced with black velvet, a round hat half worn, and common shoes and stockings. He ran away some time ago, when he worked on board a bay craft by the name of Thomas Webster.——WATT a stout Negro fellow, remarkably black, about 35 years of age, has lost some of his foreteeth, which in some measure affects his voice, has had cross paths lately shaved on his head, to conceal which he will probably shave or cut close the rest of his hair. He is an artful fellow, has a down look, and seems confused when examined: He took with him a brown cloth coat, a pair of black breeches, and a variety of clothes not known. They will perhaps change their names and pass for freemen; and it is probable they may have a forged pass.——They will probably make for the Eastern-Shore, or for the State of Delaware or Pennsylvania. The above reward, or five pounds, for either of them will be paid for delivering them to the subscribers; or for securing them in any gaol and giving us notice, so that we get them again, and if brought home all reasonable charges paid.
GEORGE MASON,
GEORGE MASON, jun.
N. B. All Captains or Skippers of vessels and others are hereby forewarned, at their peril, from taking them on board, or employing them.
September 30, 1786.

Two years later, George Mason IV and his son George, placed an ad for runaways Dick and Watt in the Virginia Journal & Alexandria Advertiser on 30 September 1786. Dick may have been recovered from his first elopement in 1784, but had fled again.

---

[306] *Virginia Journal and Alexandria Advertiser*, September 30, 1786.

FIVE POUNDS REWARD.

RAN away, in the latter end of epteminer laft, from the fubfcriber. iving in Fairfax county, Virginia, DICK, a very lufty mulatto fellow, about twenty five years of age, as bufhy hair or wool, which he generally combs back, large natural and ey s, a grum down look, and frowns when fpoken to, is a lufbtie artful fellow, and well acquainted both in Virginia and Maryland, having been formerly a waiting-man; he is fond of drefs, and took with him a variety of cloaths; he will change his name and pafs for a free man, and may have a forged pafs; he will make for the eaftern fhore or Pennfylvania, or he will attempt to get on board fome veffel, probably a bay craft, as he worked on board one by the name of Thomas Webfter in his laft runaway trip, when he commonly wore a fhort canvas fhirt over his other cloaths. The above reward will be paid for delivering him to the fubfcriber, or for fecuring him in any gaol, and giving notice fo that his mafter gets him again, if brought home all reafonable charges paid.

GEORGE MASON, jbh.

N. B. All captains or fkippers of veffels, and others, are hereby fore-warned, at their peril, from taking him board or employing him.

Still seeking to recover Dick, George Mason V placed an ad in the Maryland Gazette on 15 March 1787 for his slave Dick. He had been gone for almost six months at this point.

change his name, to use a forged pass in an attempt to pass as a freeman, and to head for the Eastern Shore, Delaware, or Pennsylvania. Mason cautioned that, "All Captains or Skippers of vessels and others are forewarned at their peril" from taking him on board or employing him.

Dick's determination was much stronger now. He was very "artful" and "plausible." In other words, Dick, a cunning young man, told a believable story. It is also likely that he planned more carefully how to navigate along the busy coastline area of the upper Chesapeake Bay and learned how to "blend in" and disappear among the large and growing free black populations there. Did he make it to freedom this time?

The answer appears to be yes!

The pass that William Smoot wrote for Dick stated that he was "Thomas Webster," a "Freeman in Fairfax County Virginia." Dick had apparently adopted the name from the vessel *Thomas Webster* on which he worked after his elopement as both the 1786 and 1787 ads stated.

The first United States Census taken in 1790 identifies a free man, "Mulatto Thomas Webster," living in Charles [County], Maryland. This man, Thomas Webster, in all probability the mulatto man formerly known as slave "Yellow Dick" to the Mason family, had apparently managed to establish himself as a free person on the Maryland shore of the Potomac River. There are three free persons listed in his household (including himself) in the census. Did Dick (now known as Thomas Webster) run away because he was anxious to be with someone he loved? Did he run away because the promise of freedom in the Revolutionary Age enticed and encouraged him? Very likely it was both reasons. Dick, this rebellious mulatto man, took his chances not once, but twice, to escape the bonds of slavery and "free himself." His determination and his knowledge of the local waterways and the Chesapeake area gave him the tools to succeed. Unquestionably, Dick wanted his freedom; it appears he achieved it as Thomas Webster.[307]

Each of the ads for Runaway Dick (1784 and 1786) listed a second runaway. When Dick ran away in 1784, **Clem** accompanied him:

> CLEM, a well, [sic] set black negro lad, of about 19 years of age, has a remarkable large scar of a burn which covers the whole of his knees... I am told they have stolen a variety of cloaths [sic] since their elopement.[308]

According to the description in the ad, Clem was born about 1765, but he has uncertain origins in the Mason records. It is possible that his father was an Eilbeck slave named Clem (born about 1743).[309] If so, the younger Clem may have been moved (or sold) to the Virginia properties of George Mason after William Eilbeck's death in 1765, but before 1773. Sarah Eilbeck apparently gave her grandson, George Mason V, two (unnamed) slaves. George Mason IV later exchanged these two slaves with his son for Liberty and Tom when he wrote his will in 1773. Those two "exchanged" slaves may be Clem and Watt. George Mason IV's will stated:

---

[307] Charles Simms Papers, Reel 61, Item 34619. United States Federal Census, 1790, Charles County, Maryland on Ancestry.com, Provo, Utah. This first census gave limited information and listed the head of the household, the number of free white males and females, the number of other free persons, the number of slaves, and the town or district of residence. Thomas Webster, a mulatto, appears in the census of 1790, but does not appear in the census of 1800 or 1810. A number of reasons for this are possible. He may have been captured and returned to slavery after 1790; he may have changed his name again; or he may have fled to another state where he and his family felt safer.
[308] Virginia Journal and Alexandria Advertiser, July 15, 1784.
[309] Charles County Inventories, Charles County, Maryland, 1753-1766, pp. 449-455.

[I confirm to George Mason V] his right and title to two other negroe men named Tom and Liberty, exchanged with him by me for two other negroe men given him by his Grand Mother Mrs. Eilbeck...[310]

No documentation reflects Sarah Eilbeck's gift. But perhaps these two slaves and other slaves as well were purchased or moved between the Eilbeck and Mason families. Also, William Mason inherited his grandfather Eilbeck's plantation, increasing the possibility that some slaves may have been purchased or exchanged on Mason properties. Clem may also have made it to freedom. The 1790 census for Charles County, Maryland records a Clem Egeton (a mulatto) as a free person.[311]

The second runaway ad placed in 1786 advertised for the slave Watt who was described as:

...a stout Negro fellow, remarkably black, about 35 years of age, [who] has lost some of his foreteeth, which in some measure affects his voice, has had cross paths lately shaved on his head, to conceal which he will probably shave or cut close the rest of his hair. He is an artful fellow, has a down look, and seems confused when examined....[312]

Watt was probably the slave listed in William Eilbeck's Maryland inventory; he was 19 years of age (born about 1746). Like Clem, he may be one of two slaves Sarah Eilbeck gave to her grandson, George Mason V. George Mason IV, exchanged them for Tom and Liberty with his son in the 1773 as George Mason IV's will noted. If so, Watt and Clem were property of George Mason IV now.

Watt is listed among slaves living on the Hallowing Point quarter in 1797; his age is given as fifty years old in that inventory. Three documents place his birth between 1746 and 1751 raising the probability he is the same person in all of them.[313]

Why did Watt run away from Virginia? Did he still have family and loved ones in Maryland he wanted to see? Was Watt caught after he ran away? Did Watt run

---

[310] Rutland, *Papers of George Mason*, 151.The other slave is possibly Watt. See Appendix F.
[311] United States Federal Census of 1790, Charles County, Maryland at *Ancestry.com*, Provo, Utah. Several Clem or Clemens (first names) are listed in Charles [County], Maryland leaving open the possibility that he managed to remain in Maryland and blend in as a free person of color.
[312] *Virginia Journal and Alexandria Advertiser*, September 30, 1786.
[313] See Appendix: F, L.

away and then have second thoughts and return on his own? Mason's Hallowing Point, Virginia community of nineteen slaves included five men, six women, and eight children in 1797. Perhaps Watt had a wife and children on this quarter and decided it was better to return to Virginia.

Runaway slaves caused great frustration to slave owners. Most owners placed ads and offered rewards for the return of their property. Some, like the Masons, continued pursuit and filed charges against those who aided slaves in their attempts to escape. George Mason IV, with the help of his son-in-law Daniel McCarty, Jr., filed charges against William Smoot in Charles County, Maryland for aiding Runaway Dick. In a deposition, Smoot acknowledged that he wrote a pass for Dick in 1784 which stated:

> I hereby certify that the Bearer Thomas Webster is a Freeman in Fairfax County Virginia and that any Person that wants to hire him need not be afraid of doing it, as to my certain knowledge he is free, and that I myself hired him, and kept him in my Vessel, The Success.[314]

The record is incomplete and does not show what punishment or fine was imposed on Smoot. He was sympathetic to slaves, but also may have used Dick to his own advantage, possibly hiring Dick for low wages until Dick had earned enough money to move out of the area. It appears that Dick and Clem had parted company once they crossed the river into Charles County, Maryland. Clem disappears from the records. He may have made it to freedom on his first attempt. Dick did not, but very likely learned from his mistakes. Knowing whom to trust was a tricky game....

Nancy Mason's Slaves: Keeping Property Together

George Mason IV's oldest daughter Ann, or "Nancy," was the last of his children he would see get married. Thirty-four years old when she wed Rinaldo Johnson, Nancy's personal property – her slaves willed to her by her two grandmothers and her father – were secured to her in a marriage contract written by George Mason

---

[314] Charles Simms Papers, Library of Congress, Reel 61, Items 34619-34620.

in 1789. Seventeen slaves are listed in that document; it includes two slave women and all their known children plus three other slave women. Missing from the contract are two slaves originally willed to Nancy by her father: Mulatto Priss (daughter of Jenny) and Nell (daughter of Occoquan Nell). Mulatto Priss is presumed deceased when the contract was written in 1789. The fate of Nell, however, appears more complicated. Perhaps through an oversight on the part of George Mason when writing the contract for his daughter, Nell's name was not listed as one of the named slaves. When George Mason died in 1792, Nell now became the property of Nancy's husband, Rinaldo Johnson. Nancy was a *feme couvert* and the property not listed in the contract of 1789 was not preserved to her under the law.[315] Johnson sold Nell. Although he made provisions to "replace" Nell with another slave named Henna and her increase (Betty age 4 and Bob age 9 months), Nancy Mason Johnson must have been highly distressed at this turn of events and the loss of a woman who was a Mason slave from birth.[316]

When Nancy Mason Johnson wrote her own will in 1804, she passed down the slaves she had clear ownership of to her children. These documents from 1763 to 1804, reveal a history of almost forty years for these slaves and their families. (See Table Nine.)

Bess and her family:

Bess, the daughter of Cloe, had at least eight children: **Frank, Lizzy, Dick, Chloe, Nancy, Margaret, Priss,** and **Delia.** Bess may be the slave originally given to Mary Mason Seldon by Ann Thomson Mason. After Mary's death in 1757, redistribution of some slaves seems to have occurred. It is plausible that Ann Thomson Mason repurchased or in some other way reclaimed this slave Bess. If so, Bess came into George Mason IV's hands and he then willed Bess to Nancy in 1773. In the ensuing sixteen years, Bess had eight children. All of these individuals were listed in the

---

[315] A *feme couvert* gave her legal right to her husband upon marriage to manage her property unless it was otherwise secured to her. Salmon, *Women and the Law of Property,* v.
[316] Archives of Maryland (Biographical Series), Ann E. Johnson MSA SC 5496-050748. See *msa. maryland.gov.* There is an error in the biography, however. It states that the slave Nell who was sold by Rinaldo Johnson was the daughter of Gunston Nell. George Mason's 1773 will bequeathed Occoquan Nell's daughter to Nancy Mason. The slave known as Gunston Nell – not Occoquan Nell – was a midwife. Martin Cockburn Account & Ledger Book, 13 April, 1790, 30 November 1790.

marriage contract George Mason wrote when Nancy Mason married Rinaldo Johnson in 1789. Following Nancy's marriage, Bess's enslaved family was moved to Prince George's County, Maryland to the Johnson's home. One of Bess's daughters, Margaret, apparently died before 1804, but seven additional slaves are included in this family group when Nancy Mason Johnson wrote her will that year. **Mary, Ned, Louis, Salisbury, Beatty, Sall,** and **Anna,** probably Bess's grandchildren, are now with her. Thus, Bess, her children and her grandchildren can be traced across a 31-year span of her time. Ann Thomson Mason favored this young enslaved girl in 1757. Nancy Mason Johnson continued that favoritism and provided protection for Bess and her "increase" for the next three decades. *See Appendix C, D, G, I, and O.*

Arecasa and her family:

Arecasa, Arecajah, or Cage – Arecasa was born about 1751 and was fourteen years old when William Eilbeck's Maryland inventory was taken in 1765. By 1775 she had a son named **Nace.** Sarah Eilbeck willed both Arecasa and Nace to her granddaughter Nancy Mason. Also known as Arecajah or (more often) as Cage, her name may reflect an African naming pattern meaning Monday. It is possible she was a newly imported slave from Africa, purchased by William Eilbeck, or that she was given her name to retain African heritage within the slave community at Mattawoman.[317] Nace may have been named for the slave man named Nacy on the Eilbeck property who is possibly his father.

Between 1780 and 1789, Cage and Nace lived in Virginia at Gunston Hall where Cage gave birth to three more children: **Kate, William, and Sarah.** After Nancy Mason married Rinaldo Johnson in 1789, Cage and her four children moved back to Maryland with the Johnsons. Cage's family grew larger. By 1804, it included Kate, Sall (possibly Sarah's a nickname), Nace, Bill, **Chansy** or **Chansey** (probably another daughter, but possibly the wife of one of her sons) and Chansey's two daughters, Mary Ann and Juda. **Mary Ann** and **Juda** are listed as Cage's granddaughters. Two generations of this slave family have been kept together for twenty-four years and a third generation has been added. It is not known what skills or jobs anyone in Cage's family has. All eight members of this family were willed to Nancy Mason Johnson's daughter in 1804. See Appendix: F, G, H, I, and O.

---

[317] Sobel, *The World They Made Together*, 158.

Three other slave women:

Penny or Penelope – Penny was given to Nancy Mason by Grandfather Eilbeck and moved to Virginia when she was perhaps eight years of age. Isolated from her own family, Penny adapted now to a family of "fictive kin," those slaves living at Gunston Hall where she now resided. Penny became a playmate, personal servant, traveling companion, and possibly a confidant to Nancy over the years. When Nancy married Rinaldo Johnson in 1789 and settled at Aquasco, his Maryland property, Penny moved with her.[318] Now, after a quarter of a century away, Penny once again lived closer to members of her family. Nancy Mason Johnson included "Penny or Penelope" in her 1804 will at which time she would have been approximately fifty years old. If Penny had any children, they did not survive to be recorded in any of the known documents. See Appendix: E, F, G, I, and O.

Lizzy (a mulatto) and **Nan** (a mulatto) – Both of these slave women appear for the first time in Nancy's marriage contract of 1789. By 1804 when Nancy Mason Johnson wills them to her daughter Ann Eilbeck Mason Johnson, four boys have been born to these women: Charles, Henry, James, and David. The document only indicates these boys are the sons of the two slave women, but does not specify which. Both "Yellow Lizza" and "Yellow Nancy" are "house servants." See Appendix: I, O.

The Closing Years

The decade of the 1780s, filled with important family milestones and a foray into the federal political arena that took him to Philadelphia (the furthest that George Mason ever traveled from home), was coming to a close. He successfully contributed to the writing of the Constitution of the United States in the summer of 1787, but saw the work undermined by a behind-the-scenes bargain late in the proceedings. Mason fumed over the agreement for retention of the slave trade in America for at least twenty more years and a reduction to only a majority vote of the states (versus two-thirds) in the regulation of America's foreign commerce.[319] These concerns would become two of his sixteen points in his "Objections" to the

[318] Copeland and MacMaster, *Five George Masons*, 241.
[319] Rutland, *Papers of George Mason*, 966, 989-990.

Constitution. In September, George Mason refused to sign the document.[320] Mason believed the work on the Constitution was not complete. He (and others) wanted the document offered to the States for review, to be followed then by a second convention before ratification. It was not to be.

The final fight during the Ratification Convention in Virginia in 1788 brought some belated satisfaction that amendments would be quickly proposed to help remedy a few of Mason's major concerns, particularly a lack of a "Declaration of Rights." James Madison took the list of Virginia's "Proposed Amendments," drawn up by Patrick Henry, George Mason, and others to the first session of Congress.[321]

The gratification of seeing the first ten amendments added to the Constitution of the United States was evident in Mason's letters. In writing to Samuel Griffin, a member of the House of Representatives in 1789, Mason wrote:

> I have received much Satisfaction from the Amendments to the federal Constitution....With two or three further Amendments... I cou'd chearfully [sic] put my Hand & Heart to the new Government.[322]

The first ten amendments to the Constitution of the United States of America were ratified by the States in December 1791. The "Bill of Rights" as they became known collectively, was finally secured in the overarching federal document. George Mason was vindicated in his argument for their inclusion.

Plantation business continued to occupy Mason's last few years. Although retired from public duties, he nonetheless viewed the world through the correspondence he carried on with many, especially his son John living and working in Bordeaux, France. George Mason corresponded frequently with him in France. John's partnership in Fenwick and Mason provided a market for George Mason's wheat crop and a means for purchasing his favorite wines. John also kept his father

---

[320] Ibid., 991-994.
[321] Miller, *Gentleman Revolutionary,* 297. There was a twenty man committee appointed, but the proposed amendments submitted were primarily the work of George Mason and Patrick Henry.
[322] Ibid., 1172. Mason's comments to Griffin were written in September 1789 after the House of Representatives passed the Amendments. They had yet to pass the Senate and be ratified by the States. Mason lived to see the "Bill of Rights," the first ten Amendments to the Constitution ratified in December 1791.

informed of the events leading up to the French Revolution before he returned home to Virginia in 1792 and settled in Alexandria.

In his last known letter to John written on September 10, 1792, George Mason related that the late summer was a sickly one for many in the family. He himself suffered from fevers and a "troublesome Cough." His second wife, Sarah Brent Mason, was recovering from an injured (perhaps broken) leg. John's sister Elizabeth and brother William were recovering from the "Fever of the Season." And he added, "Our Servants are almost all laid up with bad Fevers; there are not enough of them well, to take Care of the Sick. I hardly remember so sickly a Season."[323]

Thomas Jefferson, one of the last visitors George Mason saw, stopped at Gunston Hall on his way north on September 30, 1792. Having returned from France, Jefferson wanted to hear about the Constitutional Convention first hand from his friend and correspondent. The two men – though seventeen years apart in age – were like-minded on many subjects. In Jefferson's notes about their conversation, he related that Mason told him about the "bargain" that was struck between the three New England states (Massachusetts, Connecticut, and New Hampshire) and the two southern states (South Carolina and Georgia). Now slavery would continue for "some years" and only a simple majority was necessary for the enactment of import and export duties in the House of Representatives.[324] Mason told Jefferson that, "Under this coalition the great principles of the Const[itutio]n were changed in the last days of the Convention."[325]

Jefferson saw that Mason was growing weak. This conversation would be one of the last in Mason's final few days. George Mason died at his home at Gunston Hall on 7 October 1792 and his body was interred in the family burial ground – next to his first wife, Ann Eilbeck Mason – on the plantation.

---

[323] Rutland, *Papers of George Mason,* 1273. Earlier in 1792, George Mason carried out the inoculation of 49 slaves for smallpox. One child died as a result, but all others were successfully treated. Unpublished letter: George Mason IV to John Mason, 18 June, 1792. Gunston Hall Library, Mason Neck, Virginia.
[324] Miller, *Gentleman Revolutionary,* 253-254.
[325] Rutland, *Papers of George Mason,* 1275-1276.

Sarah Brent Mason did not inherit any of Mason's property. She had dower rights and could have remained at Gunston Hall for the rest of her life, but instead took a financial settlement that George Mason V offered. She probably returned to the Dumfries, Virginia area to be nearer her sister, Jean Brent Graham.[326] The final distribution of George Mason's property was made to his nine children as laid out in his will of 1773. His slaves and their "increase" now had new owners.

---

[326] Copeland and MacMaster, *Five George Masons*, 239.

Chapter Five

Mason's Growing Idealism and Changing Attitude in the Revolutionary Period

From the porch on the river side of Gunston Hall, the Masons and guests could view the garden and glimpse the Potomac River.

*V*irginians' idealism charted the course of America before, during, and after the American Revolution. Virginia, the most populous of the thirteen colonies, produced eloquent voices, talented writers, and strong political leadership. Thomas Jefferson's words in the *Declaration of Independence,* "that all men are created equal," set the stage for a new nation founded on freedom, republicanism, and "unalienable rights." Paradoxically, the new nation began on a foundation of slave labor. Virginia, which held the largest number of slaves of any of the colonies, also generated some of the institution's loudest critics of slave labor. This contradiction of "American Slavery, American Freedom," of our nation's foundation has been the focus of historical inquiry for the last half century.[327]

The idealism of the Revolutionary period also fostered a strong abolitionist impulse – in both the northern and southern states – although only the North would fulfill the promise of freedom for slaves in the decades following independence. Slave owners in the lower South quickly subdued abolitionist sentiments, but as a result of several pressures, both Virginia and Maryland in the Chesapeake region began to loosen the bonds of enslavement and allow masters to free individuals. Religious denominations, especially the Quakers, Methodists, and Baptists, agitated for antislavery reform. Abolitionist societies grew in numbers and size and pushed for liberal manumission laws.[328] Such movements gave hope and optimism to all who were still enslaved, but the idealism faltered all too soon. Before the close of the eighteenth century, Virginia's legislature rejected a proposed plan for gradual abolition. By the beginning of the nineteenth century, Virginia's government began to enact additional laws to restrict and control freed blacks, and, in 1806, it reinforced the requirement that newly manumitted persons to leave the commonwealth.[329]

Edmund Morgan, Ira Berlin, Gary Nash and others have examined this rapid retreat from abolitionist tendencies in the Chesapeake region. While the population of free blacks tripled in the two decades between 1790 and 1810, most large slave

---

[327] Edmund S. Morgan, American Slavery, *American Freedom* (New York: W.W. Norton & Company, 1975), 5.
[328] Ira Berlin, *Slaves Without Masters* (New York: The New Press, 1974) 20-35, 79-85.
[329] Ibid., 92, 104-105; Gary B. Nash, *Race and Revolution* (Madison: Madison House, 1990), 151-158.

holders "displayed little enthusiasm for manumission."[330] George Washington, in Fairfax County, probably the most famous person to manumit his slaves, freed more than one hundred slaves in his will in 1799.[331] Robert Carter, of Westmoreland County, freed all of his 509 slaves in 1791.[332] These men were among the exceptions. John Tayloe II, the largest slave owner in Richmond County with 700 slaves, freed only two.[333] Most efforts of manumission came from small to middling slave holders who chose to follow their conscience or religious convictions and who lived in urban rather than rural settings in the Chesapeake region. Many of the abolitionist societies and those who raised voices for change in laws also came from these small and middling slave holders. By 1810, one third of all the free blacks in America lived along the upper reaches of the Chesapeake Bay, the Eastern Shore, and along the south-side of the James River or in cities such as Baltimore, Norfolk, Richmond, or Petersburg. But the power of legislation rested primarily with the gentry – the largest slave holders. In Virginia they ultimately used that power to retain slavery.[334]

George Mason freed none of his slaves yet wrote that "all men are created equal" and called all owners of slaves "petty Tyrants." The paradox he presents demands exploration. Across the decades, historians and biographers, while noting this discrepancy of Mason's words and his lack of action, have done little more than give it passing comment. In his introduction to *The Papers of George Mason*,

---

[330] Richard S. Dunn, "Black Society in the Chesapeake, 1776-1810," in *Slavery and Freedom in the Age of the American Revolution* (Chicago: The University of Illinois Press, 1986), 72-75.

[331] Edna Greene Meford, "Beyond Mount Vernon: George Washington's Emancipated Laborers and Their Decendants," in *Slavery at the Home of George Washington* (Mount Vernon, Virginia: Mount Vernon Ladies' Association, 2001), 137-157. Washington's will freed 124 slaves, but not until Martha's death. Washington was concerned that intermarriage with Martha's dower slaves – and their subsequent dispersal on her death – would cause disruptions in the slaves' lives twice unless all done at the same time. Martha chose to free her husband's slaves, however, in her lifetime.

[332] Louis Morton, *Robert Carter of Nomini Hall* (Williamsburg, Virginia: Colonial Williamsburg, Incorporated, 1945), 251-269. Carter established a plan for the gradual manumission of his slaves, but whether all received their freedom is doubted by Morton. Richard S. Dunn notes, however, that in 1810 there was no slave gang at Nomini Hall and there were 621 free blacks in Westmoreland County, one of the largest free black populations in a Virginia County. See footnote 330 above. Andrew Levy, in a more recent study of Robert Carter's manumission plan or Deed of Gift, argues strenuously that the plan succeeded, but has been forgotten in the sweeping history of the antebellum period. Andrew Levy, *The First Emancipator, The Forgotten Story of Robert Carter* (New York: Random House, 2005), 174-195.

[333] Richard S. Dunn, "Black Society in the Chesapeake," in *Slavery and Freedom* 74.

[334] Ibid., 75-82; Berlin, *Slaves without Masters*, 79-86.

biographer Robert A. Rutland states that Mason showed a "chronic uneasiness" and an "intellectual discomfort" regarding slavery. He adds, "Entrapped by the system Mason sensed what should be done about slavery but would not tread beyond denunciations and clairvoyant pronouncements."[335] In *The Five George Masons*, Pamela C. Copeland and Richard K. MacMaster write, "The paradox was not without its own significance.... Mason's experience with slave labor made him hate slavery[,] but his heavy investment in slave property made it difficult for him to divest himself of a system that he despised."[336] Peter Wallenstein, in an article entitled "Flawed Keepers of the Flame," while concerned about this paradox, focused greater attention on the overall interpretation of Mason's attitudes on slavery. He states that as historians and interpreters "...perhaps we can do better than is sometimes done to make sense of how [Mason] saw his world, what he wanted to change, and what he wanted to keep."[337] And Jon Kukla also reinforces in "The Irrelevance and Relevance of Saints George [Mason] and Thomas [Jefferson]," that the eighteenth-century slave holders' world was extremely complicated; that the issue of slavery was far from clear cut. While many in the Chesapeake region pushed toward abolition, slave owners in some Virginia counties petitioned against even "modest antislavery measures" or the liberalization of manumission laws. But Kukla also reminds us that historians must be careful not to read history backward.[338] From our vantage point today, we must not arbitrarily dismiss or forgive people of the past for not seeing what the future held. Instead, we must look at the age and time of the circumstances. We must attempt to see the world through eighteenth century eyes and look at how and why men like George Mason made the decisions they did.

These historians recognized the problem of an individual slave owner born into an institution he did not create, but they failed to look deeper. While these writers acknowledge a discrepancy in the words in opposition to slavery and the inaction of George Mason to emancipate any slaves, none look carefully at all of the arguments he consistently made and what he argued *for* as much as *against*.

---

[335] Ibid., cxv,cxvi.
[336] Copeland and MacMaster, *The Five George Masons*, 162.
[337] Peter Wallenstein, "Flawed Keepers of the Flame, The Interpreters of George Mason," *The Virginia Magazine of History and Biography*, 102 (April 1994), 259.
[338] Jon Kukla, "The Irrelevance and Relevance of Saints George and Thomas," *The Virginia Magazine of History and Biography*, 102 (April 1994), 264, n. 9.

Reexamining Mason's Words

Mason's first written opinion denouncing slavery came in 1765 during the Stamp Act crisis. This crisis prompted his active role and he outlined a method for circumventing the need for some taxed documents. In his paper titled a *"Scheme for Replevying Goods and Distress for Rent"* he also interjected a paragraph on the subject of slavery, commenting that it had "never been duly considered" before. He bluntly stated:

> The Policy of encouraging the Importation of free People & discouraging that of Slaves has never been duly considered in this Colony, or we shou'd not at this Day see one Half of our best Lands in most Parts of the Country remain unsetled [sic], & the other cultivated with Slaves; not to mention the ill Effect such a Practice has upon the Morals & Manners of our People: one of the first Signs of the Decay, & perhaps the primary Cause of the Destruction of the most flourishing Government that ever existed was the Introduction of great Numbers of Slaves – an Evil very pathetically described by the Roman Historians – but 'tis not the present Intention to expose our Weakness by examining this Subject too freely.[339]

Mason, angry with Britain's Stamp Act thrust on the American colonies, became a frontline activist for the first time in his life. Although his plan proved unnecessary as the Stamp Tax was quickly repealed by Parliament, Mason and many others guardedly began to watch Britain's next moves. But why did Mason begin this "Scheme" with a paragraph denouncing the slave trade? Did he know from personal conversations that other gentry planters were becoming disaffected by slavery in Virginia? Or, was he "feeling out" a mood or sentiment to see if others responded to his concerns? Whatever the reasons, Mason's initial paragraph brought the topic into the forefront for all who read it. The subject was now on the table as far as Mason was concerned.

The American Colonies would see other taxes imposed when the Stamp Tax was repealed. One method of combat against Great Britain's "taxation without

---

[339] Rutland, *Papers of George Mason*, 61-65.

representation" was the process of non-importation – or economic retaliation – which Mason supported. He wrote George Washington and sent his review and some "Alterations" to what became *The Virginia Nonimportation Resolutions of 1769.* This document specifically stated in its fifth resolution: "That they [Virginians] will not import any Slaves, or purchase any (hereafter) imported untill [sic] the said Acts of parliament are repeal'd."[340] Hitting merchants – and British slave traders – in the pocketbook might bring attention in Parliament; the British slave trade was an important financial concern to many.

At about the same time as the *Resolutions* were drafted, an essay appeared in both the Maryland and Virginia *Gazette* newspapers in which "Atticus" argued for the support of the non-importation of goods from Great Britain. Atticus noted that, "If we were to desist purchasing Slaves, and making Tobacco, we shou'd have a Number of Spare Hands to employ in Manufactures, and other Improvements...." Biographer Robert Rutland and other historians have attributed the Atticus letter to George Mason.[341]

As Treasurer of the Ohio Company, Mason also turned his energy and concern to the process of acquiring land in the west. At the close of the French and Indian War in 1763, Great Britain curtailed settlement to lands west of the Allegheny Mountains. With vested interest in that territory as an officer of the Ohio Company which speculated on lands there, Mason began to address the problem of gaining clear title. He carefully studied the Virginia land laws. In 1773, while annotating his "Extracts from the Virginia Charters," a document that traced the legal authorization of headrights and substantiated the territorial limits of Virginia, George Mason again interjected his sentiments about slavery. He wrote:

> [Slavery is] that slow Poison, which is daily contaminating the Minds & Morals of our People. Every Gentlemen [sic] here is born a petty Tyrant. Practiced in Acts of Despotism & Cruelty, we become callous to the Dictates of Humanity, & all the finer feelings of the Soul. Taught to regard a part of our own Species in the most abject & contemptible Degree below us, we lose that Idea of the Dignity of Man, which the

---

[340] Ibid., 105.
[341] Ibid., 106-109.

Hand of Nature had implanted in us, for great & useful purposes. Habituated from our Infancy to trample upon the Rights of Human Nature, every generous, every liberal Sentiment, if not extinguished, is enfeebled in our Minds. And in such an infernal School are to be educated our future Legislatures & Rulers. The laws of impartial Providence may even by such Means as these, avenge upon our Posterity the Injury done a set of Wretches, whom our Injustice hath debased almost to a Level with the Brute Creation. These Remarks may be thought Foreign to the design of the annexed Extracts – They were exhorted by a kind of irresistible, perhaps an Enthusiastick [sic] Impulse; and the author of them conscious of his own good Intentions, cares not whom they please or offend.[342]

This strong statement revealed insight into how slave masters lived and reacted within the Great Houses of the slave plantations. They were literally tyrants to their slaves who were considered low forms of humanity, or brutes. Moreover, the children of these masters (who would become the future governing members of society) learned attitudes from their fathers, mothers, uncles, or grandfathers and adopted their practices. Mason, obviously giving considerable thought to this issue of slavery in America, now emphatically stated what was on his mind – whether the reader liked it or not.

Throughout the decade leading up to the decision for independence, George Mason mulled over the problem of slavery in America. He talked with and corresponded with Virginia's gentry leaders and brought the issue of slavery into discussion. He undoubtedly knew the sentiments of his peers – those who agreed with his beliefs and those who disagreed. When Mason's leadership was sought by the Virginia Convention in drafting the Virginia Declaration of Rights in May 1776, he opened the first paragraph with a statement that expressed an idealistic and underlying mood rooted in those discussions: *"That all Men are born equally free and indepen-dent, and have certain inherent natural Rights, of which they can not [sic] by any*

---

[342] Ibid., 173. George Mason began accumulating headright certificates (to acquire more land in the Ohio territory) which precipitated his interest in the laws and early charters. The document he wrote would hopefully benefit himself and the other land speculators of the Ohio Company of which Washington was a member.

Compact, deprive or divest their Posterity...."[343] On 27 May, the Committee's draft of George Mason's document was modified slightly, but his first words remained unaltered: *"That all men are born equally free and independent, and have certain inherent natural rights, of which they cannot, by any compact, deprive or divest their posterity...."*[344]

The draft was now debated in the full Convention. It hit an immediate snag. On 1 June, Thomas Ludwell Lee wrote his brother Richard Henry Lee, "A certain set of Aristocrats, for we have such monsters here, finding that their execrable system cannot be reared on such foundations, have to this time kept us at bay on the first line, which declares all men to be born equally free and independent." Robert Carter Nicholas openly opposed the phrase "born equally free" as a threat to the slave holders and stated that it could potentially be "the forerunner of ...civil convulsion."[345] Edmund Pendleton, President of the Convention, is credited with the modification and insertion of the phrase "...when they enter into a state of society...." Thus, the final draft of the Virginia Declaration of Rights as it was approved on 12 June now began: *"That all men are <u>by nature</u> equally free and independent, and have certain inherent rights, of which, <u>when they enter into a state of society,</u> they cannot by any compact, deprive or divest their posterity...."*[346] These changes obliterated the meaning of George Mason's idealism. Known for his acute distaste of committee wrangling, Mason must have been gravely disappointed – if not furious – at the outcome of this compromise. But there was more work to be done and the drafting of a constitution for the newly formed Commonwealth of Virginia began. Mason was a principle architect of that document as well. Both documents, the Virginia Declaration of Rights and the Virginia Constitution of 1776, were approved by the Convention by 29 June, 1776. Virginia moved fully into the American Revolution.

George Mason accepted a greater role in Virginia's government. He served as a colonel in the Virginia militia working to procure men and materials for anticipated conflict. He took a more active political role and became a member of the Fairfax

---

[343] Rutland, *Papers of George Mason,* 276-278.
[344] Ibid., 282-286.
[345] Ibid., 289.
[346] Ibid., 287-291. Underlined words are the changes from the first two drafts.

Committee of Safety and he participated in drafting the "Fairfax Resolves." This document, which placed the Virginians squarely in opposition to the slave trade, stated defiantly that "no Slaves ought to be imported into the British Colonies on this Continent; and we take this Opportunity of declaring our most earnest Wishes to see an entire Stop for ever put to such a wicked[,] cruel[,] and unnatural Trade."[347] The Virginia General Assembly, of which Mason also became a member, enacted the necessary legislation to end the importation of slaves into Virginia in 1778.[348] Mason assisted Virginia in carrying out this first step in changing the institution of slavery after repeatedly arguing for the closure of the external trade to Virginia for more than a decade.

Soon after the Revolutionary War, Mason retired to his preferred private station as a planter. His retirement lasted only a few years, however, and he returned to service for Virginia once again in 1787. The Articles of Confederation, the document that barely held the United States together during the war, now proved ineffective in peacetime as well. Agreements on trade between Maryland and Virginia, navigation on the Potomac River, and fishing rights were snarled. George Washington, encouraging Virginia to participate in discussions with neighboring Maryland, held a conference at Mount Vernon when an initial meeting in Annapolis failed. But the need for discussion was bigger than just these two states, and a proposal to include all of the states and to meet in Philadelphia was planned. George Mason served as one of seven Virginia delegates who attended the Philadelphia meeting in the late spring of 1787. In that session that lasted four months, the Articles of Confederation were abandoned by the delegates and a Constitution for the United States was drafted in its place.

As a delegate to the Constitutional Convention (as it became known), Mason applied his considerable knowledge of the English Constitution, Virginia law, and territorial law in these sessions. Although not a lawyer, he had expansive knowledge and masterful use of legal terminology, understanding of legal precedence, and was "cogent in argument."[349] He was an ardent participant during the entire convention. On multiple occasions, he also broached the subject of slavery, using

[347] Ibid., 199-201, 207.
[348] Ibid., 966. See also, Copeland and MacMaster, The Five George Masons, 166.
[349] Miller, Gentleman Revolutionary, 333.

his well-honed arguments to urge closure of the external slave trade for the entire new nation. He also sounded a warning:

> This infernal trafic [sic] originated in the avarice of British Merchants. The British Gov[ernmen]t constantly checked the attempts of Virginia to put a stop to it. The present question concerns not the importing States alone but the whole Union....Every master of slaves is born a petty tyrant. They bring the judgment of heaven on a Country. As nations can not [sic] be rewarded or punished in the next world they must be in this. By an inevitable chain of causes & effects providence punishes national sins, by national calamities....it [is] essential in every point of view that the Gen[era]l Gov[ernmen]t should have the power to prevent the increase of slavery.[350]

The Convention worked through debate after debate in the sweltering heat of the summer. They made progress in fits and starts, but the last few days of the Constitutional Convention frustrated Mason immensely. He was dismayed that a bargain had been struck – behind closed doors – that gave the northern states (or Eastern states as they were called) an advantage on commercial regulation and retained the external slave trade (for at least twenty more years) to the benefit of the two most southern states.[351] Mason was stunned and furious. Now, he became more outspoken and his objections on many points mounted: *There was no declaration of rights. How was the executive to be chosen? The process of amending the document was cumbersome. There was a need for a second convention. And much more...*

Mason continued to vocalize his objections to slavery. He wanted the slave trade into all of America abolished, but he harbored a fear that slaves - the "property" many already held - were not "secured" to the slave owners. Could tariffs or taxes be imposed on slaves to the point where slave owners could not afford to keep them and have to manumit them? Mason stated:

> And though this infamous traffic be continued, we have no security for the property of that kind which we already have. There is no clause in

---

[350] Rutland, *The Papers of George Mason,* 965, 966.
[351] Ibid., 993. Miller, *George Mason Gentleman Revolutionary,* 277-283.

this constitution to secure it; for they may lay such a tax as will amount to manumission....I have ever looked upon [slavery] as a most disgraceful thing to America. I cannot express my detestation of it. Yet they have not secured us the property of the slaves we already have. So that "they have done what they ought not to have done, and left undone what they ought to have done".[352]

During the final hours of the Constitutional Convention in 1787, George Mason grew angrier. He believed that the problem of slavery was a *national* problem and one that necessitated a strong federal government to create the "power to prevent the increase of slavery." The fact that the new federal legislature was "restrained from prohibiting the further importation of slaves for twenty odd years" greatly dismayed him.[353] He supported the idea of a second convention to work out further details and suggestions of the States; he moved to include a declaration of rights in the document. These concerns, and others as well, fell on deaf ears. In mid-September 1787, as the Convention concluded, he listed his objections on the back of his copy of the Constitution. Then, at the final hour, George Mason refused to put his signature on that document.[354]

Mason suffered an accident en route home to Gunston Hall. Near Baltimore his coach turned over and both Mason and his driver were hurt. About three weeks later, Mason wrote to George Washington (enclosing a copy of his objections to the Constitution) and told him, "I got very much hurt in my Neck & Head, by the unlucky Accident on the road; it is now wearing off; tho' at times still uneasy to me."[355] Now, home again at Gunston Hall, Mason discovered that his "Objections" had circulated among many without his knowledge. They became the basis for the Anti-Federalist arguments and were printed in newspapers, sent in letters, and discussed up and down the seaboard as states prepared for ratification conventions.

---

[352] Ibid., 1086. Rutland notes that the quotation is a passage from the Anglican Church Book of Common Prayer.

[353] Mason listed sixteen objections to the Constitution on the back of his copy of the Committee of Style Report. They found their way into print – without Mason's "Approbation, or Privity" and became the basis for the Antifederalist arguments against the Constitution. Rutland, *The Papers of George Mason*, 991-994.

[354] Elbridge Gerry of Massachusetts and fellow Virginian, Edmund Randolph, also did not sign the document.

[355] Rutland, *Papers of George Mason*, 1001-1002.

Mason's first objection on his list was, "There is no Declaration of Rights" which was echoed in virtually all of the conventions. Another of Mason's "Objections" was that "the general legislature is restrained from prohibiting the further importation of slaves for twenty odd years...."[356]

Despite the campaigns, discussions, and arguments about the newly proposed Constitution that went on in all of the states, the rule for the ratification conventions was to <u>adopt</u> or <u>reject</u> the document as it was presented – not suggest changes. Nonetheless, all of the states, argued for the inclusion or modification of statements, many reflecting Mason's ideas and concerns. The need for a "declaration of rights" statement in the new federal constitution was repeated continuously. But those amendments would have to come after ratification.

Virginia's Ratification Convention was held in June, 1788 in Richmond. Mason attended and provided considerable comment and concern throughout the debate. Again, he adamantly opposed the continuation of the slave trade.

> ...The augmentation of slaves weakens the states; and such a trade is diabolical in itself, and disgraceful to mankind. Yet by this constitution it is continued for twenty years. As much as I value an [sic] union of all the states, I would not admit the southern states into the union, unless they agreed to the discontinuance of this disgraceful trade, because it would bring weakness and not strength to the union...I have ever looked upon this [slavery] as a most disgraceful thing to America. I cannot express my detestation of it...[357]

George Mason believed that the southern states of South Carolina and Georgia (or any others) should *not* be admitted into the union under this new Constitution *if they refused to curtail the external slave trade.*[358] His words were strong. He wanted their feet "held to the fire" on this matter. Mason put his sentiments out in front for all Virginia to see.

---

[356] Ibid., 993.
[357] Ibid., 1086.
[358] The external trade refers to the importation of slaves from Africa (or the West Indies).

After heated debate, the Virginia delegates accepted the Constitution by a vote of eighty-nine for ratification and seventy-nine opposed.[359] Virginia was the tenth state to ratify. The Constitution had already become law with the vote to ratify in New Jersey held just days before. Virginians, however, secured the assurance of James Madison that he would present amendments at the first session of Congress. George Mason and Patrick Henry were among the twenty-man group tasked to prepare a list of suggested amendments for Madison. A large portion of the committee's recommendation came from George Mason's Virginia Declaration of Rights from 1776.[360]

In the end, the Constitution of the United States did not enact any measures to oppose slavery; in fact, the word slave was avoided in the entire document. Slavery was merely implied in Article One, Section 9 as it stated:

> The Migration or Importation of such Persons as any of the States now existing shall think proper to admit, shall not be prohibited by the Congress prior to the Year one thousand eight hundred and eight, but a Tax or duty may be imposed on such Importation, not exceeding ten dollars for each Person.

The importation of slaves into the United States would continue for twenty years as the "bargain" Mason so strenuously objected to in Philadelphia allowed.

Some states individually began to take steps to curtail importation, to allow manumission, or to begin a process for abolition. The steps were small and slow, however. The strongest sentiments opposing slavery and favoring abolition flourished in the northern states. Pennsylvania began a policy of gradual abolition in 1780.[361] In the Chesapeake region, Virginia closed the external slave trade and both Virginia and Maryland enacted laws for manumission. As a result, tens of thousands of newly freed blacks swelled the communities in and around Baltimore, the Eastern Shore of the Chesapeake Bay, and the south side of the James River over the next

---

[359] Rutland, *The Birth of the Bill of Rights*, 174. Mason voted against ratification. In a disappointing turning point, Edmund Randolph defected from the anti-federalist side to vote for ratification.
[360] Miller, *Gentleman Revolutionary*, 297.
[361] James Oliver Horton and Lois E Horton, *In Hope of Liberty, Culture, Community and Protest Among Northern Free Blacks*, 1700-1860 (New York: Oxford University Press, 1997), 71-75. Pennsylvania was the first state to pass legislation that provided for the gradual abolition of slavery.

two decades.[362] However, closing the external slave trade into America was paramount in taking further steps toward abolition. The slave trade into the United States would continue until at least 1808. George Mason did not live long enough to see it end in the United States.

In 1782, the Virginia Assembly returned the power for manumission to the hands of the individual slave owners, no longer leaving it solely for the governor and council as it had been in the colonial period. But the new law included caveats to prohibit slave owners from deserting old or indigent slaves and children; Virginia's law allowed freedom only for self-sufficient adult slaves.[363]

Abolition was on the minds of many. Virginian St. George Tucker, lawyer, jurist, and an early analyst of the Constitution, wrote and presented to the Virginia's General Assembly in 1796 a plan for the abolition of slavery, *A Dissertation on Slavery: With a Proposal for the Gradual Abolition of It, in the State of Virginia*. The legislators listened politely, but dismissed his plan. Historian Edmund Morgan reflects that it was "too dangerous to receive serious consideration."[364]

George Mason argued that training and education were the necessary first steps that needed to be taken before the vast majority of slaves could understand and accept the responsibilities of their freedom. Mason believed (as did others at the time) that African American slaves were inherently lazy and did not want to work. But he believed that providing education and skills could bring about a sense of self-pride or self-fulfillment and reduce this perceived tendency. Philip Mazzei, an Italian doctor, diplomat, and American sympathizer, spent several years in the colonies. In his conversations with many Virginia leaders during the Revolutionary period, he discussed the problems of slavery. Of his conversations with Mason, Mazzei wrote:

---

[362] Gary B.Nash, *Race and Revolution* (Madison: Madison House,1990), 13-20. North Carolina did not enact a manumission law.

[363] Hening, *Statutes*, 11:39-40. Freed slaves "above the age of forty-five years, or being males under the age of twenty-one, or females under the age of eighteen, shall be respectively supported and maintained by the person so liberating them...."

[364] Morgan, *American Slavery, American Freedom*, 385.Historian Clyde Wilson further argues that St. George Tucker did not use the United States Constitution as a "rationalization in defense of slavery." Wilson believes that is a "misunderstanding of conventional accounts of American history." See Clyde N. Wilson, ed., *View of the Constitution of the United States with Selected Writings* (Indianapolis: Liberty Fund, Inc., 1999), vii-xvii, 402.

Mr. George Mason...showed the necessity of educating [the slaves] before taking such a step [as manumission] and of teaching them how to make good use of their freedom. "We all know," he said, "that blacks consider work a punishment," pointing out that unless previously educated, the first use they would make of their freedom would be to do nothing and that they would become thieves out of necessity.[365]

Mason argued against allowing newly freed blacks to remain in Virginia. Certainly the fears of retaliation against former masters generated concern among the slave holders, but he also believed that this newly freed labor force created competition with the lower class of white workers. Slaves "...prevent the immigration of Whites, who really enrich & strengthen a Country."[366] Whether Mason advocated that freed blacks should return to Africa or not is unknown, but he did support laws that they should leave Virginia after obtaining freedom.[367]

Mason also believed that owners should receive compensation for their slaves if manumitted on a broad scale. Money was a crucial issue. Slaves and land were the two primary components of wealth for the southern gentry. Gary Nash argues that the idealism of abolition gained force during the period of the American Revolution in part because of the acquisition of western land in the Ohio Territory. Land became a source of payment for debts – including the possibility of exchange

---

[365] Philip Mazzei, Translated by S. Eugene Scalia, Edited by Margherita Marchione, *My Life and Wanderings* (Morristown, New Jersey: American Institute of Italian Studies, 1980), 223, 285-286. Philip Mazzei, an Italian physician, agriculturalist, and self-styled diplomat, came to Virginia in 1773 to introduce cultivation of grapes, olives, and silk in America. He purchased land near Monticello and befriended Thomas Jefferson and soon began enlisting subscribers for the establishment of vineyards. Jefferson, George Washington, George Mason, and others purchased shares in this venture. It ultimately failed, but the events leading up to the American Revolution drew Mazzei into ardent patriotism with these Virginians. In his memoirs of this period, he reflected on the ideas and sentiments of many of the men he met and conversed with and recorded them. He lived in Virginia from 1773-1779 and again in the 1780s. In 1783, Mazzei dined with George Mason at Gunston Hall and spent the night before going on to George Washington's. While at Mason's he met a Mr. Brent, possibly one of the nephews of Sarah Brent Mason. Mazzei organized "The Constitutional Society" in 1784 and anticipated it would become a forum for regional discussion on matters of legislative concern in America. See also, Margherita Marchione, ed., *The Constitutional Society of 1784* (Fairleigh Dickinson University, 1984).
[366] Rutland, *The Papers of George Mason,* 965-966.
[367] Ibid., 1086. A proposed bill considered in 1788 to revoke the freedom of newly manumitted slaves if they did not leave Virginia within twelve months did not pass the House of Delegates. Mason voted for the passage (with the minority) of this law. See also: Commonwealth of Virginia Journal of the House of Delegates, 1786-1790. 128-129.

or remuneration for slave property. Western land resources also doubled as a place for resettlement of freed blacks, or at least some postulated that it could. Mason might have agreed with those possibilities.[368]

Opening up the western territories could also provide a way to "dilute" slavery in some people's estimation. Many thought slavery would eventually dissipate or die out. Oliver Ellsworth from Connecticut remarked in debate at the Constitutional Convention, "Slavery in time will not be a speck in our Country."[369] Thomas Jefferson's Northwest Ordinance of 1784 forbade slavery in its vast territory, covering land from the Great Lakes to the Gulf of Mexico. However, the revised version of the ordinance did not pass into law until 1787 and in this version the reduced territory covered only land above the Ohio River. As a result, slavery was not excluded in the southern most region of Jefferson's plan.[370]

Mason's Changing World View

George Mason's experiences as a slave owner challenged and altered his world view across the middle decades of the eighteenth century. Dealing with runaways and day-to-day passive resistance taught him he was dealing with human beings. Ordering punishments to be inflicted (or doing the punishing himself) Mason became one of those "petty tyrants" trying to enforce the behavior he wanted from these people. He felt the use of the power he held and he did not like the role he was playing. He became sensitive to the broader picture of slavery and its moral

---

[368] Nash, *Race and Revolution,* 36-38.

[369] Rutland, *Papers of George Mason,* 966.

[370] Other unforeseen events put an end to the possibility that slavery would go away gradually on its own. The invention of the cotton gin in the mid-1790s facilitated expansion of cotton and the need for more slave laborers. Plus, the unexpected Louisiana Purchase 1803 opened a flood gate for southern planters' expansion. The hope that slavery would simply die out ended.

Along with those two events, several serious slave rebellions brought fear to the white population and stringent new laws and stronger enforcement throughout the south. Gabriel's Rebellion in 1800 in Richmond was a catalyst for the retrenching of manumission laws by 1806. Nat Turner's Rebellion – even more serious and widespread – saw dozens of innocent blacks convicted and executed, fear rise among whites, and strident enforcement of slave laws. Immediately following it in 1832, Virginia outlawed a slave's opportunity to learn to read or write, believing those skills could breed conspiracy among slaves. All of this came long after George Mason died. The optimism of his lifetime and much of his generation in the Chesapeake died shortly after he did.

destruction of "all the finer feelings of the soul." Mason's mother, mother-in-law, wife, and oldest daughter, Nancy, repeatedly encouraged him to look at ways that might alter or mitigate the difficulties of some slaves' lives - within the legal structure of the time. By placing slaves in protected situations through wills, deeds of gift, or contracts (such as Nancy's marriage contract) some - enslaved women and their children - were shielded provided with advantages. At least they were in his mind.

More importantly, George Mason's expanding world view throughout these years grew more insightful. He became aware that true freedom could not exist in America if its labor base included slavery. In his lifetime, Mason did not just argue against slavery. He argued *for* change that would lead to dissolution of the institution. He wanted closure of the slave trade at the national level as an initial step; he argued for the need for education and training for slaves to prepare them for freedom; and he saw the need to resolve the issue of property rights. Mason clearly believed that the *nation* - not states or regions - needed to consider the problem of slavery. Not to do so would bring a "national calamity" on the young country. Mason fearfully said, "By an inevitable chain of causes & effects[,] providence punishes national sins, by national calamities." Unfortunately, he was right. Because of steps *not* taken during the building of our new nation, in 1861 his prophecy came true.

Concluding Thoughts

James, possibly serving George Mason as a butler at Gunston Hall, could see approaching visitors or travelers from the land front windows in the central passage

$\mathcal{A}$s a young, enthusiastic gentry planter in the 1750s, George Mason's world view reflected that of other men who entered into the "Golden Age" of Chesapeake planters before him. As part of the world-wide British Empire, growth, trade, and expansion generated optimism for opportunity and success. As part of the Virginia gentry, Mason's perspective included a secure social status among the elite, an extensive classical education, and significant family assets as he arrived at his majority and stepped onto the Virginia landscape. He viewed that landscape from a position of power and prestige.[371]

But over the next several decades, Mason's world view changed. Events and personal interactions created challenges to this English-based Virginia lifestyle. Mason's own personal introspection of this lifestyle caused him to question the morality of slavery. Moreover, he began to visualize Virginia in a larger world context as part of a new nation set on a global stage. Several key factors created and shaped this new world view in George Mason's mind.

The first of these factors involved the way in which English law recognized inheritance. George Mason's father died intestate. The lack of a will invoked the English laws of primogeniture and left all of the accumulated Mason family land holdings to young George Mason IV, the oldest son. Through careful management, his mother Ann Thomson Mason made provisions for both of his younger siblings, Mary and Thomson, to receive gifts of land, slaves, or money to compensate for the lack of an actual inheritance. George Mason IV recognized his mother's efforts.

The importance of inheritance laws surfaced again in Mason's lifetime and caused him personal and sudden concern. On the death of his wife, Ann Eilbeck Mason, in March 1773, George Mason was faced with the realization of having no will of his own. Life took unexpected turns; his own children could face laws invoking primogeniture if he did not take swift action to create a will. John Mason remembered that after his mother's death "...my father for some days paced the

---

[371] Walsh, *Motives of Honor*, 394-395.

rooms or from the house to the grave (it was not far) alone."[372] Within two weeks of Ann's death, Mason wrote his will. Recorded in the Fairfax County Will Book, the document required twenty-four pages to transcribe it. He laid out in great detail everything he wanted each of his nine children to receive: land, slaves, money, and possessions. During those two mournful weeks of pacing he contemplated and planned. Thoughts of the laws of primogeniture undoubtedly sparked his concern and determination to produce this document. Without a will to direct his wishes for his assets, laws could destroy the future, plans, and expectations of eight of his young sons and daughters.

Mason took his role as a father and sole parent of his children seriously. Although some criticized him during the Revolutionary years for his reluctance to accept greater public commitment, Mason's remarks about leaving behind nine "orphaned" children in order to do so rang true in his mind. He saw his role as the only parent of this large family as his primary responsibility even while playing a significant role in the American Revolution. In a letter Mason wrote in October 1778 to an unidentified friend, he described what the family members were presently doing and added

> ...and I have the Satisfaction to see them [his children] free from Vices, good-natured, obliging & dutiful....if I can only live to see the American Union firmly fixed, and free Governments well established in our western world, and can leave to my children but a Crust of Bread, & Liberty, I shall die satisfied....[373]

Second, George Mason's evolving world view was greatly influenced as he learned what it was like to be a slave master from his own first-hand experience as well as his observation of other slave owners. During the early years as a planter and slave master, Mason strove to have an efficient system of labor. Through trial and error, he used punishment to instill the behavior he wanted from his slaves. Sometimes it backfired as with Dick who had his ear cut off for stealing in 1754, then ran away, and later died. Mason, frustrated with punishments (most likely whip lashing) on the plantation that failed to change Dick's behavior, invoked the

---

[372] Dunn, ed., *Recollections,* 49.
[373] Rutland, *Papers of George Mason,* 433-434.

law to show his power and force as a master over his slave. He learned the strength of Dick's anger toward slavery and his determination to free himself. Mason pursued other runaways to the full extent of the law into the 1780s, but it was a time consuming and frustrating process. Mason learned that slaves were *real people* and using punishment and the legal tools at his disposal did not always reign in the behavior from them that he wanted.

George Mason's mother, Ann Thomson Mason, and his mother-in-law, Sarah Eilbeck, encouraged him to look at the ways in which they treated some of their slaves and the ways in which these two women sought to "protect," or at least ease, the difficulties of life for some slaves. Ann Thomson Mason and Sarah Eilbeck each used their legal position as a *feme sole* to control what would happen to their property after they were gone. They used the legal power at their disposal to make decisions about the lives and futures of enslaved individuals. Some slaves were highly favored (most likely because of proximity to their mistresses) and gained considerable security and protection through the administration of wills and deeds of gift. Ann Thomson Mason, for example, painstakingly arranged and rearranged legal documents to provide the best future for Nan Oldgate, Letty, and Letty's son, Jamey. This may have been a three generational family. Poignantly, Ann Thomson Mason charged George Mason to carry out her wishes toward Nan Oldgate. In a codicil to her will, she instructed her son to keep Nan Oldgate, now "past labor," at Gunston Hall and to "use her with Humanity."

Sarah Eilbeck willed her special servant Bess with her four daughters to her grandson William Mason along with Mattawoman Plantation, enabling these slaves to remain together where they lived all their lives. Although Bess's sons had been separated from her, Sarah Eilbeck provided security for Bess so that she, all her daughters, and their children would remain together – at least for the foreseeable future.

George Mason's wife, Ann Eilbeck Mason, left only subtle clues as to her attitude and treatment of the slaves at Gunston Hall, but they, too, are insightful. John Mason in his Recollections noted that even as a young boy of seven, his mother charged him with indelible words on her death bed that he "be kind to the servants." John also remembered

...that I was led clothed in black to her grave, that I saw her coffin lowered down into it by cords covered with black cloth, and that there was an assemblage of friends & neighbors of every class and of the slaves of the estate present; that the house was in a state of desolation for a good while; that the children and servants passed each other in tears & in silence & spoke in whispers...

George Mason's entry in the family Bible at Ann's death provides a beautiful and lengthy eulogy to her, saying in part, "She was bless'd with...a gentle & benevolent Heart...with an even[,] calm & chearful [sic] Temper to a very unusual degree [,] Affable to All....[and] an humane Mistress...."[374]

Each of three these women influenced George Mason's behavior and attitude toward slavery and the enslaved.

In 1789, Mason wrote a contract for his daughter Nancy prior to her marriage to Rinaldo Johnson. While he sought to protect her property from Johnson's debts, the contract went further; it consolidated and preserved numerous slave families (mothers and their children) from the possibility of separation. Nancy Mason Johnson carried that protection on in her will in 1804. Her document secured those same (now) multigenerational slave families from separation once again. Thus, George Mason's daughter, Nancy Mason Johnson, learned from all of them - her parents and both grandmothers. She learned the importance of law in preserving property to a married woman; she learned the power of making decisions; she saw humanity in the way slaves were treated; and she learned compassion and concern for slave women as mothers. Through Nancy, this life-long understanding kept two multi-generational slave families together and protected several others from unknown change through a half century.

George Mason found ways to reward his favored slaves on a day-to-day basis, too. As Virginia's agriculture depended almost solely on its slave laborers, Mason provided consideration to some in his slave work force in various ways. Some individuals worked harder, gained his trust, or, at least, caused him less trouble. These slaves he rewarded. His manservant James and "some of the carpenters"

---

[374] Dunn, ed., *Recollections,* 49. Rutland, *Papers of George Mason,* 481-482.

(probably Aleck, Liberty, and Tom) lived at Log Town with their families in a separate community, away from work and supervision. They were given autonomy. These families were not under a watchful eye of the master or an overseer. They were able to talk and live freely in the confines of their community at Log Town. James also acquired a broader world view while traveling with George Mason to Williamsburg, Richmond, and Philadelphia; and he undoubtedly shared his experiences with other slaves in the community and expanded their understanding of life beyond Gunston Hall as well.

George Mason recognized Nace's skill in handling horses, his trust worthiness, and his dependability; at some point, Mason made Nace the overseer at the Occoquan Quarter, probably providing him (and his family) with extra rations of food or clothing – or perhaps paying Nace in cash or in shares of the crops made. Additionally, the children of favored house servants, skilled slaves, and others went to Mason's own children in his will. Great Sue, Lucy, Jenny, Bess, Cloe, Occoquan Nell, and others had children that benefited from some consideration – or what Mason likely saw as a reward for "good" service.

Third, and most importantly, the impact of the American Revolution brought the moral dangers of slavery home to George Mason more clearly than anything. The reality of England "enslaving" the American colonies struck hard in Mason's mind. He accepted the need for independence from the "mother country" very early and was a firm patriot to that cause. But, in forming the new nation, Mason also reflected on the demise of the Roman Empire and saw its root cause as slavery. Over the years as a slave master himself, he had first-hand experience being a "petty tyrant" and saw the personal destruction of "the morals and manners" slavery caused. He blamed the "avarice" of the British merchants who be believed foisted slaves on the planters in the first place. George Mason detested slavery.

Although the manumission law changed in Virginia in 1782 to allow individual masters to free slaves, Mason freed none of his. His earlier will in 1773 stated that each of his nine children was to receive his or her inheritance at the time of their marriage or on coming of age. This process began the next year in 1774 when George Mason V reached his age of majority (twenty-one). Nancy, William, and Thomson all reached their majority before 1782 and Sarah married Daniel McCarty, Jr. in 1778. Mason's wishes in part were invoked well before 1782. Slaves now given those children were no longer George Mason's property. Additionally, manumitting other slaves or adding a codicil to his will in 1782 would have unfairly removed bequests from the other children in his family. In other words, it would retract his gifts.[375]

George Mason continued to think about slavery in the broader picture. By the 1780s, Mason's world view had expanded greatly. He saw Virginia as part of a new nation. And he believed that the United States could – and should – step over the threshold as a new nation by beginning to divest itself from slavery. His own state of Virginia had already acted to stop the external slave trade; Mason believed that the United States should do the same. Slaves could – and should – be educated so they would understand the benefits of freedom and not all necessarily "become thieves" as many feared. Slave owners could – and should – be compensated for their "property" if manumission occurred. Outright manumission without this was not acceptable to him. Lands in the western territories might provide a real means to this end.

Mason's participation in the American Revolution and the development of a national government brought him into contact with men whose ideals were different from those of many of the Virginians he knew and associated with. At the Constitutional Convention in Philadelphia in 1787, he felt the full force of the determination that some South Carolina and Georgia delegates had in keeping the slave trade open. Mason was in total opposition to this. He angrily realized he had no way to argue against them when they negotiated a "behind closed doors" deal with the New England states. Mason later very forcefully stated that those states not accepting a policy of closure of the slave trade should not be admitted to the union.[376]

George Mason and many other founding fathers began to expand their ideas and world view. Benjamin Franklin, Thomas Jefferson, James Madison, George Washington, and so many others believed in a bright future and great possibilities for the new nation. Mason's vision included a United States without slavery. But

---

[375] Mason also knew that although manumission was possible, it did not guarantee a slave's residence in the state. Laws required (if enforced) that a freed slave leave Virginia. Hening, ed., *Statutes*, 3:86-88.
[376] Rutland, *Papers of George Mason*, 1086,

no one foresaw the impact of the invention of the cotton gin in 1794 or the expansion of American soil with the Louisiana Purchase in 1803. The South was transformed by these events into the Cotton Kingdom early in the nineteenth century and the demand for slaves as laborers soared beyond the imagination of anyone in the eighteenth century. Although the slave trade into the United States did end in 1808, the demand for slaves in the new South and the agricultural downturn in the upper South created a burgeoning internal slave trade between states and devastated the vast majority of slave families that managed to survive the eighteenth century traumas of enslavement.[377]

Many slave owners in the Revolutionary period believed that slavery as an institution would die out. Jefferson's Northwest Ordinance provided a frontier where America could grow without slavery. Perhaps Mason thought that slavery would be "diluted" (as some others believed) and finally dissipate. Perhaps he was encouraged by the abolitionist ideals forming in the North during those few months he resided in Philadelphia in 1787. If he did have thoughts about any of these ideas, they have not come to light in his surviving documents.

George Mason, seven years older than George Washington, seventeen years older than Thomas Jefferson, and twenty-six years older than James Madison, was coming nearer to the end of his life. The torch was being passed to the next generation. In so many ways they carried it well. But they did not heed the concerned and passionate voice of George Mason who so forcefully opposed slavery on the national level. The nation would pay a hefty price.

---

[377] Richard S. Dunn, *A Tale of Two Plantations* (Cambridge, Massachusetts: Harvard University Press, 2014), 45-61. Richard Dunn describes in detail the movement of the hundreds of Tayloe slaves in the nineteenth century from Virginia to Alabama. Some of these slaves were ultimately reunited with family members which is the unique situation in this study. More typically, slaves were forcefully removed (often by trickery) then sold to remote geographical locations. See also Maurie D. McInnis, *Slaves Waiting for Sale* (Chicago: The University of Chicago Press, 2011), 55-83. McInnis researches and presents the internal slave trade process through the nineteenth century painting of Eyre Crowe entitled "Slaves Waiting for Sale." Richmond, Virginia had one of the largest and most profitable sales areas in the mid-nineteenth century. Crowe witnessed a slave auction in that city in 1853. The artist's depiction and the author's research in this book reveal the trauma of separation of slave families. McInnis writes of the callous nature of the process and its business character in Virginia's capitol city: "If Main Street could be described as the retail district, Wall Street was at the center of what could be called the slave-trading district. There were numerous businesses that supplied the trade with necessary items such as clothing and shoes....In Richmond, the slave trade was interwoven into the fabric of the city, close to the state's governmental center, its religious structures, and its retail district, yet was simultaneously concealed."

The exploration of slavery at Gunston Hall in this book provides a way of examining how George Mason's experiences as a slave master transposed his views into his growing opposition to slavery. Researching the primary sources to find out more about the lives of enslaved individuals owned by George Mason's family also adds to a growing understanding of African American life in bondage in the eighteenth century Chesapeake region of North America. In addition, a few rare tracings of Mason slaves beyond that world into the nineteenth century have emerged. Hope yet remains that the oral traditions of some African American families may here find clues to their ancestors.

Epilogue

Syllabub was a favorite dessert of wine, cream, sugar, lemon and other flavorings. All whipped together, then poured into glasses, the cream rose to the top, separating from the wine. When served, it provided an attractive – and tasty – dessert.

*I*n the winter of 2013, I participated in Gunston Hall's annual "Seeds of Independence" program entitled: "The Past and the Present Meet on Mason Neck." In part, this program was a genealogy workshop and a presentation of how the surviving Mason documents can help to identify slave family members. The focal point of the afternoon's program, however, was the premier of a video entitled "A 200-Year Journey: Mattawoman Plantation to Mason Neck - The Descendents of George Gant, The Ancestors of Gladys Cook Bushrod."

Gunston Hall Plantation is located in Fairfax County, Virginia on the peninsula to-day known as Mason Neck. The region is home to many residents with an African American heritage and many families hold oral traditions of being descended from slaves. One of those residents was Gladys Cook Bushrod. On 9 February 2012, Gladys celebrated her 103rd birthday and that summer, the Seeds of Independence Committee made the video about her descendents. It traced Gladys' family genealogy and explored her family's oral history that her great-grandfather, George Gant, was a slave owned by the Mason family.

As the story of Gladys' family unfolds, we learn about her mother, Mary Bertha Rosa Gant who married George Cook. The couple made their home near Gladys' maternal grandparents, Rosetta (Rose) Maskins Gant and George Washington Gant. Gladys was only seven years old when her mother Bertha died. Gladys and her sister Laura now went to live with their grandparents while the girls' father worked in Alexandria and returned to Mason Neck to spend the weekends with his family. Gladys' grandmother Rose was a midwife. Gladys remembered that she and Laura often went with their grandmother in the middle of the night when she delivered babies - both black and white - across all of Mason Neck.

The oral tradition among the children of Gladys Cook Bushrod has held that George Gant (her great-grandfather), the father of George Washington Gant, was born enslaved in Charles County, Maryland about 1800. Their oral tradition also relates he was owned by the Mason family. At the Seeds of Independence program that afternoon, I presented the documentation - through an examination of Mason family inventories and wills - of a strong link for this oral history.

William Mason, George Mason IV's second son, inherited his grandfather Eilbeck's Charles County, Maryland plantation known as Mattawoman. This inheritance included land and numerous slaves. In 1817, William Mason divided his property between his two sons in his will. In that document, his son, George Mason [of Maryland], inherited a slave named George. (See Appendix: P.) About 1848, George Mason [of Maryland] purchased the property known as Hollin Hall in Fairfax County, Virginia and moved his family and his slaves there. He now became known George Mason of Hollin Hall.[378]

The United States Federal Census Slave Schedules for 1850 and 1860 provide lists of male and female slaves with ages, but no names. However, a male, age 50, appears in the 1850 census belonging to George Mason [of Hollin Hall], living in Fairfax County, Virginia. In the 1860 census, a male, age 62, belonging to Gee [Geo?] Mason is living in Fairfax County, Virginia. It seems probable that both of these entries reference the enslaved man, George, moved from the Maryland property.[379]

The United States Federal Census of 1870 reveals the first names of all family members, their ages, and race. The family of George [Washington] Gaunt [Gant], age 35, along with his wife Rose, age 25, four sons, and [his mother] Charlotte, age 60, are living in Fairfax County, Virginia. They lived beside the Thomas Chapman family for whom George Gaunt worked as a farmhand.[380]

Taken together, these documents (wills, inventories, and census records) give supporting evidence that a slave named George was born in Charles County, Maryland on the plantation of William Mason, the son of George Mason IV, and was later brought to Fairfax County, Virginia. Thus, the Gant family has a strong and plausible link to George Mason of Gunston Hall through its oral history tradition. Gladys Cook Bushrod died in 2013. Her family's ancestry is as follows:

---

[378] Hollin Hall was originally the property built by George Mason IV's son Thomson.
[379] United States Federal Census Slave Schedules, 1850 and 1860, Fairfax, Virginia, (Slaves of George Mason), *Ancestry.com*, Provo, Utah. (It is of note that in each of these census records, a male slave of the approximate age of George Washington Gant is apparent.)
[380] United States Federal Census 1870, Fairfax County, Virginia. *Ancestry.com*, Provo, Utah. Young Maria Gaunt, age seven, lived with the Chapmans and was employed as a "domestic." Bertha Gant was not born until 1886.

Gladys Cook Bushrod (1909-2013)

George Cook (1867-1947) — m. Bertha **Gant** (1886-1916)

|

George Washington **Gant** (1836-1914)
m. Rosetta Maskins (1846-1918)

|

George **Gant** (c. 1800-c. 1870)
m. Charlotte (1810-1889)

Acknowledgements

Archeologists at work under the direction of David Shonyo at the slave quarter site on the east side of the mansion in the late spring of 2016.

The seeds of an idea often germinate over a long period of time. So it is with this book which has been germinating for over twenty-five years. I am deeply indebted to Susan Borchardt, who, as Gunston Hall's Curator and Assistant Director, inspired my interest in historical research, offered opportunities, and continually encouraged me to set goals to bring my ideas to life. My sincere thanks go to Susan, a true mentor and friend.

The offices of the educational staff, formerly housed on the second floor of the Hertle Building at Gunston Hall (the area that I often referred to as "the attic"), was a close-knit environment where ideas were bantered about, planning for events took place, and much camaraderie was built. I am greatly indebted to Mickey Crowell, Linda Hartman, Denise McHugh, and Susan Borchardt who welcomed me into many discussions there. Your encouragement and support furthered my quest to learn more about George Mason and slavery at Gunston Hall.

I owe thanks to three Gunston Hall librarians who provided much assistance along the way. Anne Baker, Kevin Shoup, and Mark Whatford were incredibly helpful across the years and constantly supportive of searches and questions. Kevin and I formed a unique bond additionally through the Ph.D. Program at George Mason University. My good wishes go to him in completing that goal! I also spent many hours in the Rockefeller Library at the Colonial Williamsburg Foundation and thank all of the staff there for their consistent smiles, cheerful help, and incredible resources.

Gunston Hall's Docents have been overwhelmingly supportive of my study of slavery. I have greatly appreciated the many opportunities to take part in their training sessions across the years. They provided me with opportunities to hone my thoughts and present new research. They challenged me with their questions and eagerness to learn more about the complicated and sensitive subject of slavery in America. Thank you to all who have been part of that organization and made me feel welcome and included.

In my long association with Gunston Hall, the Historical Interpreters represented a corps of highly skilled and enthusiastic educators who form the front line of the museum staff. Offering visitors the history of George Mason's family and con-temporaries, emphasizing his contributions to human rights, and placing him in context with America's Founding Fathers, the Interpreters continue to function as the lynch pin of the site and the primary contact that guests have during a visit to the museum. Most importantly, visitors are provided with a "real person" to learn about eighteenth century history and to have the opportunity to ask questions. I like to say that the Interpreters pull George Mason out of the "footnotes of history" and put him squarely on the page where he belongs. I am extremely proud to have been a part of this corps of dedicated men and women. I have loved working with each of you. Gunston Hall Plantation truly has been my "home away from home" for almost thirty years.

No book comes into being without the help of editors and technical supporters. I am so grateful to have had three incredible editors read and advise this project as it has progressed. Michelle Rudolph and Chris Vile provided their valuable time to read, suggest, and make recommendations on this book. Michele's insights into the "woman's" side of this story and my daughter Chris's strong background in eighteenth century slavery and knowledge of George Mason brought important discussions forward for consideration in this book. I cannot thank them enough for their input to this project. My third editor, my husband, Keith A. Dunn, has read more drafts than anyone can count and discussed more ideas than anyone should be expected to. Saying thank you is barely enough to show my appreciation for his talents, abilities, education, and experience – and his tireless devotion to me and my project. But they are special thanks to him for his help and belief in me. My critical need for technical support was fulfilled by my son Drew Dunn and without him this would probably have been a hand written document. I thank him for the years of patient teaching to help me acquire new skills and the confidence to use them. Most of all, I thank each one of you for helping me over hurdles and pushing me to do better.

Thanks to David Shonyo, Gunston Hall Archeologist, whose time and discussions about the important and exciting discoveries helped me add to the documentation about slavery in the Chesapeake region. I hope his reward comes in the discovery of Log Town at some time in the near future!

Arlene Fabbri, historian, artist, and long time esteemed friend brings her talent to this book with her illustrations and firsthand knowledge of Carter's Grove Plantation. I thank her for her wonderful contributions.

My friend and fellow historian, Jackie Geschickter, provided a "wayside tavern" for me countless times. I thank her (and Emma and Darcy) for the comfortable accommodations and the opportunity to reflect and discuss George Mason and his contemporaries with her.

I was extremely fortunate to have my graduate experiences at George Mason University enriched by Dr. Roy Rosenzweig and Dr. Lawrence W. Levine. Roy's critiquing of the earliest drafts for the ideas for this book helped me rewrite and reformulate what I wanted to say all along. His early personal encouragement and written comments kept this project buoyant for me. Larry's remarkable insight into American slavery sparked deeper interest for me into the cultural aspects and transformation of Virginia's enslaved people in particular. The incredible discussions in his office reflected his place in the first generation of historians who dug deeper into the story of American slavery. Larry and his generation of historians broke ground for others who refined the understanding of enslavement from "the bottom rail." I am indebted to both Roy and Larry and only wish I had told them in person.

I am extremely grateful to Betsy Hodges, the graphic designer who truly made *Among His Slaves* come alive with her creative talents, editing skills, and keen eye for detail. I cannot thank her enough for her incredible patience and dedication to this project. It has been delightful to work with her.

Last, I want to pay tribute to a feline chum. Hobo made his residence at Gunston Hall for many years. All of us who knew him, I think, believed that he understood the place far better than any of us.

Terry Dunn
Williamsburg, Virginia
September 2016

Appendix

Mason and Eilbeck Wills and Inventories

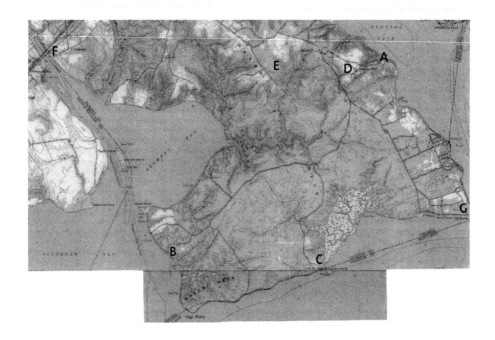

This 1950 topographical map of Mason Neck serves a base for locating several key properties of Mason family members. Historian Robert Moxham examined the extant record of patents, surveys, and land boundaries of the Masons. George Mason IV's holdings included all of the southern most part of what is today known as Mason Neck. The Occoquan, Dogues Neck, and Hallowing Point Quarters were probably along the Potomac River and Occoquan Bay, while the Pohick Quarter was likely closer to Gunston Hall. See Robert Morgan Moxham, The Colonial Plantations of George Mason (North Springfield, Virginia: Colonial Press, 1975), passim.

 A. Newtown
 B. Home of George Mason II
 C. Dogues Neck Plantation
 D. Gunston Hall Plantation
 E. Lexington Plantation
 F. Occoquan Ferry
 G. Hallowing Point

Appendix A

1735 Inventory of George Mason III, Charles County, Maryland

Slaves:	Value (£):
Judith (30)	20
Peg (16)	23
Sue (8)	6
Dick (4)	6
Jenny (2 ½)	4
Priscilla (1 ¾)	4
Beck (1)	3
Frank (10) [female?]	10
Isaac (7)	6
Sarah (6)	6
Nan (26) & her 1 day old child	25
Frank (30, a woman)	10
Will (30)	26
Bridget (14)	14
Kit (15)	15
Virgin (40)	12
Jo (50)	20
Rush (30, ship carpenter)	30
Dublin (30, ship carpenter)	30
Dick (30, shoemaker)	30
Gambor (26)	25

Indentured Servants:		Time left to serve:
Daniel Davey (30)	6	6 years
Cha[rles] Dougherty (21)	4	4 years
James Cody (24)	6	6 years
Rich[ar]d Wote (no age given)	6	6 years
Alex[ande]r Young (35, carpenter)	6	1 ¾ years
John Davis (24)	10 shillings	3 months

Source: Maryland Archives, Annapolis Maryland: Charles County Inventories, 1735-1752, f. 13-15, 3.

Appendix B

1735 Inventory of George Mason III – Prince William County, Virginia

Slaves:		Value (£):
Parus	Negro man	20
Job	Negro boy	10
Lucey	Negro girl	6
Jenny	Mulatto girl	4
Stephen	Negro boy	12
London	Negro man	22
Nan Wilson	Mulatto woman	19
Winsor	Negro man	22
Matt	Negro man	22
Jack	Negro boy	14

Servants:		
James	Serv[an]t man	7
John Webb	Servant man	5
Morgan Carpenter	Servant man	7

Source: Prince William County, Virginia, Will Book C, 1734-1744, 49-50.

Appendix C

1756 Deed of Gift – Ann Thomson Mason to Mary Mason Seldon:

Sampson	Pegg	*Slaves already in her possession:*	
George	Hannah	Will	Bess
Charles	Poll	London	Lucy
Peter	Nan Oldgate	Limerick	Judy
Job	Letty	Sue	Esther
Rush		Grace	

Addendum: slaves transferred to grandson Samuel Seldon after the death of Mary Mason Seldon:

Sampson	Peg
George	Hannah & Thomas her child born since
Charles	Pete
Peter	Nan Oldgate
Rush	

1760 Will of Ann Thomson Mason to George Mason IV:

Bridgett	Lucy
Ancilla	Alice
Anthony	Milly
Sabrina	Letty and Jamey her son

1762 Codicil to Will of Ann Thomson Mason to grandson Samuel Seldon:

Letty and her son Jammy - in trust with George Mason

1762 Codicil to Will of Ann Thomson Mason to George Mason:

"It is also my earnest request & desire, that the Mulatto Wench named Nan Oldgate who has been a useful Slave in the family may not be sold, or exposed to Hardship as she is past her Labor & that if possible she may be allowed to live with my Son George Mason who I hope will use her with Humanity."

Source: Stafford County, Virginia Deeds, Liber O, 1748-1767, 433-456.

Appendix D

1763 Inventory of Ann Thomson Mason

Fairfax County

Slaves:		Value (£):
Mouses [Moses?]	man	70
Corraga	woman	55
Jemima	girl	40
Bridgett	woman	45
Ancilla	girl	55
Lucy	girl	23

Stafford County

Slaves:		Value (£):
Letty	woman	75
James, Letty's mulatto son	boy	30
Anthony	boy	45
Alice	girl	30
Milly	girl	35
Phill		50
Sarah		60
Peter		40
Daphne		36
Hannah		35
Milly		25
Priscilla		20
Jallow		50
Ned		60
Mary		50
Jack		40
Betty		40
Rachael		45
Pegg		40
Scipio		60

Appendix D, *Continued*

1763 Inventory of Ann Thomson Mason

Stafford County, *Continued*

Slaves:	Value (£):
Jane	60
Anthony	40
Jack	35
Grace	25
Tom	20
Rachael	60
Daniel	60
Nase	60
Kato	40
Miles	50
Phil	40
Will	45
Bess	40
Dublin	45
Tom	40

Source: Stafford County, Virginia Will Book Liber O, 1748-1767, 456-462.

Appendix E

1763 Will of William Eilbeck, Charles County, Maryland

To my Grand Son George Mason, Jr. [V] - slave Dick
To my Grand Daughter Ann - slave Penny
To my Grand Son William - slave Cato
To my Grand Son Thomson - slave Cupid
To my Grand Daughter Sarah - slave Priss
To my Grand Daughter Mary - slave Nan

Source: Charles County, Maryland Wills, 1753-1766, 315-318.

Appendix F

1765 Inventory of William Eilbeck of Charles County, Maryland

Slaves:	Age:	Value (£):
Ben (carpenter)	24	70
Sam	31	54
Penroth	40	40
Charles	40	38
Clem	22	54
Harry	26	54
Watt	19	54
Peter	16	45
Mattawoman Kate	45	35
Beck	28	40
Bessie with child	25	50
Jenny	19	40
Moll	21	40
Doll	18	40
Cage	14	38
Milly	12	32
China	11	30
Frank	8	25
Jack	7	18
Patt	4	14
Dick	16	15
Cato	9	26
Cupid	8	25
Priss	7	18
Nan	5	15
Hector	59	28
Jack	very old	5
Nacy	27	54
Jerry (weakly)	20	45
Sue	37	35

Continued on page 172

Appendix F, *Continued*

1765 Inventory of William Eilbeck of Charles County, Maryland

Slaves:	Age:	Value (£):
Nell	27	38
Molotto Poll (lost one Eye)	19	32
Pamonkey Kate	very old	5
Stephen	14	35
Bob	4	14
Sampson	3	13
Joe	1 yr 7 mo	8
Sue	2	11
Vicky	0.8	5

"1 Negro Girl Penny mentioned in Mr Eilbecks Will but not a part of his Estate having been given several Years ago to his Grandaughter Ann Mason & ever since in her possession"

Source: Charles County Maryland Inventories, 1753-1766, 449-455.

Appendix G

1773 Will of George Mason IV

To George Mason V:
Alice
Bob Dunk
Yellow Dick
Bob (son of Occoquan Nell)
Peter (son of great Sue)
Judy
Lucy
Dick (given by Grandfather
  Eilbeck)
Tom
Liberty

To William Mason:
Milly (daughter of Kate)
Sampson
(son of Mrs. Eilbeck's Bess)
Cato (given by Grandfather
  Eilbeck)

To Thomson:
Sally (daughter of Lucy)
Joe (son of Mrs. Eilbeck's Bess)
Cupid (given by Grandfather
  Eilbeck)

To John:
Harry (son of House Poll)
Peg (daughter of Chloe)

To Thomas:
Jack (son of House Nell)
Daphne (daughter of Dinah)

To Ann [Nancy]:
Bess (daughter of Cloe)
Frank (Bess' child)
Mulatto Priss (daughter of Jenny)
Nell (daughter of Occoquan Nell)
Penny (given by Grandfather
  Eilbeck)

To Sarah:
Hannah
Venus (daughter of Beck)
Mulatto Mima (daughter of Jenny)
Priss (given by Grandfather
  Eilbeck)

To Mary:
Ann
Nell (daughter of House Nell)
Little Jenny (daughter of Jenny)
Nan (given by Grandfather
  Eilbeck)

To Elizabeth:
Vicky (daughter of Occoquan Nell)
Sarah (daughter of great Sue)
Rachel (daughter of Beck)

Source: Fairfax County, Virginia Will Book F-1, 95-119. See also: Robert A. Rutland, *The Papers of George Mason* (Chapel Hill: University of North Carolina Press, 1970), 147-161.

Appendix H

1780 Will of Sarah Eilbeck

To grandson William Mason:

Ben	Peter	Doll	Henny (daughter of Bess)
Penrith	Clem	Milly	Beck (daughter of Bess)
Frank	Jack	Nell (daughter of Bess)	
Will	Bess	Kate (daughter of Bess)	

To grandson John Mason:
boy Tom (son of Bess)

To grandson Thomas Mason:
boy James (son of Moll)

To granddaughter Ann Mason:
Arecasa and her son Nace

To granddaughter Sarah Mason:
Jenny and her children
    Sue
    Robin
    Jesse

To granddaughter Mary Mason:
Moll and her son Billy

To granddaughter Elizabeth Mason:
China and her daughter Patt
girl Hannah (daughter of Moll)

Note: George Mason V was bequeathed a diamond ring and Thomson Mason was to receive £25 to purchase a watch. Neither received any slaves in her will.

Source: Charles County, Maryland Wills, Liber AF, No. 7, 582-585, 578.

Appendix I

1789 Contract – George Mason IV to Ann [Nancy] Eilbeck Mason

Lizzy (a mulatto)
Nan (a mulatto)
Bess and her eight children
    Frank
    Lizzy
    Dick
    Chloe
    Nancy
    Margaret
    Priss
    Delia
Penny
Arecajah and her four children
    Nace
    Kate
    William
    Sarah

Source: Fairfax County, Virginia Deed Book R-1, 336-340.

Appendix J

1792 Inventory of George Mason IV – Stump Neck, Maryland

Slaves:	Age:	Value (£):
Benjimin	58	20
Charles	48	48
Frederick		not worth one farthing
Nancy	18	50
Cloe	60	12
Moll	55	17.10
Lett	45	22.10
Sary	12	25
Charity	5	15

Source: Charles County, Maryland Inventories, 1791-1797, 139-140.

Appendix K

1795 Will of George Mason V

To wife Elizabeth:
Sarah
Phillis
Betty
Cooke Charles
Jerry (son of Occoquan Nell)
George (son of Phillis)
Negro lad Jacob (who worked in the garden) [added in codicil]

To daughter Betsy:
Priss and Will her child   Matilda
Nathan   Lett (daughter of Ancilla)
Bess

To daughter Nancy:
Cloe and Kate her child   Henry (son of Phillis)
Alice (daughter of Phillis)   Dennis (son of Phillis)
Jeremy (son of Phillis)

To daughter Sally:
Case and her child Sall   Hagar (child of Milly)
Frank   Tony (child of Milly)
Sam (son of Winey)

To his unborn child:
Nell and her increase
boy Jeremy
Sarah (on his wife's death)
Phillis (on his wife's death)

Source: Fairfax County, Virginia Will Book G-1, 253-259.

Appendix L

1797 Inventory of George Mason V

At Lexington Plantation

Slaves:	Age:	
Aleck	40	carpenter
Liberty	50	carpenter
Tom	50	carpenter
Isaac	56	blacksmith
Anthony	22	blacksmith
Jim	24	
Bob	32	
Lewis	18	
Jacob	18	
Jerry	18	
Charles	40	cook
George	20	waiter
Aaron	18	waiter
Grandison	12	
Sarah	30	maid
Jine	9	Sarah's child
Humphrey	7	Sarah's child
Bill	7 months	Sarah's child
Nell	25	maid
Tom	1	Nell's son
Matilda	16	maid
Kate	50	half-blind
Beck	50	
Betty	30	
Mary	50	nurse
Philis	40	
Dennis	5	Philis' son
Henry	3	Philis' son
Davy	1	Philis' son
Jeremy	14	

Appendix L, *Continued*

1797 Inventory of George Mason V

At Dogue Neck Plantation

Slaves:	Age:	
Peter	30	
Daniel	25	
Will	25	
Peter	Past labor	
Jerry	14	
Ancilla	45	
Juda	40	
Scipio	10	
Nancy	7	
Lucy	38	
Stace	18	
Minta	24	
Sarah	3	Minta's daughter
George	1	Minta's son
Cloe	22	
Kate	3	Cloe's child
Eliza	2	
Bess	19	
Old Susan	Past labor	

1797 Inventory of George Mason V, continued on page 178

Appendix L, *Continued*

1797 Inventory of George Mason V

At Pohick Plantation

Slaves:	Age:	
Kingston	58	
Phill	45	
Will	30	
Harry	23	
Frank	26	(a woman)
Winny	24	
Sam	7	
Betty	5	
Phill	3	
Charles	1	
Alexander	18	
Lucy	2	Alex's child
Amy	12	
Lett	10	

At Occoquan Plantation

Slaves:	Age:	
Nace	50	Black overseer
Nace	30	
James	22	
Charles	19	
Case	20	
Lett	22	
Nathan	13	
Jenny	6 months	Lett's child
Sall	3	Case's child
Jerry	1	Case's child
Hogar	10	Son of Milly
Doll	Past labor	

Appendix L, *Continued*

1797 Inventory of George Mason V

At Hallowing Point Plantation

Slaves:	Age:	
Watt	50	
Charles	29	
Stephen	30	
Dumfries	30	
Ben	19	
Barbary	9	
Silvy	18	
Milly	40	
Tony	8	child of Milly
Bridgett	6	child of Milly
Peg	4	child of Milly
Cilla	2	child of Milly
Patience	20	
Jesse	2	child of Patience
Priss	20	
Bill	3	
Beck	14	
Dinah	55	
Winny	Past labor	

Source: Fairfax County, Virginia Will Book H-1, 38-52

Appendix M

1797 Will of Thomson Mason of Hollin Hall

To his wife Sarah McCarty Mason:

Jesse	
Charles	son of old Let
Bob	son of old Let
Cupid	
Will	son of old Lilia
Old Let	
Long Sall	
Phillis	
Mulatto Let	
Old Nell	
Nell	Old Nell's daughter
Black Poll	
Nan	daughter of old Delia
Pamela	
Alice	
Robin	
James	
Jesse	son of Jenny

To his daughter Sarah Chichester:

Priss	daughter of Black Poll
George	son of Black Poll
Nell	daughter of Long Sall
Liszey	given by Grandfather Chichester

To his daughter Elizabeth:

Tom	son of Jenny
Winney	daughter of Winney
Monima	daughter of yellow Hannah

Appendix M, *Continued*

1797 Will of Thomson Mason of Hollin Hall

To his daughter Ann Eilbeck:

Jenney	daughter of Yellow Hannah
Case	daughter of Long Sall
Peggy	daughter of Phillis

To his son Thomson:

mulatto boy Bill	given by Grandfather Chichester

Source: Fairfax County, Virginia Will Book M-1, 1820-1822, 130-136.

Appendix N

1800 Inventory of Thomas Mason

Slaves:	Age:		Value (£):
Cyrus	65		No value
Jacob	40		80
Sam	24		90
James	22		80
Mulatto Jack	30		90
Frank	30		90
Jack (a rough carpenter)	32	(lost sight of one eye)	82
Will (a rough carpenter)	26		90
Jeremiah	18		70
Charles	16		50
James Clark	14		50
Joe Clark	12		40
Lame Will	12	(lost a leg)	20
Jenny Roley	30		50
Polly	25		50
Lucy	35		40
Molley	18		50
Daphne	28		40
Alice	45		35
Milley	15		50
Pompey	10		36
Ancilla	6		20
Nancy	3		15
Bill	3		15
Sam Montjoy	4		15
Sam	6		20
Bob	5	(sickly)	5
Milly	10		30
Lucy	7		15
Anne	3		10

Appendix N, *Continued*

1800 Inventory of Thomas Mason

Slaves:	Age:	Value (£):
Henry	1	5
Dinah	6 months	5
Winny	6 months	5

Source: Prince William County, Virginia Will Book I, 1803-1809, 123-141.

Appendix O

1804 Will of Ann [Nancy] Eilbeck Mason Johnson

To her son Thomas Rinaldo Johnson:

Negro Bess	Dick	Frank
Black Lizza	Ned	Salisbury
Black Nancy	Delia	Beatty
Priss	Louis	Sall
Mary	Chloe	Anna

To her daughter Ann Eilbeck Mason Johnson:

Negro Caga
Kate
Sall
Chansy
Mary Ann (Chansy's daughter)
Juda (Chansey's daughter)
Nace (Caga's son)
Bill (Caga's son)
Yellow Lizza (house servant) and
Yellow Nancy (house servant)
    And their sons:
    Charles
    Henry
    James
    David
Penny or Penelope

Source: Prince George's County, Maryland Wills, Recorded March 12, 1816.

Appendix P

1817 Will of William Mason

To his son William (all now in his possession):
Mat
Toney
Gus
Louis
Abram
Lucy
Nelly
Eleanor
Leannah
Mathelda
Joshua
Henny

To his son George (all now in his possession):
George
Harry
John
Henry
Peter
Anne
Mary
Hannah
Liza
Ciatha
Lilly
Fanny (daughter of Hannah)

Source: Charles County, Maryland Wills, H.B. No. 14, Fol. 51, 43-51.

Appendix R

1819 Inventory of William Mason - Charles County, Maryland

Slaves:	Age:	Value ($):
Joseph (carpenter)	40	600
Glasgow (carpenter)	50	500
Moses	45	350
Ben	40	450
Bob	30	350
Nace	37	400
Davy	30	450
Daniel (Blacksmith)	30	600
Ben (miller)	30	550
Joe	17	500
Tom	65	100
Len	15	350
Isaac	14	350
Sam	15	350
Manuel	15	350
Bartlet	15	350
Sam	13	350
Sampson	10	275
Ned	9	275
Ben	9	275
John	8	250
Antony	7	150
Nat	6	200
Gusty	5	150
Edward	4	150
Nathan	3	100
Osborn	3	100
Adam	3	100
Calvert	3	100
Jonathan	2	100
Frank	60	100

Appendix R, *Continued*

1819 Inventory of William Mason - Charles County, Maryland

Slaves:	Age:	Value ($):
Cato	56	000 00
Tom	17	500
Jes	50	200
Dennis (cripple)	17	000 00
Let	75	000 00
Hanna	50	25
Henny	45	100
Beck	40	100
Eliza	40	150
Rachel	40	100
Nel	25	200
Molly	30	250
Betty	24	250
Fanny	16	300
Kitty	16	300
Nelly	20	300
Philicia	16	350
Letty	14	250
Luthira	10	200
Betsy	8	175
Milly	8	175
Lucinda	7	150
Sophia	5	125
Dolly	2	75
Sally	2	75
Cazy	2	75
Caroline	4	100
Peter	1	100
Aaron	1	100
1 male Infant	2 months old	75
1 male Infant	3 weeks old	75

Source: Charles County, Maryland Inventories, 1825-1829, 70-75.

Appendix S

1821 Inventory of Thomson Mason - Fairfax County, VA

Slaves:	Age:	Value ($):
Bob	55	100
Lawrence	30	325
Alec	23	350
Len	17	320
Delia & infants	33	300
Winney & 1 yr old child	26	300
Charlotte with infant & 3 yr old	24	300
Helen	18	275
Rutha	16	250
James	46	225
Charles	43	250
Poll & child 4 & child 6	48	475
Pamela	45	200
Alice	38	200
Priss & child 2 yrs old	28	300
Anne & child 2 & child 3	27	400
Caroline	15	275
Rosena	10	220
Edward	10	250
George	21	350
Dennis	11	250
William	10	200
Ben	8	175
Isaac	7	150
Mat	10	250
Jacob	4	120
Sarah	60	120
Kizzey	12	250
Judy	12	230
Jenny	9	175
Sarah	9 since dead	

Source: Fairfax County, Virginia Will Book N-1, 387-389.

Tables

Bricks were made on site with local clay dug and mixed with water to a workable consistency. They were formed in a wooden mold and allowed to sun dry. The hardened clay bricks were piled to form a kiln with multiple channels for fires. Once lit, the firing process required constant tending day and night and took about a week to complete. Photos taken at Colonial Williamsburg, Brickyard Site, 2016.

Table One: A Summary of Some Pertinent Virginia Slave Laws

1639 - All persons except Negroes to be provided with arms and ammunition (1:226)

1644 - All Negro men and women and all other men ages 16 to 60 adjudged tithable (1:292)

1662 - Negro women's children to serve according to the condition of the mother (2:170)

1663 - Servants not to go abroad without a "lycense" (2:195)

1667 - Baptism of a slave does not exempt him/her from bondage (2:260)

1669 - Death of a slave during punishment not deemed a felony (2:270)

1672 - Birth of Negro and mulatto children to be recorded in church parish (2:296)

1672 - Legal to wound or kill a slave resisting arrest (2:299-300)

1679 - Offences for hog sealing: 1st offence, 39 lashes; 2nd offence, ears nailed to the pillory for 2 hours and then cut off; 3rd offence, felony prosecution (2:440)

1680 - Ages of Negro children imported into Virginia to be adjudged within 3 months of their arrival (2:479-480)

1680 - Negroes forbidden to carry weapons (2:481-482)

1680 - Negroes forbidden to lift a hand against a Christian (2:481-482)

1691 - Master required to transport an emancipated slave out of the colony within six months (3:86-88)

1705 - Mulatto defined as the child, grandchild, or great-grandchild of a Negro (3:252)

1705 - Slaves adjudged to be real estate (3:333-335)

1705 - It is not a felony if a slave dies while being punished ((3:447-462)

1705 - Dismemberment made a legal punishment for "incorrigible" slaves (3:447-462)

1705 - If a slave put to death as punishment, master reimbursed with public funds (3:447-462)

1723 - No slave shall be set free except for some meritorious service to be adjudged by the Governor and Council (4:126-134)

1754 - Slave patrols required to visit all slave quarters once a month (6:421-422)

1778 - Act to end the importation of slaves into Virginia (9:471-472)

1782 - Act authorizing manumission of slaves in Virginia (11:39-40)

Source: William Walter Hening, ed., *The Statutes at Large; Being a Collection of All the Laws of Virginia, From the First Session of the Legislature, in 1619.* 13 Volumes (Richmond, New York, and Philadelphia, 1819-1823).

Table Two: Profits for the Virginia Dower Estate of Ann Thomson Mason

1736: "This year no Crop made but the Negroes would have brought the Estate considerably in debt if any account had been made for their maintenance... except for London & Parus."

"London this year worked in Maryland & made for his share Nett £18.1.7"

"Parus in Virginia for his share £9.9.0"

1737: "London in Maryland made 707 [pounds of tobacco]"

"Parus, Windsor, Matt & Jack in Virg[ini]a made 2658 [pounds of tobacco] Nan Wilson Sick. The rest unable to work."

1738: "London & Matt in Maryland made 2806 [pounds of tobacco]

Parus, Windsor, Nan Wilson[,] Jack & Stephen 4 shares 3500 [pounds of tobacco] The rest unable to work[.] Nan Wilson mostly sick."

1739: "London & Matt in Maryland made 3436 [pounds of tobacco]

Parus, Windsor, Nan Wilson, Jack & Stephen in Virg[ini]a 4 shares made 4547 [pounds of tobacco]"

"...there is no charge of Cloathing or maintaining the Negroes or for their Bedding..."

1740: "London & Matt in Maryland this year made 2804 [pounds of tobacco]

Nan Wilson, Parus, Windsor, Jack & Stephen 4 shares made in Virg[ini]a 4236 [pounds of tobacco]"

1741: "London & Matt in Maryland this year made 2032 [pounds of tobacco]

Nan Wilson, Parus, Windsor, Jack & Stephen 4 1/2 shares made in Virg[ini]a 5080 [pounds of tobacco]"

"no Charge of Cloathing[,] maintaining the Negroes or for their Bedding[,] tools[,] Levies &c..."

Note: Payments were made on two occasions to Drs. Tenant and Brown for "medicines for Nan Wilson" during these years.

Source: Prince William County Virginia Will Book C, 275-290, 367-375.

Table Three: Value of Rents Received in Virginia

Year	Money Received	Pounds of Tobacco
1735	£26.7.8	11,390
1736	20.0.0	13,166
1737	20.0.0	10,801
1738	22.0.0	12,383
1739	22.10.0	19,035
1740	20.6.0	17,438
1741	13.7.7 1/4	16,825

Source: Prince William County Virginia Will Book C, 275-290, 367-375.

Table Four: Profits for the Maryland Estate of George Mason IV

Year	Pounds of Tobacco Produced
1735	1,749
1736	4,686 $\frac{1}{2}$
1737	3,930
1738	4,153
1740	3,315
1741	5,985
1742	2,928

Source: Prince William County, Virginia Will Book C, 275-290, 367-375.

Table Five: 1753 List of Slaves Adjudged for Their Ages

Oronoko	12 years
Synharp	11 years
Juba	11 years
Kato	10 years
Beck	9 years
Jenny	8 years
Agniss	8 years

Source: Fairfax County, Virginia Order Book 1749-1754. 436. 12 August 1753.

Table Six: Slave children willed to his grandchildren by William Eilbeck 1763

Slave name:	Willed to:
Dick (14)	George Mason V (10)
Penny	Ann [Nancy] Mason (8)
Cato (9)	William Mason (6)
Cupid (8)	Thomson Mason (4)
Priss (7)	Sarah Mason (3)
Nan (5)	Mary Mason (1)

Note: Ages of the slave children taken from William Eilbeck's Inventory on 7 November 1765. The inventory states: "1 Negro Girl Penny mentioned in Mr Eilbecks [sic] Will but not a part of his Estate having been given several Years ago to his Grandaughter Ann Mason & ever since in her possession"

Source: Charles County, Maryland Wills, 1763, 316-317; Charles County, Maryland Inventories, 1753-1766, 449-455.

Overview of Tables Seven, Eight, and Nine

Tables Seven, Eight, and Nine each include some of the known or highly likely slave family connections in the appendix documents. Additional mother-child connections are revealed in individual wills or inventories, but are not included here. These tables attempt to define relationships across time.

In **Table Seven,** the Mason's ownership of the slave families of Nan Old Gate, Bridgett, Sue and Peter, Jenny, Beck, Occoquan Nell, Nace, Dinah, and Gunston Nell stretch across multiple documents. Survival of some members in each of these slave families helped to retain namesakes and memories even though in bondage.

Table Eight looks principally at Sarah Eilbeck's slave woman Bess and her seven children that are documented through more than a half century. Many in this slave family remained together on the Charles County, Maryland property where they were born. George Mason referred to her as "Mrs. Eilbeck's Bess" in his 1773 will. Bess, the most highly valued female slave on William Eilbeck's inventory of 1765, possibly served as the cook, the most important domestic trade on a plantation.

Table Nine examines the combined Mason and Eilbeck slaves that were willed to Ann Eilbeck [Nancy] Mason Johnson by her father, grandfather, and both grandmothers. Documentation reveals that Nancy's efforts kept those slaves and progeny together for more than forty years. It also reflects the Mason and Eilbeck family attitude to protect some slaves from separation.

Throughout these tables:
- Parentheses ( ) indicate an age given in a document.
- Brackets [ ] indicate a calculated age.
- Brackets [?] with a question mark indicate a possible family connection.
- Added notations in Appendix L by the letter L, O, H, D, or P refer to the farm or quarter a slave was living on. (Lexingtion, Occoquan, Hallowing Point, Dogues' Neck, or Pohick quarter).

Table Seven: Some Identified Slave Families of George Mason IV

Appendix A George Mason III 1735	Table 4 Slaves Adjudged 1753	Appendix C Ann Thomson Mason 1756-1762	Appendix D Ann Thomson Mason 1763	Appendix G George Mason IV 1773
Nan (26) and 1 day old child		Mulatto Nan Oldgate		
		Letty	Letty	
		Jamey her son	James her mulatto son	
Bridgett (14)		Bridgett	Bridgett (woman)	
		Ancilla	Ancilla (girl)	
		Anthony	Anthony (boy)	
			[Anthony man?]	
Lucy (girl)		Lucy	Lucy (girl)	Lucy
				Sally (daughter of Lucy)
		Alice	Alice (girl)	Alice
		Milly	Milly (girl)	

Table Seven: Some Identified Slave Families of George Mason IV

Appendix K George Mason V 1795	Appendix L George Mason V 1797	Appendix M Thomson Mason 1797	Appendix N Thomas Mason 1800	Appendix S Thomson Mason 1821
		[Old Let ?]		
		[James ?]		
	Ancilla (45) D			
			Ancilla (6)	
Lett (daughter of Ancilla)	Lett (10) P			
	Lucy (38) D		Lucy (35)	
			Lucy (7)	
			Alice (45)	
	Milly (40) H			
Hagar (Milly's child)	Hogar (son of Milly) O			
Tony (Milly's child)	Tony (8) (child of Milly) H			
	Bridgett (6) (child of Milly) H			
	Peg (4) (child of Milly) H			
	Cilla (2) (child of Milly) H			
		Milley (15)		
		Milly (10)		

Table Seven: Some Identified Slave Families of George Mason IV

Appendix A George Mason III 1735	Table 4 Slaves Adjudged 1753	Appendix C Ann Thomson Mason 1756-1762	Appendix D Ann Thomson Mason 1763	Appendix G George Mason IV 1773
Sue (8)		Sue	Peter	
				Sarah (daughter of Great Sue)
				Peter (son of Great Sue)
Jenny (8)		Mulatto Priss (daughter of Jenny)		
		Mulatto Mima (daughter of Jenny)		
		Little Jenny (daughter of Jenny)		
	Beck (9)			
		Venus (daughter of Beck)		
		Rachel (daughter of Beck)		
		Bob (son of Occoquan Nell)		
		Nell (daughter of Occoquan Nell)		
		Vicky (daughter of Occoquan Nell)		
			Nase	

Table Seven: Some Identified Slave Families of George Mason IV

Appendix K George Mason V 1795	Appendix L George Mason V 1797	Appendix M Thomson Mason 1797	Appendix N Thomas Mason 1800	Appendix S Thomson Mason 1821
	Old Susan (past labor) D			
	Peter (past labor) D			
	Peter (30) D			
	Beck (50) L			
	Bob (32) L			
	Nace (50) Black Overseer O			
	Nace (30)			

Table Seven: Some Identified Slave Families of George Mason IV

Appendix A George Mason III 1735	Table 4 Slaves Adjudged 1753	Appendix C Ann Thomson Mason 1756-1762	Appendix D Ann Thomson Mason 1763	Appendix G George Mason IV 1773
				Daphne (daughter of Dinah)
				Jack (son of Gunston Nell)
				Nell (daughter of Gunston Nell)

Summary:

Nan, Letty, and James, Letty's mulatto son, are intertwined in the documents of Ann Thomson Mason as discussed in pages 60-65. Although it is speculative, James later may have become the property of Thomson Mason, George Mason IV's son. The will of Ann Thomson Mason provided that in the event of the death of Samuel Seldon, Jr. (and other contingencies), Thomson Mason would become heir to this slave. Stafford County, Virginia Will Book O, 1748-1767, 433-439.

Bridgett is likely the mother of one or more of the following slave children: Ancilla, Anthony, Lucy, Alice, and Milly. The close connection of family names reveals intergenerational links. Milly has three children, Bridgett, Cilla, and Tony; Ancilla also has a daughter Lett, a possible familial link to Letty (above).

Sue and Peter are the likely parents of Peter and Sarah. All of these individuals were living on the Dogue Neck Quarter in 1797 except Sarah. Sarah was most likely moved to King George County when Elizabeth Mason married.

Jenny and Beck, two of the slaves whose ages were adjudged in 1753, both had children who were separated from them in the 1773 will of George Mason IV. Beck appears to have outlived Jenny; Beck is estimated to be fifty years old in 1797.

Table Seven: Some Identified Slave Families of George Mason IV

Appendix K George Mason V 1795	Appendix L George Mason V 1797	Appendix M Thomson Mason 1797	Appendix N Thomas Mason 1800	Appendix S Thomson Mason 1821
	Dinah (55) H			
			Dahpne (28)	
			Dinah (6 mo.)	
			Jack (32) a "rough carpenter"	

Occoquan Nell's three children were separated in the 1773 will of George Mason IV. Only Bob can be traced to the Lexington Plantation in 1797.

Nace, the black overseer at the Occoquan Quarter, has a son named Nace on the same property in 1797. Martin Cockburn, who paid Nace to break horses on his Springfield Plantation, owned a slave Nace in his 1822 inventory who was valued highly at $350. This is possibly the son named Nace (or perhaps a third generation with the same name). "Nase," on Ann Thomson Mason's inventory in 1763, is probably the elder man Nace in the Occoquan inventory in 1797.

Dinah's daughter Daphne was given to Thomas Mason. In 1800, Daphne is estimated to be twenty-eight years old. Six month old Dinah is very likely her daughter, named for her grandmother.

Gunston Nell, or House Nell as she may also have been known, had two children. They were separated from her in George Mason's 1773 will. Jack, a "rough carpenter" who "lost sight of one eye," and is 32 years old in 1800 is likely her son. Nothing more is known of her daughter Nell.

Table Eight: One slave family of Sarah Eilbeck

Appendix F William Eilbeck, 1765	Appendix G George Mason IV, 1773	Appendix H Sarah Eilbeck, 1780	Appendix R William Mason, 1819
[Sam (31) Father?]			
Bessie (25) with child		Bess [40]	
		Nell	
			[Nel (25)?]
			[Nelly (20)?]
		Henny [6]	Henny (45)
Beck (28)			
		Beck [1]	Beck (40)
		Tom	[Tom (65)?]
			[Tom (17)?]
	Mrs. Eilbeck's Bess' Sampson [11]		
Sampson (3) Joe (1 yr. 7 mo.)	Mrs. Eilbeck's Bess' Joe [9]		
			Joseph (40) Carpenter
			Joe (17)
			[Sampson (10)?]
			[Sam (13)?]
			[Sam (15)?]
Mattawoman Kate (45)			
Pamonkey Kate (very old)			
		Kate	

Table Eight: One slave family of Sarah Eilbeck

Summary:

Bess was born circa 1740 and had at least seven children. They include: Sampson, Joe, Tom, Nell, Henny, Beck, and Kate. Sampson (born c. 1731) may have been Bess' husband – or, at least, the father of her son Sampson. Bess' daughter Kate may have been named for Mattawoman Kate, possibly her grandmother and the mother of Bess. Bess may have had a sister Beck for whom she named a daughter Beck. Bess' daughters Henny and Beck both survived to 1819 when William Mason's inventory was taken.

The 1819 inventory includes the names and ages of slaves who may be descendents of Bess (grandchildren or great grandchildren). However, Joseph, a forty-year old carpenter is not her son, but may be related (nephew?) through other unidentified kin. Bess' son Joe was willed to Thomson Mason and does not appear in Thomson's 1821 inventory.

Likewise, Tom, age sixty-five, is not her son, but also possibly related thorough unidentified kin. Bess' son Tom was willed to John Mason.

Table Nine: Identified Slave Families of Ann (Nancy) Mason Johnson

Appendix A George Mason III 1735	Appendix E William Eilbeck, 1763	Appendix F William Eilbeck 1765	Appendix G George Mason IV 1773	Appendix H Sarah Eilbeck 1780
	Penny	Penny	Penny	
		Cage (14)*		Arecasa*
		Nacy (27)		her son Nace

Note: *Arecasa had multiple names or nicknames.

Table Nine: Identified Slave Families of Ann (Nancy) Mason Johnson

Appendix I Nancy Mason 1789	Appendix J George Mason IV 1792	Appendix L George Mason V 1797	Appendix O Nancy Mason Johnson 1804
Penny			Penny or Penelope
Arecajah* & her four children			Negro Caja*
Nace			Nace (son)
Kate			Kate
William			Bill (son)
Sarah			[Sall]
			Chansy and her children
			Mary Ann
			Juda

Table Nine: Identified Slave Families of Ann (Nancy) Mason Johnson

Appendix A George Mason III 1735	Appendix E William Eilbeck, 1763	Appendix F William Eilbeck 1765	Appendix G George Mason IV 1773	Appendix H Sarah Eilbeck 1780
			Bess daughter of Cloe	
			Frank Bess' child	
[Frank (woman) (30)]				
[Frank (10)]				

Table Nine: Identified Slave Families of Ann (Nancy) Mason Johnson

Appendix I Nancy Mason 1789	Appendix J George Mason IV 1792	Appendix L George Mason V 1797	Appendix O Nancy Mason Johnson 1804
Bess			Negro Bess
	Cloe (60)		
Frank			Frank
Lizzy			Black Lizza
Dick			Dick
Chloe			Chloe
Nancy			Black Nancy
Margaret			[Mary]
Priss			Priss
Delia			Delia
			Ned
			Louis
			Salisbury
			Beatty
Lizzy (mulatto)			Yellow Lizza
Nan (mulatto)			Yellow Nancy
			Their sons Charles James Henry David

Table Nine: Identified Slave Families of Ann (Nancy) Mason Johnson

Summary:

Penny or Penelope, the slave child given to Nancy Mason by her Grandfather Eilbeck, has the longest documented history of any of the Mason slaves. She can be traced for forty-one years. Penny had no known children.

Arecasa (or Arecajah), born about 1751, and her son Nace were given to Nancy by her Grandmother, Sarah Eilbeck. Cage, or Caja, as she was also known had at least four children: Nace, William (or Bill), Kate, and Sarah. Nace was likely named for Nacy listed in William Eilbeck's inventory, but the relationship is not known. Mary Ann and Juda are Arecasa's grandchildren; their mother, Chansy, may be another daughter of Arecasa or a "daughter-in-law."

Bess, the daughter of Cloe, had eight known children. Cloe is most likely the slave woman still living at George Mason's Maryland property known as Stump Neck when an inventory was taken in 1792. Bess' children are: Frank, Lizzy, Dick, Chloe, Nancy, Margaret, Priss, and Delia. Bess has four grandchildren: Ned, Louis, Salisbury, and Beatty. It is interesting to note that there was a slave woman named Frank and a child named Frank at Stump Neck in 1735. Bess' first child, Frank, may have been a namesake, but it is not known if Bess' child was a male or female. Chloe was likely named for her grandmother. See also the discussion on page 93 regarding Frank (Bess' child).

The two mulatto slaves that Nancy owned, Yellow Lizza and Yellow Nancy, were both house servants. They had four sons: Charles, James, Henry, and David. It is not known which mother had which son(s). As these two slave women were not named in the marriage contract by her father, Nancy Mason legally acquired them sometime after 1789.

It is of importance to note that Nancy Mason preserved these slave families of several generations that included males and females. She chose not to separate the sons from their mothers as was typically done.

Index

Corn stored for the slaves weekly rations was often held in a shed or store house within the slave quarter like this reconstructed one at Carter's Grove Plantation (circa 2001). The overseer had the key to the locked building and distributed the rations. Some tobacco might have been gleaned from the fields for the slaves use, drying wherever possible.

For individual slave names, see *Index for Mason and Eilbeck Slaves* beginning on page 218. Page number followed by a "*n*" indicate the reference is found in the footnote on the page.

Index for Mason and Eilbeck Slaves

Note: Many slaves belonging to the Mason and Eilbeck families were moved across time with the transfer of ownership through wills, deeds, and possibly verbal agreements. This index for slaves refers to pages in the text of this book. Additional references in the text lead to the Appendices and Tables for further information.

Where multiple slaves have the same name, a distinguishing characteristic is given to separate the individuals. Some names had multiple spellings. Some individuals had known nicknames.

Slaves Owned by the Mason Family

Slaves Owned by the Eilbeck Family

The restored interior of the Center Passage at Gunston Hall reveals the classical architecture designed by William Buckland. The largest room in the mansion, the Passage (or Hall) was used as a receiving and waiting area, a occasional ball room, and a seasonal summer parlor or dining room. This door opens to the land entrance of the plantation.

About the Author

Terry K. Dunn brings her varied background and long experience as a college teacher, historical researcher, and historical interpreter at The State Museum of Pennsylvania, Colonial Williamsburg, and Gunston Hall Plantation to her writing. She is editor of *The Recollections of John Mason: George Mason's Son Remembers His Father and Life at Gunston Hall.*

In her new book, *Among His Slaves,* this author considers the lives of the enslaved people owned by George Mason, draftsman of Virginia Declaration of Rights.

She holds a B.S. in Zoology from The Pennsylvania State University and an M.A. in American History from George Mason University. Terry and her husband Keith live in Williamsburg, Virginia. Their daughter and son are married. They have two granddaughters, four grandsons, one beagle, and two parrots.

About the Illustrator

Artist **Arlene Weik Fabbri** shares her artistic talent and enthusiasm for eighteenth century American history for this project. Born in Litchfield, Connecticut, she spent most of her life in Williamsburg, Virginia where she worked for the Colonial Williamsburg Foundation for more than forty years. Arlene currently lives in Richmond, Maine where she enjoys painting, meeting people, and her children, grandchildren, and great grandson.

About the Covers

Front Cover: The photo illustration includes from the top left – 1888 portrait of George Mason, courtesy Library of Congress; front of Gunston Hall, courtesy Library of Congress; illustration of slave by Arlene Weik Fabbri; field at Gunston Hall, courtesy of the author; and reconstructed slave quarter, courtesy of the author.

Back Cover: Photo of George Mason bust at Gunston Hall, courtesy of the author and illustration of slave by Arlene Weik Fabbri.

CPSIA information can be obtained
at www.ICGtesting.com
Printed in the USA
FSOW04n0449050217
30305FS

9 781943 642373